Introduction for students

You will use this Workbook with the accompanying Student's Book *Investigating Science for Jamaica, Grade 9: Biology Chemistry Physics*. You will find page references to the Student's Book (e.g. *SB9: BCP, p 2–4*) with the activities in this book.

You will be investigating science as part of STEAM (science, technology, engineering, art and mathematics).

You can use this Workbook to:

- help you plan and carry out your practical work
- help you solve problems using the scientific method
- guide you in the engineering design process (EDP)
- show you how to use art as part of STEAM
- work in a group for problem- and inquiry-based learning
- show you how and where you can use ICT in your work
- record data and write information into tables
- present results as bar charts and line graphs
- complete Worksheets for revision to summarise what you have found out
- use the completed Workbook as a record of the year's work.

You will find lots of:

- diagrams to label and explain
- checklists and ideas for projects
- multiple-choice, short-answer and essay type questions
- crossword puzzles and matching exercises on important points
- answers for some of the questions in this book and the Student's Book.

Introduction for teachers

The *Investigating Science: Biology Chemistry Physics* series has a full-colour Student's Book, this write-in Workbook and a Teacher's guide. The books are based on the Grade 9 Biology Chemistry and Physics National Standards Curriculum in Jamaica. The topics in this Workbook follow the same order and are cross-referenced to pages in the accompanying Student's Book. Workbook activities, questions and Worksheets can be used in the classroom or as homework, and are designed to complement, revise and extend the content and skills covered in the Student's Book.

There are further suggestions in the accompanying Teacher's Guide on the setting up of the various activities, background material, additional tests and answers to questions.

Contents

Introduction

Working like a scientist (3)

Biology

UNIT 16 Transport in living things

UNIT 17 Sensitivity and co-ordination

UNIT 18 Embryo development and birth control

Chemistry

UNIT 19 Chemical bonding, reactions and equations

UNIT 20 Acids and alkalis

Physics

UNIT 21 Electricity and magnetism

UNIT 22 Thermal energy

Introduction

Working like a scientist (3)

Science, technology, engineering, art and mathematics (STEAM) (SB9: BCP, Introduction p 1–4, 6–7)

Your science programme now includes technology, engineering, art and mathematics as part of STEAM.
Science is how you find out about living and non-living things and how things work.
Technology and Engineering are how you use special materials for specific purposes to make new things.
Art you use in the design process in EDP, in the choice of materials, and making sketches and drawings.
Mathematics you use for dealing with numbers and calculations, measuring and displaying information.
You also use ICT (which is part of technology) as a tool for research and to communicate with others.

1 Here are some problems. You want to:

(a) set up a watering system for a plant.

(b) make a heated box to incubate some fertile chicken's eggs.

(c) find out which of two substances dissolves most easily in water.

Discuss in your group how you could use STEAM to help solve your problems. Then fill in the table.

Science	Technology/Engineering	Art	Mathematics
(a)			
(b)			
(c)			

2 Match each way of working to its description.

(a) Investigation	....	1 You find the structure and properties of materials
(b) Scientific method		2 You decide on the question and find the answer
(c) EDP including art		3 You set up a fair test to answer a problem
(d) Problem-based		4 You design, draw, make, test, and improve a model
(e) Inquiry-based		5 You use people and paper resources and ICT
(f) Research a topic		6 Your group tries to solve a real-life problem

The scientific method (SB9: BCP, Introduction p 2–4, 7–9 and throughout your course)

You use the scientific method when you have a problem and need a fair test to find the answer. You make a hypothesis and test a prediction based on it. You should change only one variable (the independent variable) so you can find its effect (the dependent variable). The other variables you keep the same (control variables).

Steps	What it means	My activity
Problem *Ask*	What is the problem? What solutions can I suggest?	
Hypothesis *Imagine*	Do background research Can I make a general statement about what I expect to happen?	
Prediction *Plan*	What do I think will happen in this case? What is my prediction?	
Fair test	Which **one** variable will I change?	
Plan	Which variables will I keep the same?	
	What results do I expect? (Observations and measurements)	
Materials and method *Do*	What equipment and materials do I need? What will I do to solve my problem?	
Present and analyse results *Assess*	What do I find out? Observations Measurements Data display	
Write an account *Report*	Record what I have done under headings Discuss my findings with other students	
Evaluate	Have I solved my problem?	

Engineering design process (EDP) (SB9: BCP, Introduction p 2–4, 7, 10–11 and throughout your course)

You use the engineering design process when you have a problem that involves making a model or prototype or designing a new material or process. You need to brainstorm the materials you will use and how you will plan and test your ideas. You may need to plan, build, test and redesign several times before you succeed.

Steps	What it means	My activity
Engage Ask	What is the problem? What are the requirements and constraints? What materials might I need for a model?	
Explore Imagine	What are some solutions? I research and brainstorm ideas/ designs I sketch my ideas I select and compare the best two designs	
Elaborate Plan	I choose the option likely to be the best I make neat drawings I gather the necessary materials I make a detailed plan	
Execute Create	I follow my plan I write any problems and how I made changes I make labelled drawings I see how it works	
Explain Assess, improve, report	Does my design meet the requirements? I make changes to my model to improve it I repeat the 'assess and improve' steps I report to others on how my model works I repeat 'assess and improve' if necessary	
Evaluate	When I have my final model have I solved my problem?	

Using Art in STEAM (SB9: BCP, Introduction p 6, 11, 110 and throughout your course)

Tick the boxes to record in the tables below how well you can use Art during your course.

Using Art and design in the engineering design process

	How to do well
	Brainstorm design ideas.
	Think of lots of ideas to try out.
	Choose materials based on their properties.
	Research what is needed to make choices.
	Be aware of constraints, e.g. time, cost.
	Check texture, colour, strength, etc.
	Make freehand sketches with labels.
	Make accurate, measured, drawings.
	Add labels, annotations and a title.

For example: making a model of a cell:

- Research and choose materials with as many similarities as possible to the 'real thing'.
- Check colours, strength, consistency, and if it should be transparent, elastic, waterproof, etc.
- Make sketches of alternative models.
- Make scale drawings of a final design.
- Use artistic flair to make the model attractive.

Using Art to make diagrams and drawings of living things

	How to do well
	Diagrams and sketches show main features.
	They show relationships between the parts.
	They can include arrows and colour.
	They do not have to be 'life-like'.
	Drawings show the 'real thing' to scale.
	They have a clear, continuous outline.
	They show the parts in proportion.
	There is no shading or use of colour.
	Draw label lines with a ruler.
	Lines do not cross and no arrowheads.
	Print labels in lower case.
	Give a title and magnification.

For example: model of a heart:

- Make a diagram to show the compartments.
- Add tubes to show the position of vessels.
- Add arrows to show direction of blood flow.
- Add notes to help in the design process.

Using Art to draw equipment

	How to do well
	First make a sketch to show the parts.
	Then make the drawing using a ruler.
	It should show an imagined cut surface.
	It should be a good size and in proportion.
	Show tubes with two parallel lines.
	Draw a liquid surface as one straight line.
	Use arrows to show actions taken.
	Label the parts with straight label lines.
	Labels should be in lower case.
	Use colours for solutions, precipitates.

For example: mixing two solutions:

- Draw cut surfaces of the test tubes.
- Use a ruler for tubes and label lines.
- Use arrows to show the solutions were mixed.
- Add colours to show any changes that occurred, and any products, e.g. precipitate that is made.

Using Art in ICT and presentations

	How to do well
	Practise your ICT skills to include art.
	Know and use buttons to change fonts, style (bold, italic, underline), size, and colour.
	Know and use bullet points, numbered lists, lining up of text and numbers of columns.
	Know and use tables to improve display.
	Use colour, style and visual appeal in models.
	Make models attractive and marketable.
	Make flyers and magazines with DTP.
	Use attractive layouts for PowerPoint.

For example: Use Art to make a flyer:

- Make a flyer on different kinds of birth control.
- Research the information.
- Brainstorm an eye-catching presentation.
- Find images, colours, style, and fonts to use.
- Make alternative designs and choose the best.
- Make the finished flyer.

Writing a report (use the outline throughout your course to record what you did)

Heading	What it means	My report
Aim or problem	What prediction am I testing?	
	What am I trying to make?	
Materials and equipment	A list of all the things that were used	
Diagram or drawing	Equipment, living thing or a model They should be labelled	
Method or design process	What was done. Use the past tense. Did I set up a fair test? Did I choose, design and make a model?	
Results	What was found out? Observations Measurements Model and drawing	
Data display	Is a table, bar chart, pie chart or line graph needed? How do I prepare them?	
Interpretation or Discussion	What do my results mean? How can they be explained? Does my model work?	
Conclusion and evaluation	Has the aim been achieved? Do my results support or disprove my hypothesis? Have I made a model to solve the original problem?	

Problem-based and Inquiry-based learning (use this for Group work throughout your course)

Use this sheet as a checklist for your Group work. For each item mark yourself with a 0, 1, 2 or 3 points.

0 = action was not done, 1 = I sometimes do this action, 2 = I often do this action, 3 = I usually do this action.

Your teacher will observe you and also add his or her points. You can then discuss the results.

Hint	What it means	Points	
		My marks	Teacher's marks
Plan	Check the problem to be solved. Or decide on what question(s) you want to investigate. What do you need?		
Set up	Talk about and do research on how you will solve the problem. Share out the tasks to be done in the group, e.g. • Chairman (guides and makes sure everyone takes part) • Questioner (asks questions so the group is on the task) • Investigators (search to find information and materials) • Reporter (records the group's ideas and results) Arrange for different roles in different activities.		
Be curious	Show an interest in the activity being done, and what is being found out. Ask questions about anything you don't understand. Think about how the result will be useful.		
Be inventive	Use equipment and materials in safe but unusual ways. Think of new ways to find things out, including ICT. Present findings, for example, as posters and models.		
Be friendly	Use a friendly supportive tone of voice when working. Encourage the group to work together. Speak softly.		
Contribute ideas	Think about and put forward your own ideas to the group. You need to explain clearly so others understand. Be able to answer questions about what you say. Do not expect everyone else to agree with you on everything.		
Resolve conflicts constructively	Don't start a shouting match or pick a fight. It is better to say, 'We seem to have a difference of opinion', 'Let's listen quietly to both sides of the argument', 'This might be a good time to take a vote.'		
Encourage each other	Make supportive comments to others, such as 'That's a good idea', 'Yes, I agree with you', 'Please explain more about what you mean'.		
Be persistent	Continue with the work until it's finished. Repeat some activities if necessary. Keep on working, even if others have finished their activity.		
Be critical of results	Check and recheck results. Base conclusions on the evidence. Point out any contradictions in the report. Record any opinions strongly held by some of the group.		
Do your fair share	Contribute to ideas, research, activities and clearing up, etc. Do your fair share but do not try to take over.		

Evaluation for marking an oral presentation (use the scheme throughout your course)

Use this sheet to assess an Oral or ICT presentation. For each item mark with 1, 2 or 3 points.

1 = Fair but below average, 2 = Satisfactory or average, 3 = Very good or above average

Several students should mark each presentation. Then find the average marks for each part.

Hint	What it means	Assessment		
		Fair	Satisfactory	Very good
Sensible order	The presentation was arranged so that one part led into the next. There was an introduction and summary.			
Used good English	Complete sentences were used. There were no grammar mistakes or slang words.			
Spoke clearly and audibly	The mouth was open enough to form the words properly. The person spoke neither too quietly nor too loud.			
Spoke confidently	The person didn't mumble. They seemed to believe in what they were saying.			
Stood upright	The person stood with their shoulder back in a relaxed position. They did not slouch on the furniture.			
Kept eye contact	They kept their face up and looked at the audience. They did not talk into their notes.			
Kept interest	They made the talk interesting by giving examples. They used pictures and diagrams where these were useful.			
Answered questions	They were prepared to answer questions, and did this well. They did not seem to be put off by the questions.			

Using ICT for reports and research (SB9: BCP, Introduction p 13 and throughout your course)

Hint	What it means	Assessment		
		Fair	Satisfactory	Very good
Use word processing	Use word processing to type and edit (make corrections) to your reports and improve their appearance.			
Use graphics	Prepare drawings, designs or flyers with good use of style, colour and presentation.			
Use spread-sheets	Set up spreadsheets for tables and calculations and to show data as bar charts, pie charts and line graphs.			
Use Power-Point	Design slides using templates and arrange a presentation to show in class with multimedia resources			
Connect to the Internet	Know your Internet Service Provider and how to log on and log off safely and responsibly.			
Use search engines	For example, use Google to search for information on given topics by good choice of search words.			
Check several sources	Do not copy word for word. Use several sources, be critical and make your own summaries and comparisons.			
Acknowledge sources	Keep a record of where you find material so you can list your sources for text or pictures in your report.			
Use email and chat rooms	Use email to communicate your work and socially. Use chat rooms responsibly. Don't believe everything you see.			
Save work	Save your work in well-labelled files and folders.			

Using the binary code (SB9: BCP, Introduction p 12–13)

Binary code

The binary code uses two bits, 0 (off) and 1 (on). Strings of eight bits make a byte. In the binary code the column to the left has a value of twice that on the right.

2^7	2^6	2^5	2^4	2^3	2^2	2^1	2^0
128	64	32	16	8	4	2	1
0	1	0	0	0	0	0	1
0	1	1	0	0	0	0	1

In the table above:
the first byte: 01000001, represents capital A
the second byte: 01100001, represents lower case a.
The base ten value of 'A' is 64 + 1 = 65, and for 'a' it is 64 + 32 + 1 = 97

1 Add binary code and base ten value for each letter.

A	01000001	65	a	01100001	97
B			b		
C			c		
D			d		
E			e		
F			f		
G			g		
H			h		
I			i		
J			j		
K			k		
L			l		
M			m		
N			n		
O			o		
P			p		
Q			q		
R			r		
S			s		
T			t		
U			u		
V			v		
W			w		
X			x		
Y			y		
Z			z		

In Question 1 you will find that:
Capital A to Z have base ten values of 65 to 90, and lower case a to z have base ten values of 97 to 122.

These values are used internationally as part of the **ASCI** code (American Standard Code for Information Interchange).

2 The base ten values for some common symbols are shown below. Add the binary code for each one.

Symbol	Base ten value	Binary code
Space	32	
Dollar sign	36	
Comma	44	
Full stop	46	
Question mark	63	

3 Now use binary code to write a message, using capital and lower case letters, and symbols. Ask a friend to decode it and to reply to you.

4 Add what is meant by these ICT terms.

CPU	
ROM	
RAM	
VDU	
OS	
CD	
DVD	
ISP	
'hit'	
'spam'	

Units and physical quantities (SB9: BCP, Introduction p 14–17, 108–9, 163–5)

1 Look at Activity 0.4 on page 15 in SB9: BCP. Use the table below to record your measurements. Record your estimates first, and then your accurate measurements of the water and the wire. Remember to add the symbols for the quantities.

Table for recording physical quantities	
A Mass of water Estimate of mass = ... Find and record the mass of the water to the nearest gram. Mass = ...	**D Length of wire with a ruler** Estimate of length = ... Find and record the length of the wire to the nearest centimetre. Length = ...
B Volume of water Estimate of volume = ... Find and record the volume of the water to the nearest cubic centimetre. Volume = ...	**E Diameter of wire with Vernier caliper** Estimate of diameter = ... Find and record the diameter of the wire to the nearest 0.1 millimetre. Diameter = ...
C Temperature of water Estimate of temperature = ... Find and record the temperature of the water to the nearest °C. Temperature = ...	**F Diameter of wire with micrometer screw gauge** Estimate of diameter = ... Find and record the diameter of the wire to the nearest 0.01 millimetre. Diameter = ...

How good were your estimates? ....

2 Complete the table below showing important SI units. Some answers have been done for you.

Fundamental quantity	Base unit (symbol)	Base unit (name)	Other common units used
Mass			g
Length			
Time	s		min
Temperature		kelvin	

Measuring area and volume (SB9: BCP, Introduction p 16–17, 108, 165)

Measuring area

Area is a measure of the surface of an object. For regular shapes we can work out the area using a formula. For composite shapes we need to add together the areas of the parts of the shape.

1 Areas of regular shapes

Work out the areas of these shapes in cm^2

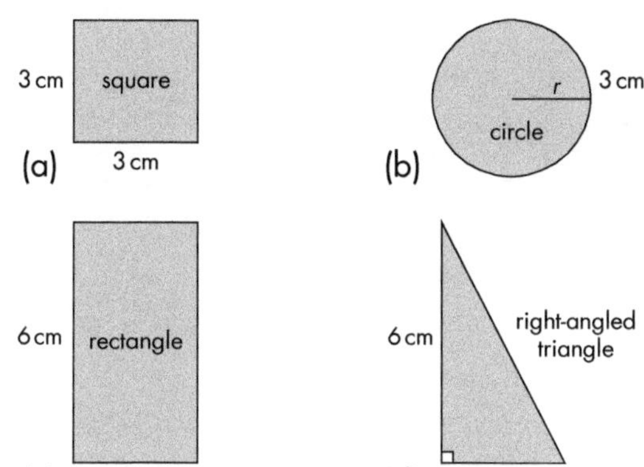

2 Areas of composite shapes

Work out the areas of the composite shapes in cm^2

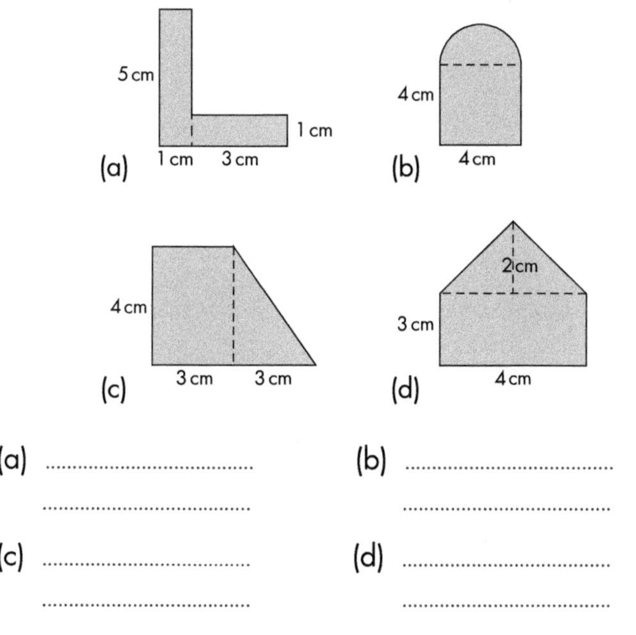

Measuring volume

Volume is a measure of the amount of space taken up by an object. For regular shapes we can work out the volume using a formula. For an irregular shape we find how much water it displaces.

3 Volumes of regular shapes

Work out the volumes of these shapes in cm^3

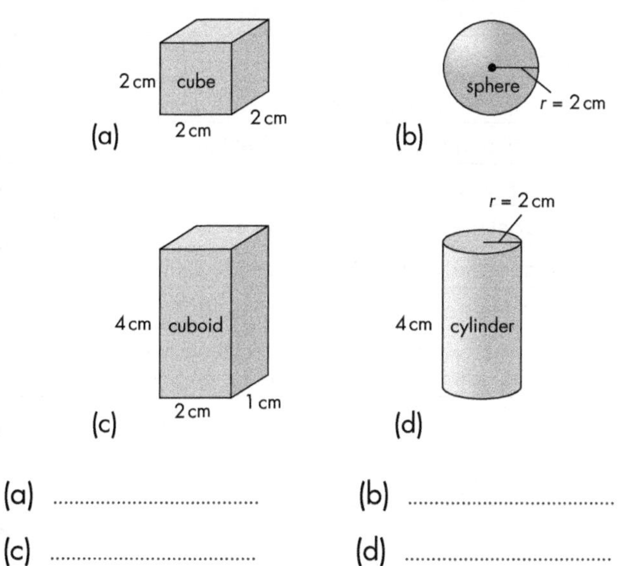

4 Volumes of irregular volumes

Different stones (A-D) were lowered into 50 cm^3 of water (V_1) in a measuring cylinder, and the new volumes (V_2) recorded in the table below.

Record the volumes of each stone.

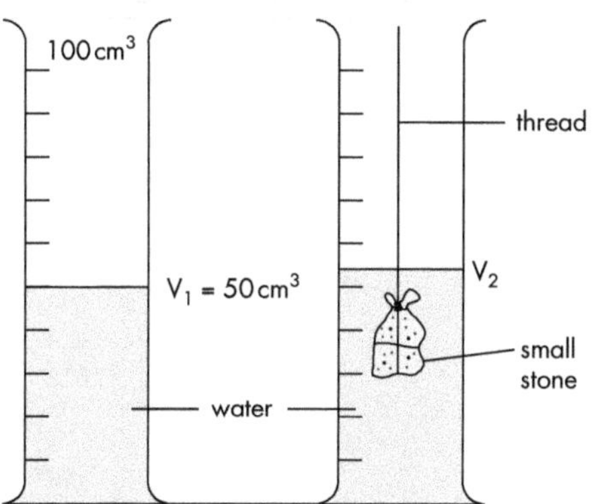

Sample	V_2	V_1	Volume
A	55 cm^3	50 cm^3	
B	65 cm^3	50 cm^3	
C	75 cm^3	50 cm^3	
D	80 cm^3	50 cm^3	

Line graphs and gradients (SB9: BCP, Introduction p 20–3)

Line graphs

We draw a line graph to show the relationship between two variables. We draw lines at right angles on graph paper, called the axes.
On the horizontal x-axis is the independent variable.
On the vertical y-axis is the dependent variable.
Draw line graphs of the following sets of data.
Questions 1–3: Mark yourself out of ten on how well you drew your graphs (one mark for each item).

Use a sharp pencil and a ruler	
Plan your graph to take as much space as possible	
Draw the axes and leave space to label them	
Choose increments of 1, 2, 5 or 10 for your scales	
Mark and label the values of the independent variable	
Mark and label the values of the dependent variable	
Add the quantities and the unit, e.g. time (s)	
Make small crosses (or dot inside a circle) where each reading on the x-axis corresponds to one on the y-axis	
Draw a line of best fit with a ruler or a curved line	
Add a title. The change in the dependent variable is written first, e.g. increase in height with time	

Total /10

1 Distance–time graph

Distance (m) and time (s) readings to plot on a graph:

m	0	2	4	6	8
s	0	1	2	3	4

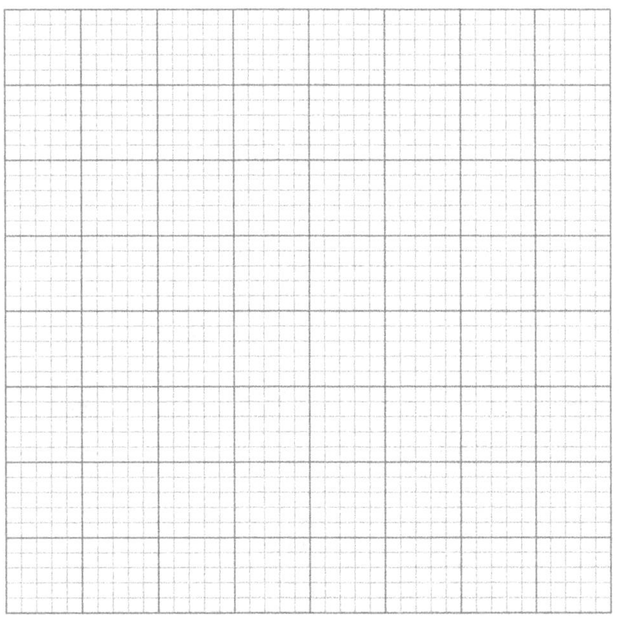

2 Velocity–time graph

Velocity (m/s) and time (s) readings to plot:

m/s	0	1	2	3	4	5
s	0	1	2	3	4	5

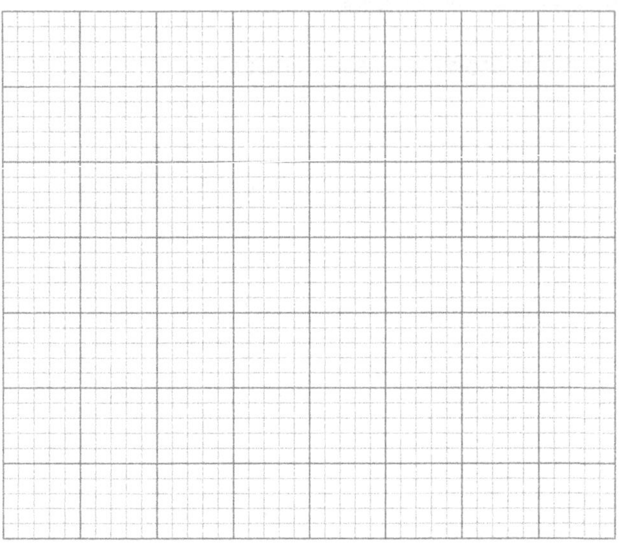

3 Velocity–time graph

Velocity (m/s) and time (s) readings to plot:

m/s	0	19	36	48	57	64
s	0	2	4	6	8	10

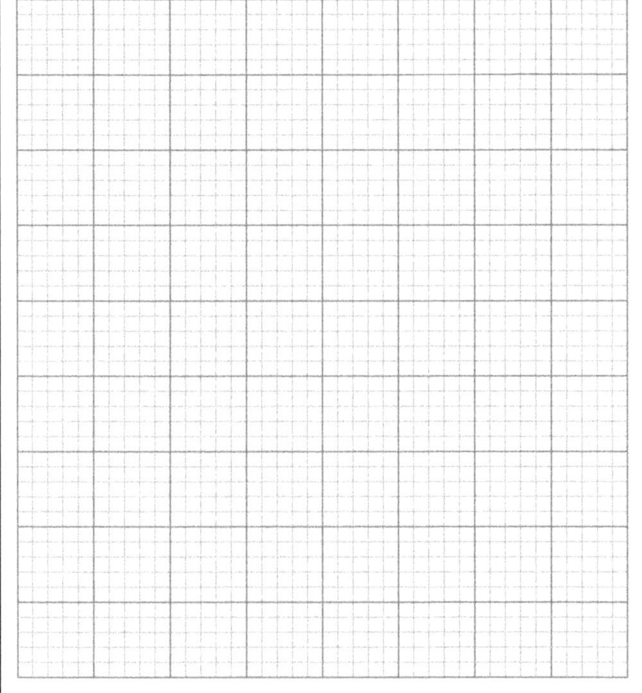

Gradients

The gradient describes the slope of the line on a line graph. The gradient is the

$$\frac{\text{numerical change on the y-axis}}{\text{numerical change on the x-axis}}$$

Note: Distance travelled is measured in metres (m)
Time taken is measured in seconds (s)
Speed is the rate of movement in m/s or ms^{-1}
Velocity is speed in a certain direction, m/s or ms^{-1}
Acceleration is how much the velocity changes each second: acceleration = velocity/ time = ms^{-1}/s or ms^{-2}

Distance–time graph (distance plotted against time)
If the distance travelled (y-axis) is 10 m, and the time taken (x-axis) is 5 s, then

the gradient = $\frac{10\,m}{5\,s}$ = speed of 2 m/s or $2\,ms^{-1}$

4 Look at the distance–time graph you drew for Question **1**.

Select two points on the best line of fit, where the slope is uniform, and draw a large triangle.

Gradient is = $\frac{\text{change on the y-axis}}{\text{change on the x-axis}}$

Work out the speed. Show the units.

Velocity–time graph (velocity plotted against time)
If the change in velocity (y-axis) is $8\,ms^{-1}$, and the time taken (x-axis) is 4 s, then

the gradient = $\frac{8\,ms^{-1}}{4\,s}$ = acceleration of $2\,ms^{-2}$

5 Look at the velocity–time graph you drew for Question **2**.

Select two points on the best line of fit, where the slope is uniform and draw a large triangle.

Gradient is = $\frac{\text{change on the y-axis}}{\text{change on the x-axis}}$

Work out the acceleration. Show the units.

Velocity–time graph (velocity plotted against time)

6 Look at the velocity–time graph you drew for Question **3**.

It shows the acceleration of a racing car at the beginning of a race.

(a) Work out the acceleration from 0 to 4 seconds. Add the units.

(b) Work out the acceleration from 4 to 6 seconds. Add the units. What do you notice?

(c) Work out the acceleration from 6 to 10 seconds. Add the units. What do you notice?

(d) Write a description of the acceleration of the racing car from 0 to 10 seconds.

7 A seedling grew 2 cm in 5 days. What is its rate of growth in mm/day?

8 A car starts up by accelerating from 0 to $30\,ms^{-1}$ in 10 s. What is the acceleration of the car? Show the units.

Prefixes

Show the value of a unit using powers of ten.

Quantities larger than the base unit

Multiple	Prefix	Symbol	Example
10^9	giga	G	gigametre
10^6	mega	M	megabyte
10^3	kilo	k	kilogram

Quantities smaller than the base unit

Multiple	Prefix	Symbol	Example
10^{-1}	deci	d	decimetre
10^{-2}	centi	c	centimetre
10^{-3}	milli	m	millilitre
10^{-6}	micro		microgram
10^{-9}	nano	n	nanosecond

1 What fraction of a gram is a
(a) centigram .... (b) milligram ....

2 How far do I move the digits relative to the decimal point so as to change from:
(a) mega to kilo .... (b) micro to centi ....
(c) deci to milli .... (d) milli to deci ....
(e) kilo to giga .... (f) milli to nano ....

Significant figures (sig figs)

Significant figures show the precision of a number.

Digits 1–9 are always significant
Zeros between digits are significant.
Zeros *before* significant figures are **not** significant.
Zeros *after* significant figures **are** significant if the numeral has a decimal point.
Zeros after significant figures are **not** significant if the numeral does not have a decimal point.

1 Which measurement is most precise?
(a) 4.2, (b) 4, (c) 4.0, (d) 4.15 ....
(e) 17.3, (f) 17, (g) 17.03 (h) 16.9 ....

2 How many significant figures?
(a) 49 cm .... (b) 54.8 m ....
(c) 0.034 .... (d) 0.502 ....

3 Add and give the answer to 3 significant figures
(a) 156 + 187.6 ....
(b) 0.56 + 0.007 ....

4 Subtract and give the answer to 3 significant figures
(a) 78.92 – 54.58 ....
(b) 0.56 – 0.003 ....

5 Divide and give the answer to 3 significant figures
(a) 5698 ÷ 43.2 ....
(b) 7832 ÷ 57.4 ....

Rounding

This is making an approximation of a number, e.g.
to the nearest 10 or 100, or
to a certain number of significant figures.

Round-up if the next digit is 5, 6, 7, 8 or 9
Round-down if the next digit is 1, 2, 3 or 4

1 What are these numbers to the nearest 10?
(a) 56 .... (b) 71.4 ....
(c) 97 .... (d) 768 ....

2 What are these numbers to the nearest hundred?
(a) 716 .... (b) 567 ....
(c) 3467 .... (d) 8359 ....

3 Round these figures to 3 significant figures
(a) 0.03289 .... (b) 437.45 ....
(c) 0.5496 .... (d) 45927 ....

4 Round these figures to 2 significant figures
(a) 43.2 .... (b) 56.97 ....
(c) 0.05648 .... (d) 0.4567 ....

Standard form

This is a numeral between 1 and 10, multiplied by a power of ten,
e.g. for large numbers: 5.6×10^4
for small numbers: 4.23×10^{-5}

1 Change these numerals to standard form
(a) 460 .... (b) 73700 ....
(c) 0.390 .... (d) 0.043 ....

2 Change these from standard form
(a) 8.9×10^3 .... (b) 5.27×10^2 ....
(c) 5.5×10^{-2} .... (d) 8.43×10^{-4} ....

3 Add in standard form
(a) $5.9 \times 10^2 + 9.73 \times 10^3$ ....

4 Subtract in standard form
(a) $5.62 \times 10^4 - 7.89 \times 10^3$ ....

5 Multiply in standard form
(a) $(4.4 \times 10^2) \times (9.82 \times 10^{-1})$ ....

6 Divide in standard form
(a) $(7.9 \times 10^4) \div (6.8 \times 10^3)$ ....

Checklist

You should know the meanings of these words (check the Glossary and Index in SB9: BCP):

acceleration, area, art, composite shape, controlling variables, density, derived unit, digits, displacement method, distance–time graph, EDP, engineering, fair test, force, fundamental quantities, gradient, hypothesis, ICT, irregular shape, line graph, mathematics, physical quantity, prediction, prefixes, precision, problem statement, regular shape, rounding, science, scientific method, significant figures, SI system, speed, standard form, STEAM, technology, unit, variable, velocity, velocity–time graph, volume

Questions

1 Technologists include
A engineers **B** ICT programmers
C inventors **D** all of the above

2 An important tool for engineers is
A the design process **B** controlling variables
C using fair tests **D** testing hypotheses

3 An important tool for scientists is
A making predictions **B** controlling variables
C using fair tests **D** all of the above

4 Germinating seeds were left, with damp cotton wool, some in the light and some in the dark. The experimenter was testing whether
A water was necessary for germination
B growth occurred in the light and the dark
C temperature was important for growth rate
D damp cotton wool encouraged plant growth

5 The binary code for a number is 101010. What is this in base ten?
A 12 **B** 41
C 42 **D** 74

6 How would I write 71 (base ten) in binary code?
A 100111 **B** 1000111
C 10111 **D** 10101

7 What is the largest number (base ten) you can make using 5 binary digits?
A 32 **B** 31
C 16 **D** 15

8 Which of these is the same as 10 g?
A 0.001 kg **B** 0.1 kg
C 0.01 kg **D** 1 kg

9 How many milligrams in a gram?
A 10 **B** 100
C 1000 **D** 10 000

10 What do we measure using cm^3?
A volume **B** length
C circumference **D** surface area

11 To change from gigabyte to megabyte I
A divide by 10^3 **B** multiply by 10^3
C divide by 10^2 **D** multiply by 10^2

12 To change from centimetre to micrometre I
A divide by 10^4 **B** multiply by 10^4
C divide by 10^3 **D** multiply by 10^3

13 How many micrometres in a millimetre?
A 10^{-1} **B** 10
C 100 **D** 1000

14 The prefix 'nano' means
A 10^{-9} **B** 10^{-8} **C** 10^{-7} **D** 10^{-6}

15 The area of a right-angled triangle is
A $a \times b$ **B** $2\,a \times b$ **C** $\frac{1}{2}\,a \times b$ **D** a^2

16 What is the area of a rectangle 7 cm by 8 cm?
A 15 cm **B** 15 cm^2 **C** 56 cm^2 **D** 56 cm^3

17 What is the volume of a cube of side 3 cm?
A 27 cm^2 **B** 27 cm^3 **C** 12 cm^3 **D** 9 cm^3

18 What is the volume of a sphere?
A $\frac{4}{3}\pi r^3$ **B** πr^2
C $\frac{1}{2}\pi r^2$ **D** $\pi r^2 \times b$

19 Which number has 3 significant figures?
A 0.56 **B** 82 **C** 0.0501 **D** 89.20

20 What is 0.6075 rounded to 3 significant figures?
A 0.607 **B** 0.608 **C** 0.61 **D** 0.600h

21 What is the 5793 in standard form?
A 5.793×10^3 **B** 5.793×10^2
C 57.93×10^3 **D** 57.93×10^2

22 What is 0.0067 in standard form?
A 0.67×10^{-2} **B** 0.067×10^{-2}
C 6.7×10^{-3} **D** 6.7×10^{-2}

23 What is 5.67×10^2?
A 5670 **B** 567 **C** 56.7 **D** 56700

24 What is 2.39×10^{-3}?
A 2.39 **B** 0.239
C 0.0239 **D** 0.00239

25 What is $5.2 \times 10^2 + 4.8 \times 10^3$?
A 10×10^2 **B** 10×10^3
C 5.32×10^2 **D** 5.32×10^3

26 What is $(5.2 \times 10^2) \times (4.0 \times 10^3)$?
A 20×10^5 **B** 2.08×10^6
C 20×10^6 **D** 20.8×10^6

27 If the distance travelled is 30 m in 15 s, what is the speed, in the correct units?
A 2 ms^{-1} **B** 2 ms^1 **C** 30 ms^2 **D** 15ms

28 In what units do we measure acceleration?
A ms^1 **B** ms **C** ms^{-2} **D** ms^2

Your turn

Work with a partner or in a small group. The aim is for you to set some questions for the other students to do. Then you mark the answers and see how well you have all done. Here are some ideas:

1. Look in the SB9: BCP p 12 for the binary code of capital and low case letters. Put these on a chart and complete the alphabet. Then write messages in binary code for a partner to 'read'.
2. Look in the SB9: BCP p 16 for the area of shapes. Use some squared paper and cut out some composite shapes. Give these to a partner to find the area (both by counting squares and by working out the areas using formulae).

Or you could try these

1. Set up two teams and have a quiz. You will need to give the answers to a quizmaster so they can decide if a team is correct.
2. Make some cards for a game of Snap or Happy Families. You could make sets of cards for physical quantities, symbols of a unit, prefix and its value, e.g. mass, g, micro, 10^{-6}.
3. Look in the SB9: BCP p 13 for the list of ICT skills. Talk about how many of these you can do and how you could develop the other ones.

Puzzle

Complete the crossword. The clues are given in the next column.

Across

5 Change in velocity (m/s) with time (s) (12)
8 Short for nanometre (2)
9 Distance (m) divided by time (s) (5)
10 Information and communication technology (3)
11 A figure in a numeral; 0 or 1 to 9 (5)
12 Added before a symbol to change its value (6)
13 There are 10 in a centimetre (2)
17 A shape made of more than one part (9)
19 The amount of substance in an object (4)
21 There are 10^3 in a gram (2)
22 Short for significant figure (6)
24 We use standard form to show low and .... numbers (4)
26 Eight bits makes one of these (4)
27 The gradient is the .... on a graph (4)
29 Engineering design process (3)
30 International system for units (8)

Down

1 Speed in a certain direction (ms^{-1}) (8)
2 An object will float if it is less .... than the liquid it is placed in (5)
3 A group of technologists (9)
4 A description for measuring a physical quantity (4)
6 Prefix meaning 1/100th (5)
7 Surface of an object, measured in cm^2 (4)
12 Part of the formula for the area of a circle (2)
13 Short for megabyte (2)
14 Pushes and pulls, measured in newton (N) (5)
15 Measured in metres and centimetres (6)
16 A condition in a fair test (8)
18 What we need to solve, often in groups (8)
20 The base unit is the second (s) (4)
23 A flat or solid regular or irregular figure (5)
25 Short for gigametre (2)
28 There are 10^4 micrometres in one of these (s)

Add the formulae for finding the area and volume of these shapes.

Shape	Area	Shape	Volume
Square		Cube	
Rectangle		Cuboid	
Circle		Sphere	
Semicircle		Hemisphere	
Right-angled triangle		Cylinder	

Unit 16

Transport in living things

Diffusion and osmosis (SB9: BCP, Unit 16 p 30–3)

1 Complete the table (see SB9: BCP, p 30) Activity 16.1.

Activity	Results and explanation
1 Air freshener	
2 Smoke	
3 Water and coffee	

2 Setting up fair tests. On page 30 in SB9: BCP, you were asked to set up fair tests to answer questions about diffusion.

(a) Use the table on page 5 in this Workbook, to plan your investigation.

(b) When your investigation is completed, use the table on page 8 to help you write up your report.

3 Self check. As you complete your activities, put a tick to show if you were a good group member.

- ☐ I gave good ideas to the group.
- ☐ I listened carefully while other people spoke.
- ☐ I respected other people's ideas.
- ☐ I expressed my ideas briefly and clearly.
- ☐ I took my fair share of responsibility.
- ☐ I did not try to take over all the jobs.
- ☐ I helped the group come to its decisions.
- ☐ I helped set up the experiments.
- ☐ I worked with due regard to safety.
- ☐ I helped to tidy up after the activity.

4 Complete the table (see SB9: BCP, p 31) Activity 16.5.

Activity	Results and explanation
1 Citrus fruit and salt	Beginning 10 minutes
2 Raisins and water	Beginning 10 minutes 2 hours
3 Potato and brown sugar	Beginning 30 minutes

5 Suggest evidence for each statement.

(a) Particles spread apart by moving.

....

....

(b) Diffusion occurs in gases and liquids.

....

....

(c) Osmosis is a special case of diffusion. It is the movement of water through a partially (selectively) permeable membrane.

....

....

Transport in plants: adaptations and transport tissues (SB9: BCP, Unit 16 p 34–41)

1 (a) Describe two adaptations of roots. Give reasons.

(i) ....

....

(ii) ....

....

(b) Describe two adaptations of leaves. Give reasons.

(i) ....

....

(ii) ....

....

2 List the substances moved around in a plant. For each one, list the tissue in which it moves and the process(es) that are most important.

Substance	Tissue	Processes
Water	Xylem	Osmosis, root push, transpiration pull

3 How does the structure of the following suit them for their functions?

Root hairs	
Xylem	
Phloem	

4 Label and annotate the diagram of a root hair to show how it takes in water and mineral salts.

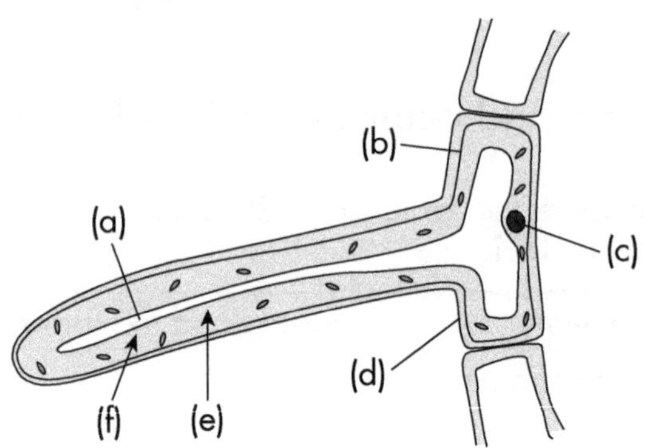

5 Label and annotate the diagram of a cross-section of a root.

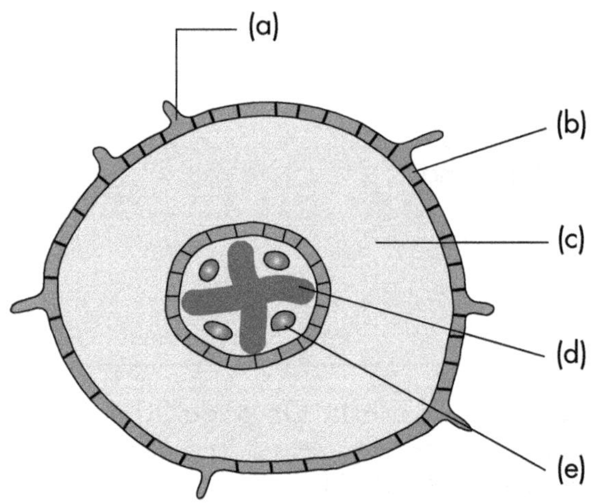

6 Label and annotate the diagram of a cross-section of a stem.

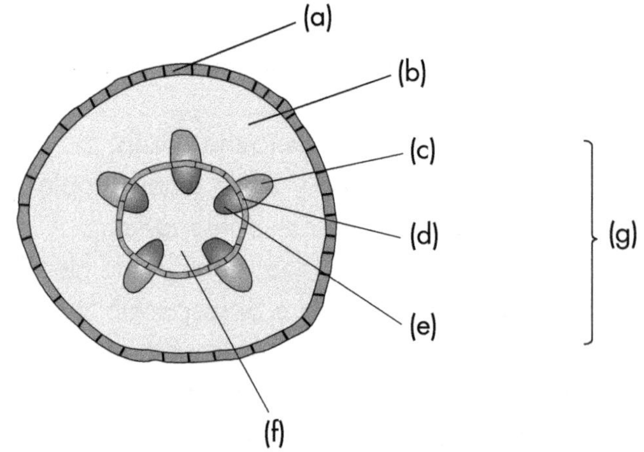

Transport in plants: water pathway (cont.)

7 Label and annotate the diagram of a section through a leaf.

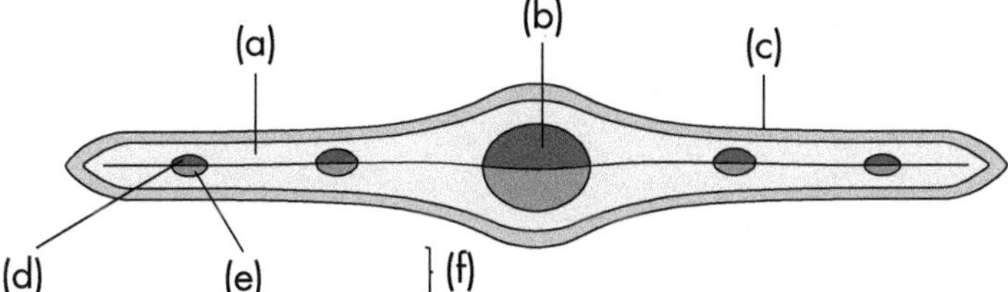

8 Design and draw your own diagram to summarise how substances enter and leave a flowering plant. Also show and label the tissues in which they move.

Projects

- Plan and design a model of the transport system of your community. Identify the items that are similar to the transport system of plants.
- Research how heat is lost by the plant as water evaporates during transpiration.

9 How is each of the properties of water important for the transport of substances around plants. The first one has been done.

Property	Importance
Water is a liquid	1 Water can flow 2
Molecules show adhesion	1 2
Molecules show cohesion	1 2
Water rises in narrow tubes	1 2
Water is a solvent	1 2
Water can carry solid substances	1 2

10 How are these processes important in a plant?

Osmosis	
Diffusion	

11 What effect do the following have on the movement of water through the plant?

Root push	
Transpiration pull	

Transport in humans: blood and blood vessels (SB9: BCP, Unit 16 p 42–7)

1 Complete the table to list the constituents of the blood, and their structure and function(s). Include simple diagrams of the constituents.

Constituents	Structure	Functions

2 Complete the table to compare the different structure and functions of blood vessels. Include simple cross-sections of the vessels.

Blood vessel	Structure	Functions

3 Take your pulse (see SB9: BCP p 45, Activity 16.25) and see how it changes with exercise.

(a) Use the table to record the pulse rate in 30 seconds when at rest (four trials).

At rest 1	2	3	4	Total

Divide total by 4, and × 2 = pulse rate per minute

....

(b) Now run around in the playground or do a similar kind of exercise for 2 minutes.

Take four readings again of your pulse rate over 30 seconds.

Exercise 1	2	3	4	Total

Divide total by 4, and × 2 = pulse rate per minute

....

(c) Wait for five minutes, and repeat all the readings again. Record them in the table.

Later 1	2	3	4	Total

Divide total by 4, and × 2 = pulse rate per minute

....

(d) Does everyone in the classroom have the same pulse rate when at rest? What is the range of readings? Make a class bar chart of the rates.

....

....

(e) How does your pulse rate compare immediately after exercise, with that at rest? Why is this?

....

....

....

....

(f) Did everyone's pulse return to pre-exercise rate when at rest after five minutes? ....

(A quick return to normal shows good health.)

4 Label the diagram of a section through the human heart. Name each compartment of the heart and the blood vessel that enters or leaves it.

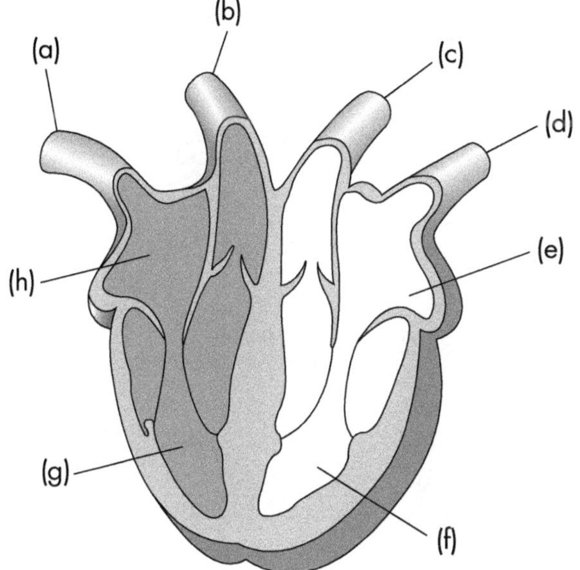

(a) What is an artery? ....

....

....

(b) What is a vein? ....

....

....

(c) What is de-oxygenated blood? ....

....

....

(d) On which side of the heart is de-oxygenated blood found? ....

(e) In which blood vessel does the blood leave the heart to go to the lungs?

....

(f) In which blood vessel does the blood return to the heart from the lungs?

....

(g) Which ventricle has the thicker wall? Why?

....

....

(h) Which chamber of the heart receives blood from the body?

....

Transport in humans: circulation and heart model (SB9: BCP, Unit 16 p 46–9)

1 Label the diagram below showing the circulation of blood. Use these labels:

capillaries in lungs, capillaries in body, artery to body, artery to lungs, vein from body, vein from lungs, heart, lot of carbon dioxide, lot of oxygen, right side, left side.

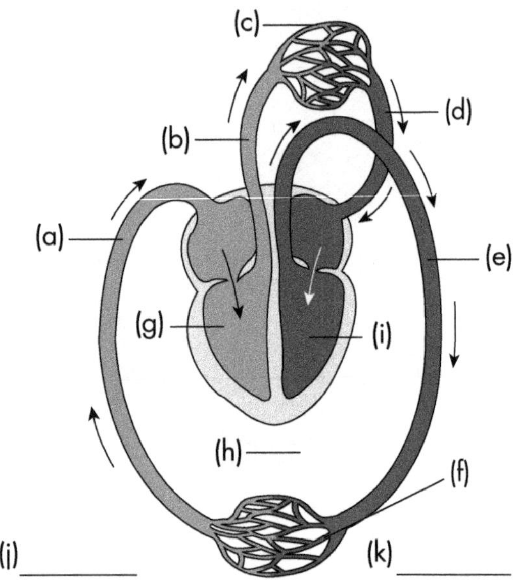

2 Make a model heart.
Materials: shoe box, pieces of red and black tubing, cardboard, ruler, glue or paper tape, scissors, pen.

(a) Cut cardboard pieces to divide the heart into right and left sides, and into top and bottom parts.

(b) On each side make a hole between the top (atrium) and the bottom (ventricle).

(c) Cut and push tubing through the sides of the heart (black on the right, red on the left).

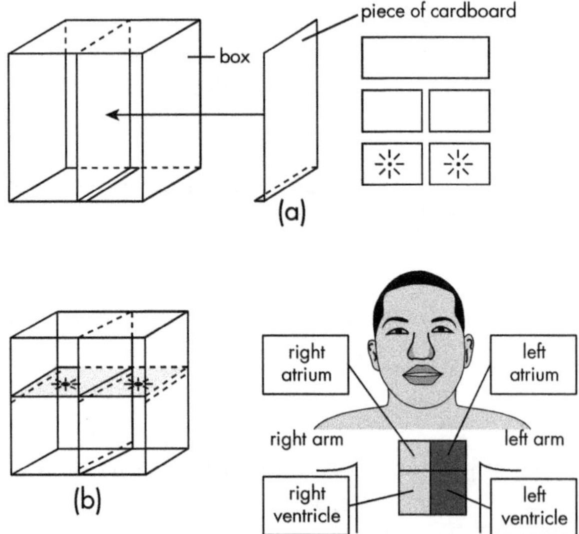

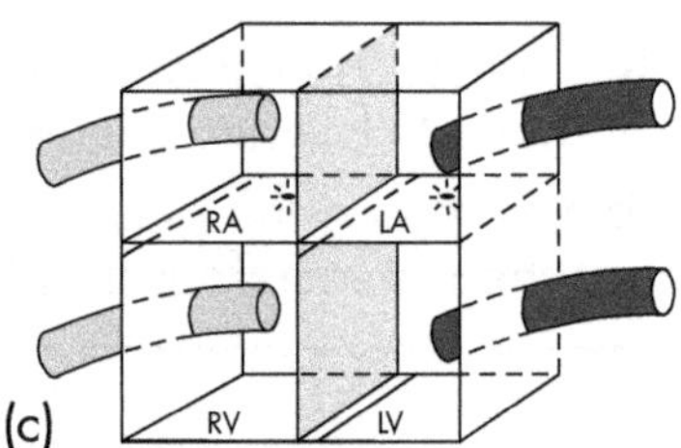

Now add coloured thread to your model heart, to show how blood travels through it.

(a) Use black thread to show blood with a lot of carbon dioxide going into the right atrium, then the right ventricle, and leaving to go to the lungs.

(b) Use red thread to show blood with a lot of oxygen returning from the lungs to the left atrium, then into the left ventricle and out to the body.

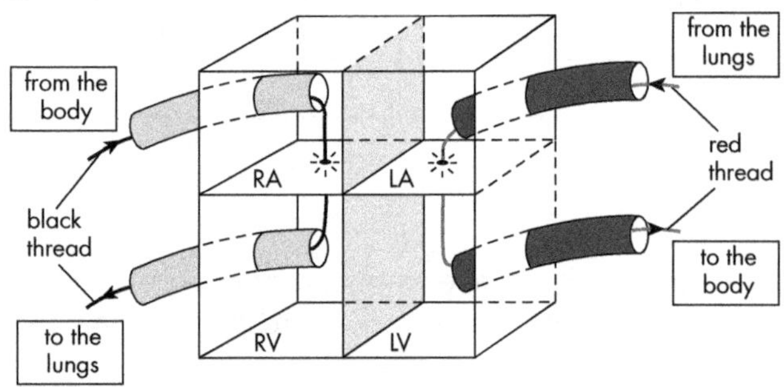

How is the model like a real heart?
1
2
3
4
5

How is the model not like a real heart?
1
2
3
4
5

Tranport in humans: circulation (cont.)

3 (a) Label the main parts of the circulatory system shown below.

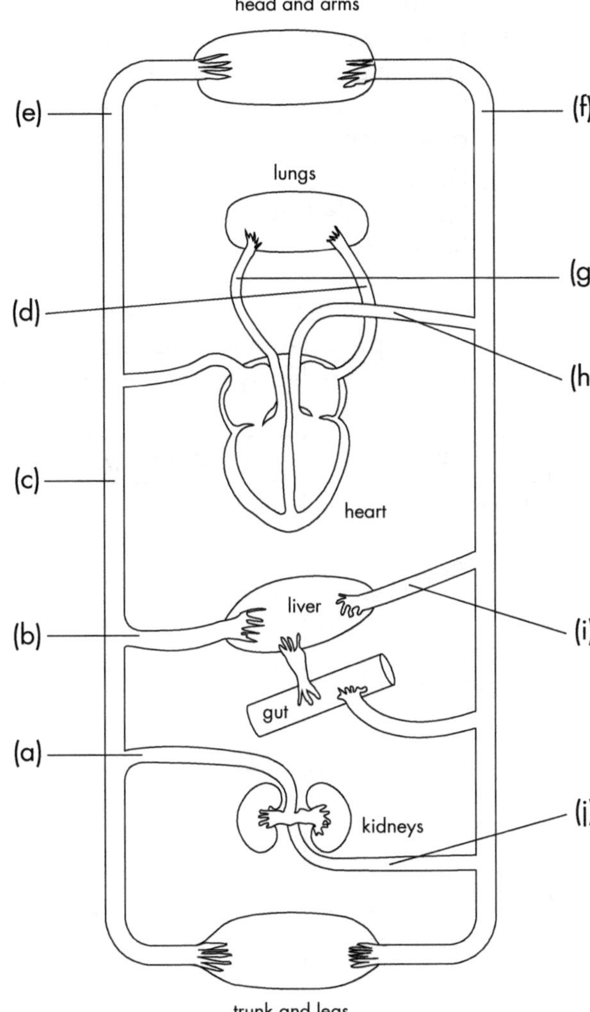

(b) Colour light blue the vessels and heart chambers that contain de-oxygenated blood.

(c) Colour light red the vessels and heart chambers that contain oxygenated blood.

(d) Add arrows to the heart to show the direction in which blood flows.

(e) Add arrows to show the direction blood flows to and from each organ.

(f) Which is the only artery that contains de-oxygenated blood? Where does it take the blood?

....

....

(g) Which is the only vein that contains oxygenated blood? Where does it take the blood?

....

....

4 Use the diagram on the left to describe the blood supply to the organs.

Name each vein, artery, chamber of the heart, and any other organ the blood passes through as it goes:

(a) from the arms to the liver.

(b) From the kidneys and back again to the kidneys.

(c) From the legs to the lungs.

(d) From the heart (right side) to the kidneys.

(e) From the liver to the legs.

7 Complete the table to list the substances lost and gained in each of the organs that are listed.

Organ	Gained	Lost
Leg		
Lungs		
Intestines		
Kidneys		
Skin		

Transport in humans: exercise and fitness (SB9: BCP, Unit 16 p 50, 53)

1 Think up a fitness programme that someone your age could do in 10 minutes each day.

- Try to include exercises to develop strength, stamina and suppleness,
- Use everyday materials, so the exercises could be done at home. Do not make them too difficult.
- Start with a 'warm-up' exercise.
- Write up your programme and show it to your teacher.
- If the programme seems safe, you can try it out for a few weeks. Make changes if necessary.

....

....

....

....

....

....

2 (a) When exercising, you are advised to stop if you feel breathless or under strain? Why is this?

....

....

....

(b) What exercise would you recommend to a person who is overweight, and used to working at a desk? Explain your answer.

....

....

....

(c) Ask a doctor or gym instructor for advice about problems with exercise, and record what they say.

....

....

....

(d) Some people take drugs to enhance their body development or achievement. What are the dangers?

....

....

....

3 (a) Work in a group. Make up a questionnaire with about ten questions that you could ask people to find out how they stay healthy.

(b) Check your questionnaire with your teacher. Then interview five people in your family and the community. Select people of different ages, occupations and appearance.

(c) Discuss the answers in your group. Do you find people have different ways of staying healthy?

4 Summarise in the table what you have learned about keeping healthy, in relation to diet, exercise, sleep, lifestyle choices and benefits.

Item	What I have learned
Diet	
Exercise strength	
stamina	
suppleness	
Sleep	
Lifestyle choices	
Benefits	

5 Are there any changes you might make to your lifestyle in order to become healthier?

....

....

....

Transport in humans: diseases and their prevention (SB9: BCP, Unit 16 p 51–3)

1 Complete the table to summarise information about diseases of the circulatory system.

Kind of disease	Named example	Cause	Symptoms	Treatment
Deficiency				
Inherited				
Parasitic				
Functional	1			
	2			

2 Give four examples of poor health care that would make it **more** likely we would suffer from disease. In each case list some diseases we might suffer from.

Poor health care	Possible diseases

Projects

- Choose a disease. Research its cause, symptoms, and possible prevention and treatment. Collect all the reports for a class book on Diseases.
- Work with your group to make a poster that informs people of what they can do to reduce their problems with circulatory diseases.

3 Complete the table

Body fighting disease	Examples

4 Tick which actions you take for staying healthy.

- ☐ I have a balanced diet.
- ☐ I do not have much saturated fat in my food.
- ☐ I do not eat too many sugary foods.
- ☐ I keep myself and my clothes clean.
- ☐ I would check if I were feeling tired or ill.
- ☐ I exercise and keep fit.
- ☐ I enjoy my activities and have plenty of sleep.
- ☐ I do not smoke.
- ☐ I do not take harmful drugs, including alcohol.
- ☐ I am responsible in my sexual behaviour.

Checklist

You should know the meanings of these words (check the Glossary and Index in SB9: BCP):

adhesion, amoeba, absorption, blood, blood vessels, cell membrane, cell respiration, circulation, cohesion, concentration gradient, deficiency, inherited, parasitic and functional diseases, diffusion, evaporation, exercise, heart, hypertonic, hypotonic, isotonic, leaves, mineral salts, osmosis, partially or selectively permeable membrane, phloem, pulse, preventive methods, root hair, root push, roots, solute, solution, solvent, stems, surface area to volume ratio, transpiration pull, vascular tissue, veins, xylem

Questions

1 Why do gases diffuse the quickest? Because
A they have most particles
B their particles move the fastest
C they are often invisible
D they have the least particles

2 Diffusion is the movement of particles from a region of high concentration to a region
A at the same concentration
B that is at a lower temperature
C of higher concentration
D of lower concentration

3 Osmosis describes the movement of
A any particles in a living thing
B water through a selective membrane
C water in a solution
D any particles in a non-living thing

4 Water would be most likely to move into living cells if they were placed in
A distilled water **B** seawater
C a sugar solution **D** a salt solution

5 Water would be most likely to move out of living cells if they were placed in
A a weak salt solution
B a strong salt solution
C distilled water
D tap water

6 To which of these is an amoeba most similar?
A phagocyte **B** lymphocyte
C red cell **D** root hair cell

7 What tissue is found in the centre of a root?
A phloem **B** xylem
C root hairs **D** root storage tissue

8 Which tissue takes water into the root?
A phloem **B** xylem
C root hairs **D** root storage tissue

9 Which forces are involved in water rising up the stem?
A root push **B** adhesion
C transpiration pull **D** all of the above

10 Which of these is NOT part of the veins in a stem?
A phloem **B** xylem
C storage tissue **D** cambium

11 In which tissue is food distributed in a flowering plant?
A phloem **B** xylem
C cambium **D** all of the above

12 Which gas(es) diffuse(s) from a leaf during the daytime?
A oxygen only
B carbon dioxide only
C oxygen and water vapour
D carbon dioxide and water vapour

13 In which of these conditions would you expect transpiration to be greatest?
A dull and calm **B** windy and cold
C dull and windy **D** windy and warm

14 Which blood cells contain haemoglobin?
A red cells **B** phagocytes
C lymphocytes **D** platelets

15 Which blood cells assist with clotting?
A red cells **B** phagocytes
C lymphocytes **D** platelets

16 White cells help protect us from disease because they
A make antibodies
B make antibiotics
C help to form clots
D all of the above

17 Which of these is not a blood group?
A group A **B** group B
C group C **D** group O

18 A person who gives blood is called a blood
A bank **B** donor
C transfusion **D** patient

19 Which blood vessel is smallest?
A capillary **B** artery
C aorta **D** vein

20 Which statement is correct? Only veins have
A muscular walls **B** valves
C inner walls **D** an outer cover

21 What produces the pulse? The
A entry of blood into the atria
B entry of blood into the ventricles
C relaxation of the heart muscles
D contraction of the heart muscles

22 De-oxygenated blood has a lot of
A food **B** pressure
C oxygen **D** carbon dioxide

23 Which blood vessel has de-oxygenated blood?
A pulmonary artery **B** pulmonary vein
C aorta **D** renal artery

24 Blood from the body is brought to the
A left atrium **B** left ventricle
C right atrium **D** right ventricle

25 Which vessel takes blood to the lungs?
A pulmonary artery **B** pulmonary vein
C vena cava **D** aorta

26 What do cells produce during respiration?
A carbon dioxide **B** water
C energy **D** all of the above

27 Which of these exercises would be least likely to develop strength?
A digging in the garden
B walking
C weightlifting
D rowing

28 Which of these would use up the most energy?
A walking upstairs **B** office work
C gardening **D** jogging

29 Which exercise would you recommend for someone recovering from a heart attack?
A nothing **B** running
C walking **D** playing football

30 Which vessel supplies the heart muscle?
A vena cava **B** aorta
C coronary artery **D** coronary vein

31 Which of these is a deficiency disease?
A haemophilia **B** malaria
C sickle cell anaemia **D** anaemia

32 Which kind of disease is sickle cell anaemia?
A deficiency **B** functional
C inherited **D** parasitic

33 Which of these is more likely if a person has high blood pressure?
A stroke **B** heart attack
C hardened arteries **D** all of the above

34 Which may cause furring up of the arteries?
A saturated fats **B** amino acids
C urea **D** all of the above

35 Which are important for healthy circulation?
A balanced diet **B** not smoking
C regular exercise **D** all of the above

Puzzle

Complete the crossword. The clues are given below.

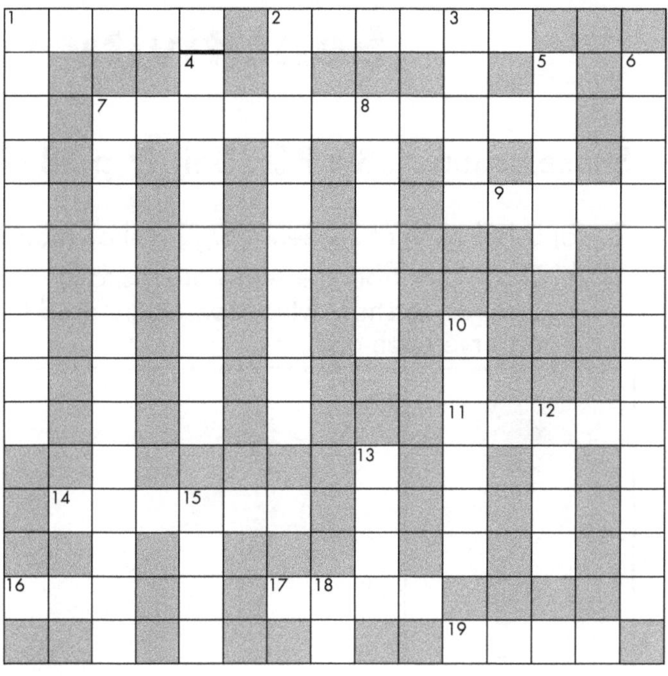

Across

1 Organ that pumps blood around the body (5)
2 A single-celled organism (6)
7 Transport system in animals, the .... system (11)
9 Carries blood back to the heart (4)
11 The main artery in the body (5)
14 Gas needed in respiration (6)
16 Blood cells that transport oxygen (3)
17 A blood disease caused by a virus (4)
19 The .... membrane is partially or selectively permeable (4)

Down

1 A .... solution is more concentrated than another one for a particular substance (10)
2 .... artery takes blood to the lungs (1,9)
3 Transport medium in animals (5)
4 Complex organisms need .... systems (9)
5 In plants, transport water and salts (5)
6 Loss of water from the leaves (13)
7 Gas produced during respiration (6,7)
8 Takes blood away from the heart (6)
10 Liquid part of the blood (6)
12 In plants, takes in water and salts (4)
13 Needed by all cells for respiration (4)
15 Capillaries .... 7 Down from the cells (4)
18 Gas in 14 Across is taken .... by the lungs (2)

Unit 17

Sensitivity and co-ordination

Sense organs (SB9: BCP, Unit 17 p 58–9, 73)

1 (a) Label each of the sense organs shown below.
(b) Draw lines from the sense organs to the pictures, to show which senses are used to observe each one.

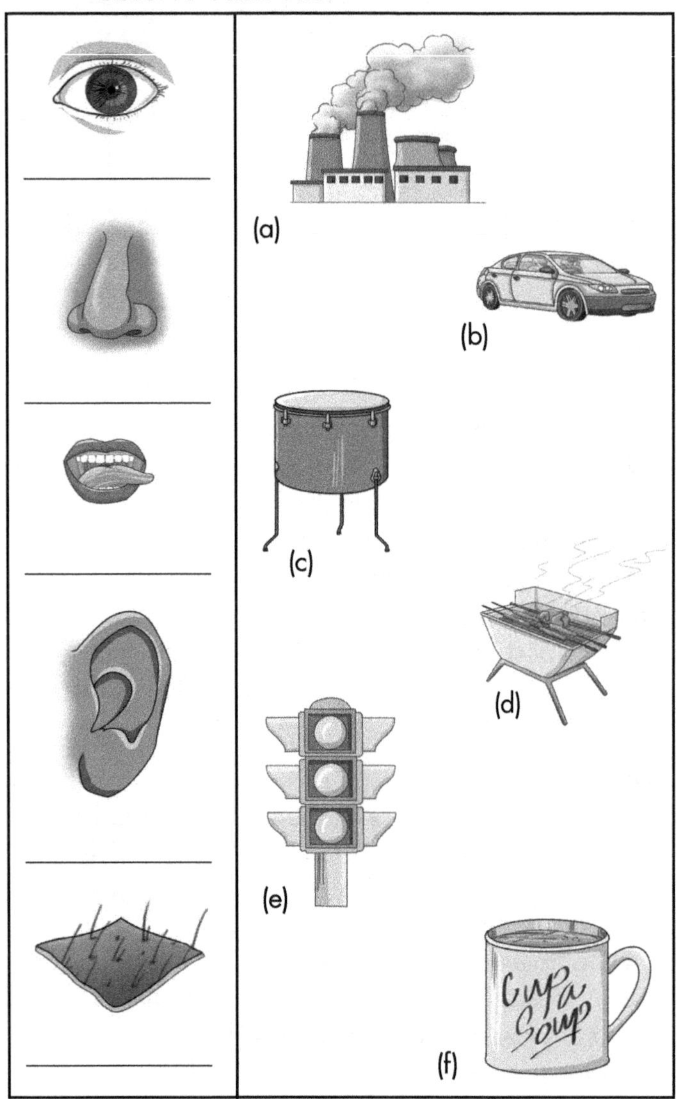

2 Complete the table for the senses in humans.

Stimuli					
Sense					
Sense organ					
Number					
Position on body					

3 The diagram shows a sensory (receptor cell) as found in the sense organs. Label the parts.

nerve endings in sense organ, impulse, nucleus, nerve fibre covered by a sheath, nerve endings in the spinal cord or brain, cytoplasm

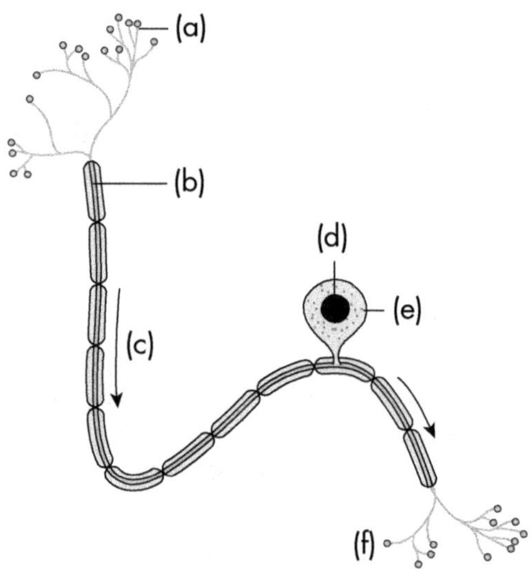

4 Fill in the words.

cord, brain, centres, sight, hearing, impulses, receptor

Impulses are sent from the sensory (a) .... cells to the spinal (b) .... in reflex actions. To appreciate touch, smell, (c) .... and (d) ...., (e) .... are sent to (f) .... in the (g) ....

Touch, taste and smell (SB9: BCP, Unit 17 p 59–62)

4 Label the parts of the section of the human skin.

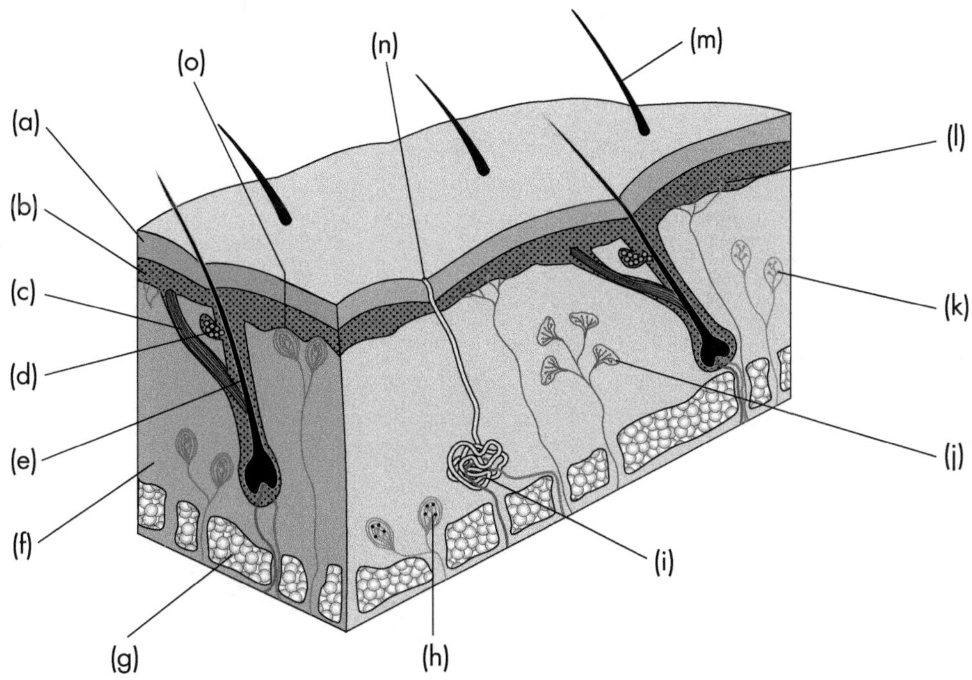

5 The number of touch nerve endings in a cm^2 of skin was found:

Back of hand: 14, fingertips: 100, arm: 24, lips: more than 100, forehead: 50.
Prepare a bar chart of this information.

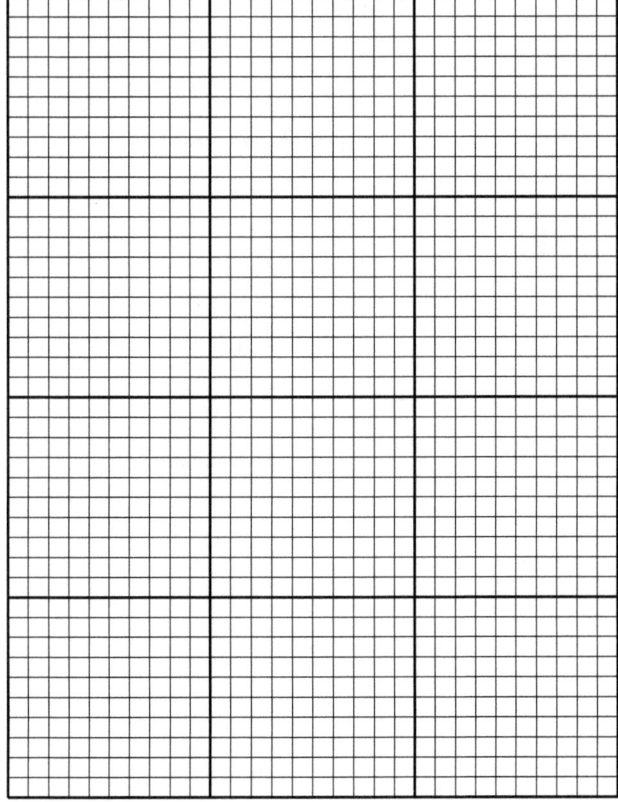

6 (a) Draw and label the structure of a taste bud and the sense organ for smell.
Describe how they are similar and different.

(b) If the tongue is only sensitive to four tastes, how do we appreciate the full flavour of our food?

....

....

....

....

Sense organs: Eye and seeing (SB9: BCP, Unit 17 p 63–7)

1 Label the parts of the longitudinal section of the human eye. Annotate each label (this means you should add a description of its function; what it does.)

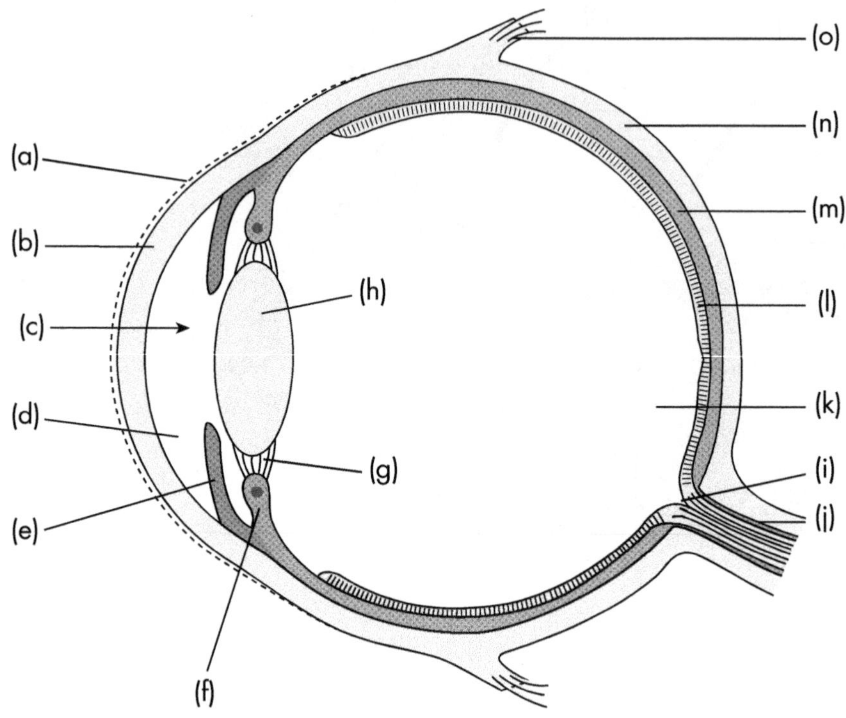

2 Within the outline below, draw your own simple diagram of the eye.

3 Add lines to show the light rays.

(a)

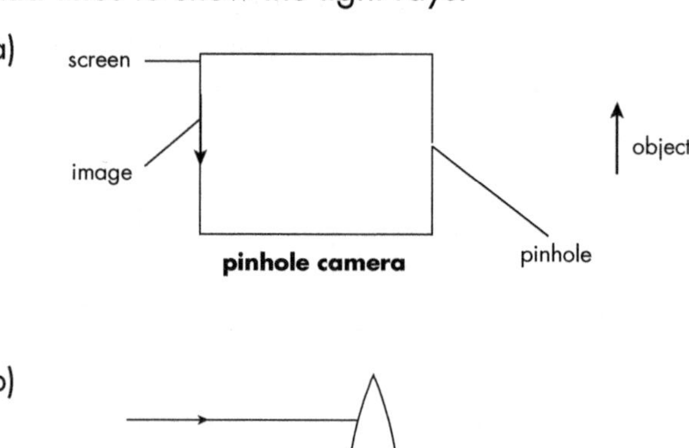

(b)

convex lens

(c)

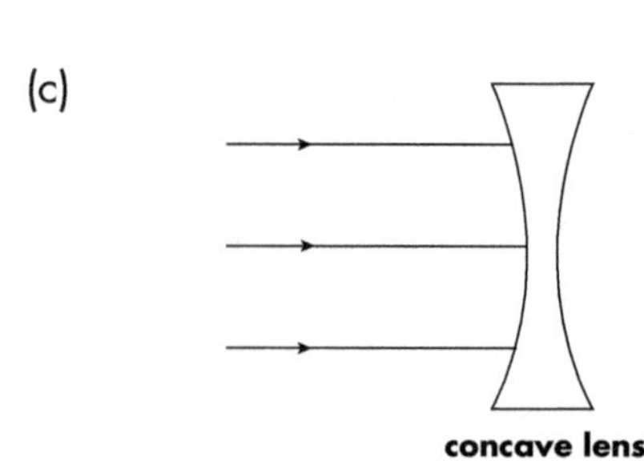

Sense organs: Ear and hearing (SB9: BCP, Unit 17 p 68–71)

1 Label the parts of the longitudinal section of the human ear. Annotate each label (this means you should add a description of its function; what it does.)

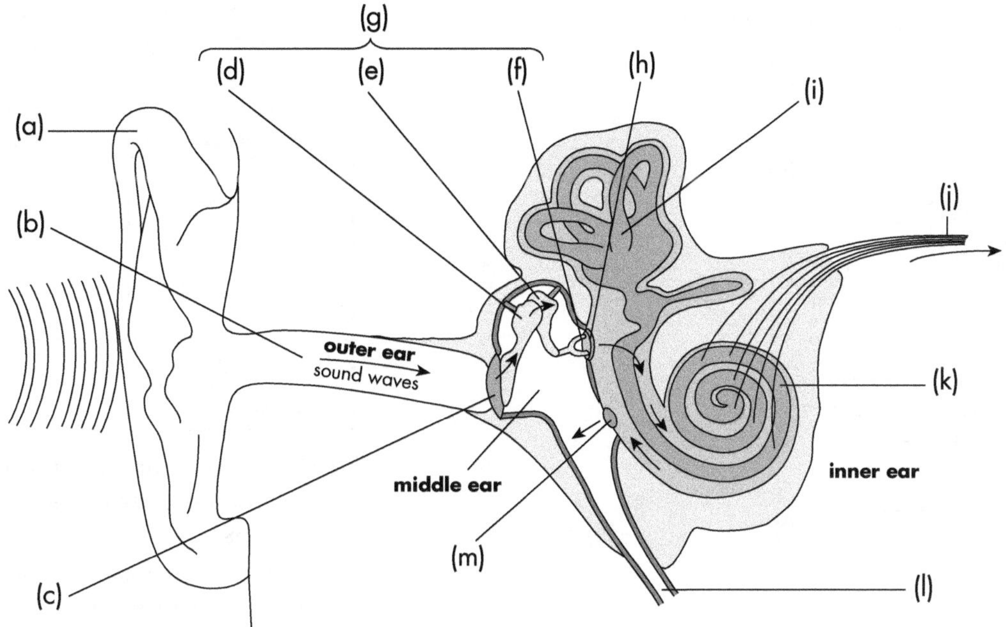

2 (a) What is a vibration?

(b) Write an account, beginning from the hitting of a drum, to our hearing the sound.

3 (a) What is amplitude?

(b) What is frequency?

4 The diagrams below show four waves.

(a) Which has the largest amplitude? ....

(b) Which has the highest frequency? ....

(c) Which was the quietest sound? ....

(d) Which sound has the lowest pitch? ....

(e) Which two have the same amplitude? ....
Which of them is higher pitched? ....

(f) Which two have the same frequency? ....
Which of them is louder? ....

A

B

C

D

Central nervous system (SB9: BCP, Unit 17 p 72–5)

1 Add the labels correctly to the diagram:

brain, spinal cord, skull, central nervous system. peripheral nervous system, vertebrae, nerves

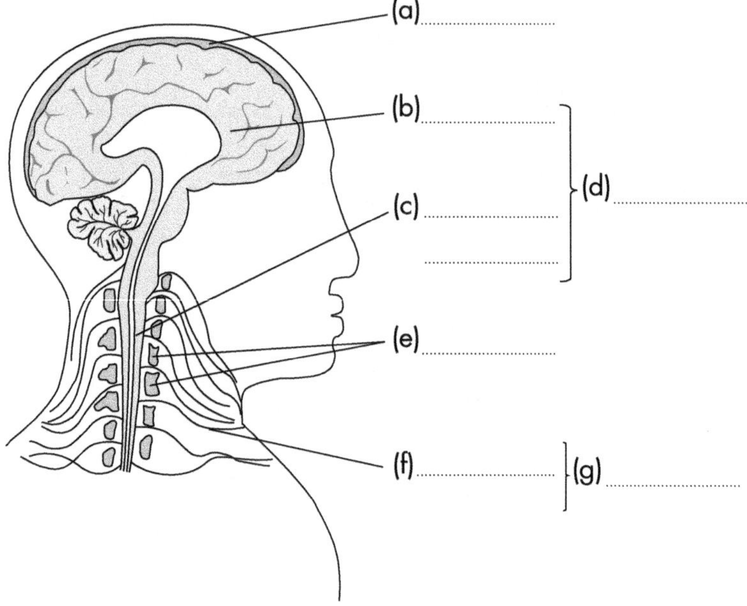

2 (a) Label the three parts of the brain. For each part add two functions.

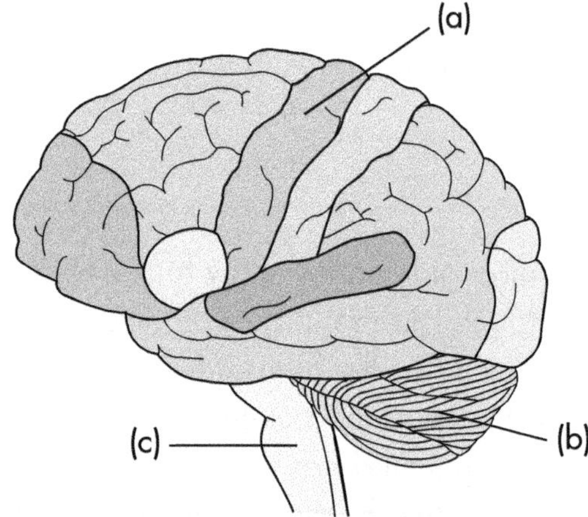

(b) Which part(s) of your brain did you use to answer this question? Explain your answer.

....

....

....

3 In SB9: BCP, p 74 Activity 17.19, you investigated reaction times.

(a) Enter the results of the reaction times of the five final measurements of yourself and your partner.

You will record the number on the ruler that is closest to the thumb. (Make sure everyone in class uses a 30 cm ruler the same way up, so that a large number shows a quick reaction time.)

Measurements	Me	My partner
1		
2		
3		
4		
5		
Average		

(b) Work out your average reaction times. Collect the average times for everyone in the class.

Put the times into a table, recording the number of students with the same reaction times.

(c) Make a bar chart of the results.

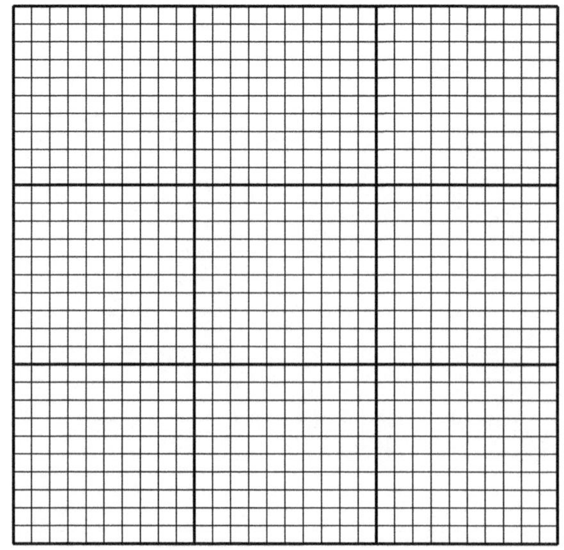

4 (a) Label the parts of a simple reflex arc. Add arrows to show the direction of nervous impulses.

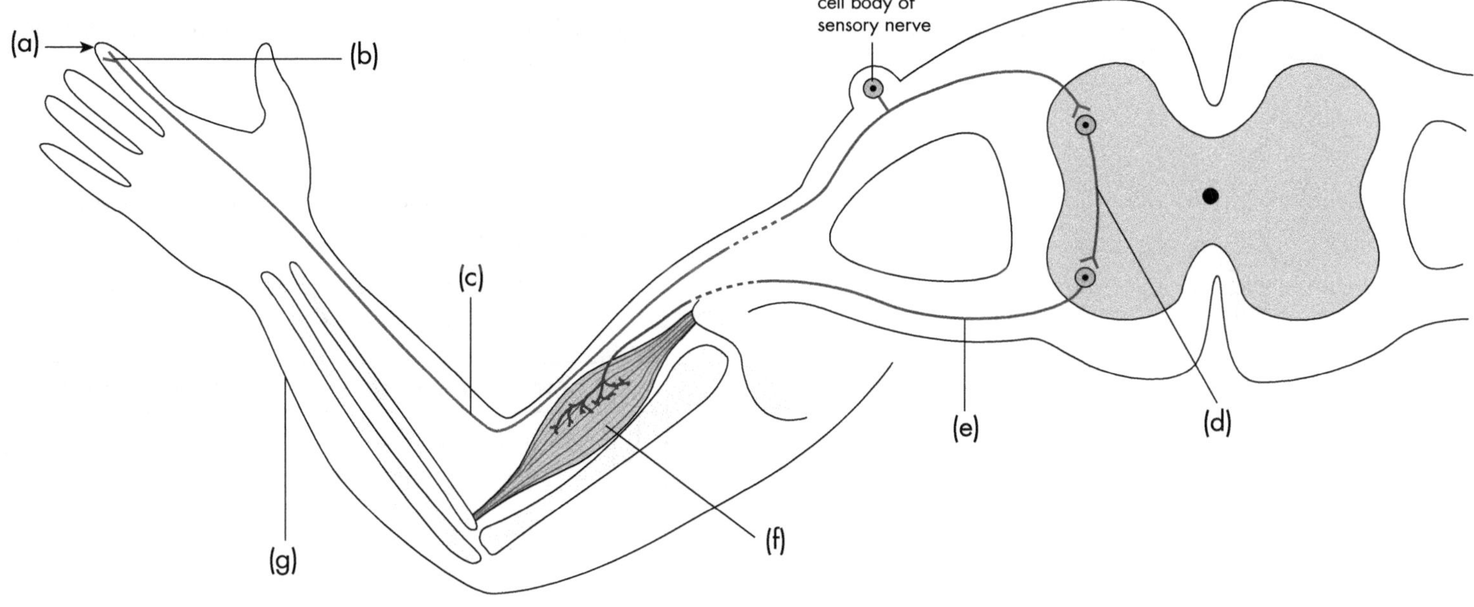

(b) In the table, describe the function of each part of a reflex arc.

Part	Function
Stimulus	Change in the environment
Receptor	
Sensory nerve fibre	
Relay fibre	
Motor nerve fibre	
Effector	
Response	

Projects

Each group makes one thing. Then connect the parts together to make a class display.

- Choose one of the sense organs you have studied. Use recycled materials to make a model. Label all the parts and include a description of how the organ works. (Include as many sense organs as possible in the class.)
- Make models of sensory nerve fibres, relay fibres and motor nerve fibres.
- Design and construct a model of a reflex arc, to include the spinal cord.
- Make a presentation to show how the central nervous system coordinates the body's response to the environment.

5 Compare involuntary and voluntary actions.

	Involuntary actions	Voluntary actions
Speed		
Purpose		
Control		
Examples		

Endocrine system (SB9: BCP, Unit 17 p 76–9)

1 Name the endocrine glands, and a hormone produced by each one.

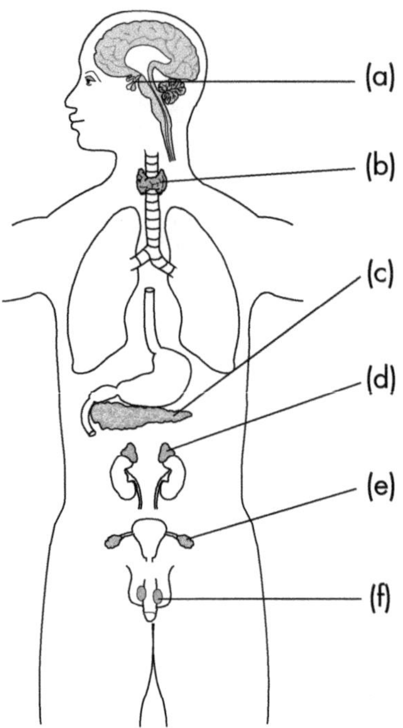

3 (a) Why are endocrine glands sometimes called ductless glands?

....

....

(b) Complete the table to compare the nervous and endocrine systems, on the following points:

1. How it works, 2. Means of transport, 3. Speed of action, 4. Importance, 5. Effect

	Nervous system	Endocrine system
1	Nervous impulses	
2		
3		
4		
5		

2 Complete the table to show the endocrine glands, their location, hormones produced, and how the body responds to normal and abnormal functioning of the gland.

Gland	Location	Hormones	Normal functioning	Abnormal functioning
Pituitary	Base of the cerebrum			

Checklist

You should know the meanings of these words (check the Glossary and Index in SB9: BCP):

amplitude, brain, central nervous system, convex and concave lenses, ear structure, effector, endocrine system, eye structure, frequency (Hz), gland, hearing, hormone, impulse, involuntary, light, long and short sight, loudness (dB), nerve, nose, pinhole camera, pupil reflex, reflex arc, receptor, respond, sense, sense organs, senses, sensory nerve endings, sight, skin structure, smell, sound, spinal cord, stimuli, taste buds, tongue, touch, voluntary

Questions

1 What is a stimulus?
A a change in conditions
B another name for a sense
C another name for a sense organ
D the change that occurs in an organism

2 Which sense organ responds to the greatest number of different kinds of stimuli?
A the skin **B** the eye
C the tongue **D** the ear

3 Which pair of senses is closely connected?
A smell and taste **B** sight and hearing
C smell and sight **D** taste and hearing

4 In bright light the pupil
A increases in size **B** decreases in size
C is not changed **D** changes colour

5 The inner layer of the eye is called the
A sclera **B** conjunctiva
C choroid **D** retina

6 When it shines onto the eye, the light first goes through the
A aqueous humour **B** conjunctiva
C pupil **D** lens

7 What energy change occurs in the rods and cones?
A chemical energy to light energy
B electrical energy to chemical energy
C light energy to chemical energy
D light energy to electrical energy

8 The image formed on the retina is
A exactly like the object
B upside-down and same size as the object
C upside-down and smaller than the object
D the right-side up and same size as the object

9 Here are a list of things: Bouncing a ball off a wall, bats finding their way, echo-sounding in the sea, using ultrasound, seeing yourself in a mirror.
What do they all have in common? They all use
A echoes **B** reflections
C light **D** sound

10 A concave lens
A is thickest in the middle
B can correct long sight only
C can correct short and long sight
D can correct short sight only

11 Sounds will travel most quickly in a
A vacuum **B** gas
C liquid **D** solid

12 The loudness of a sound depends on
A the wavelength **B** the frequency
C the amplitude **D** all of the above

13 Which of these would you find in the middle part of the ear?
A semi-circular canals
B the auditory nerve
C ear bones
D cochlea

14 Which of these is the odd-one-out?
A anvil **B** hammer
C stirrup **D** cochlea

15 Which of the following would be likely to make the loudest noise?
A a heavy lorry
B a bird singing
C an aeroplane taking off
D a person screaming

16 Which of these do NOT form part of the central nervous system?
A spinal cord
B sensory nerves
C cerebrum
D medulla oblongata

17 The impulses from the eye are interpreted in
A the cerebrum **B** the retina
C the optic nerve **D** the cerebellum

18 In a reflex arc, a stimulus acts on
A a motor nerve **B** the spinal cord
C an effector **D** a receptor

19 Which of these is an involuntary action?
A pupil reflex
B blinking
C moving the hand from a hot object
D all of the above

20 Which part controls voluntary actions?
A medulla oblongata
B cerebellum
C cerebrum
D hypothalamus

21 Which structure is called the master gland?
- **A** brain
- **B** cerebrum
- **C** pituitary
- **D** hypothalamus

22 Which gland needs a supply of iodine to make its hormone?
- **A** adrenal glands
- **B** thyroid
- **C** testes
- **D** pancreas

23 Diabetes is caused by a lack of which hormone?
- **A** insulin
- **B** growth hormone
- **C** thyroxine
- **D** adrenaline

24 The 'fight or flight' hormone is:
- **A** insulin
- **B** growth hormone
- **C** thyroxine
- **D** adrenaline

25 What is the pupil reflex?

....

....

(a) Why is the reaction in dim light important?

....

....

(b) Why is the reaction in bright light important?

....

....

(c) Explain if you think the cerebrum is involved in the reaction.

....

....

26 (a) Where are the rods and cones found?

....

(b) How do the cones differ from each other, and why is this important?

....

....

27 (a) Name a hormone and describe its action.

....

....

(b) How are problems with this hormone dealt with?

....

....

Puzzle

Complete the crossword. The clues are given below.

Across

1 They help us to see in black and white (4)
7 Place where 1 Across are found (6)
8 The distance up or down that a wave vibrates (9)
11 Focuses the light rays in the eye (4)
12 Light and sound are forms of .... (6)
13 Nerves that bring impulses in from the sense organs to the central nervous system (7)
15 A sensitive nerve ending in a sense organ (8)
17 Gland that makes testosterone in men (6)
19 An automatic response is a .... one (6)
20 Sense organs sensitive to sounds (4)
21 Part of CNS inside the vertebral column (6, 4)

Down

2 Changes in the environment (7)
3 The number of wavelengths per second (9)
4 An .... voluntary response does not require thought (2)
5 It senses four different flavours (5,3)
6 This will contract when it receives an impulse (6)
9 Light rays travelling into a concave lens will .... (7)
10 Sense organ sensitive to light (3)
13 Our sense of .... is the nose (5)
14 Two of the .... are touch and sight (6)
16 The line we draw to show how light travels (3)
18 Most sense organs are found on the .... (4)

Unit 18

Embryo development and birth control

Embryo development (SB9: BCP, Unit 18 p 84–6)

1 Label and annotate the parts of a sperm and an egg shown below.

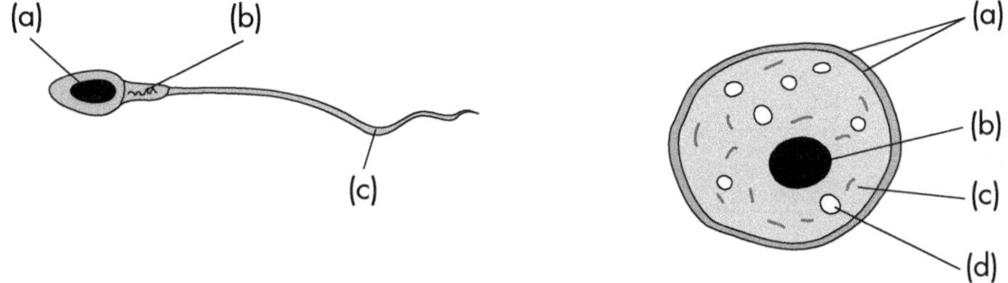

2 Draw diagrams in the spaces (a) and (b) to show how identical and non-identical twins are formed. List which sex(es) they might be, e.g. both boys.

In (c) draw two different ways in which triplets might be formed. Again, list what sexes they might be.

(a) Identical twins	(b) Non-identical twins	(c) Triplets

3 Label and annotate the diagram of the foetus in the uterus.

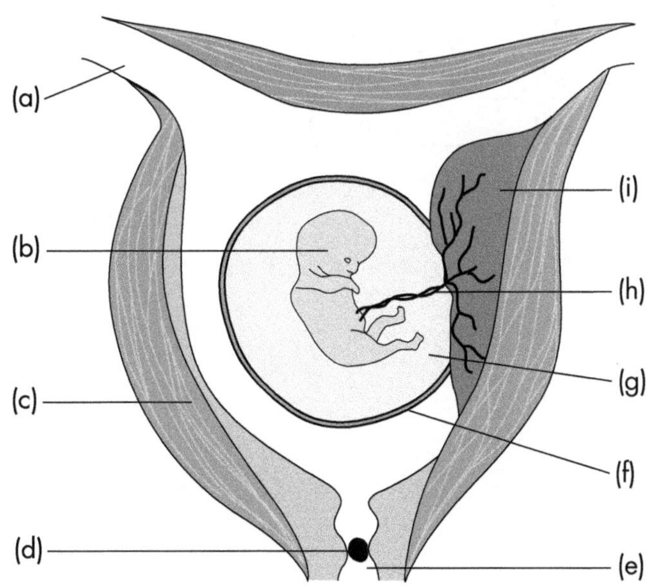

Embryo development (cont.) (SB9: BCP, Unit 18 p 86–90)

4 How are the needs of the developing foetus met, and those of a newborn baby?

Need	Developing foetus	Newborn baby
Oxygen		
Food		
Removal of carbon dioxide		
Removal of other wastes		
Steady temperature		
Protection from bumps		
Protection from diseases		

5 What happens if:

(a) an egg is fertilised? ……………………………

……………………………

(b) an egg is not fertilised? ……………………………

……………………………

6 Use these figures of the embryo and foetus to prepare a graph. When is growth greatest?

Weeks	Length	Weeks	Length
5	0.2 cm	16	16 cm
6	0.5 cm	20	25 cm
7	1.3 cm	24	33 cm
8	2.5 cm	28	37 cm
9	3.0 cm	32	41 cm
11	5.5 cm	36	46 cm
12	7.5 cm	40	51 cm

7 (a) What advice would you give on postnatal care?

……………………………

……………………………

……………………………

……………………………

……………………………

(b) Combine your points with those of others, to prepare a chart or class brochure on postnatal care.

8 (a) List the costs you identified for a baby during its first year of life.

(b) List the additional costs for schooling.

(c) Combine your findings with other class members, and prepare a chart on the cost of a child.

A healthy pregnancy (SB9: BCP, Unit 18 p 91–6)

1 Use the following guidelines to prepare a healthy diet for a day for a pregnant woman.

	Three meals	Three snacks
9 servings of bread, rice, pasta and other starches		
7 servings of fruits and vegetables		
3 servings of milk and dairy		
3 servings of meat, fish, eggs, nuts, beans		
Little fat and/or sugar		

2 Carry out research and complete the table to show the needs of a developing foetus and embryo.

Item	Function	Food source for mother
Protein		
Carbohydrate		
Fat		
Folic acid		
Calcium		
Iron		
Vitamin C		
Other vitamins		

A healthy pregnancy (cont.)

3 Complete the table to explain the possible dangers to the developing embryo and foetus of the things listed, and what can be done about them.

Possible dangers	How it might affect development	What should be done
Alcohol		
HIV		
Drugs, e.g. cocaine		
Rhesus factor		
German measles		
Smoking		

4 List some of the tests and advice that are given as part of pre-natal care, and their purpose.

Test/advice	Purpose

5 Write an essay on 'How to have a healthy pregnancy'.

....

....

....

....

....

....

....

....

....

....

....

....

Birth control methods (SB9: BCP, Unit 18 p 97–101)

1 What is meant by:

(a) Fertilisation? ....

....

(b) Implantation? ....

....

(c) Contraception? ....

....

2 Match each contraceptive method to the principle on which it works.

1. Rhythm method	(a) Sterilisation operations
2. Condom	(b) Chemical kills sperm
3. Spermicide	(c) Calculating 'safe' days
4. Diaphragm	(d) Barrier to sperm
5. Contraceptive pill	(e) Chemical stops ovulation
6. Abstinence	(f) Barrier to sperm
7. Cutting of tubes	(g) Stops implantation
8. IUD	(h) Not having sex

3 Work with a friend or in a small group. Discuss which group of people would be most likely to use each of the contraceptive methods above. List and share your reasons in class. There may be more than one answer for each group of people.

(i) Teenagers who have decided, for personal reasons, not to have sex until marriage. ....

(ii) A couple with three children who are certain they do not want any more children. ....

(iii) A working wife who wishes to delay motherhood for a few years. ....

(iv) A couple who have been told the wife runs a risk of becoming ill if she conceives. ....

(v) A couple with deep convictions that they do not want to use chemical or unnatural methods. ....

(vi) A newly qualified doctor who wants several partners before settling down. ....

(vii) A couple not wanting chemical methods and who want to delay parenthood, but would not mind if the wife became pregnant sooner than planned. ....

(viii) A teenage girl who wants to delay parenthood, but thinks she might have intercourse. ....

(ix) A woman who has been told not to use the pill, but who needs a reliable contraceptive. ....

(x) A teenage boy who wants to delay parenthood, but who thinks he might have intercourse. ....

4 Mark which of the following statements are True and which are False.

(a) A woman should not swim when she has her period. ....

(b) At birth, a baby girl already has many thousands of eggs in her ovaries. ....

(c) A hairy chest shows a man is more masculine. ....

(d) A man should feel his testicles each month to check for bumps or enlargements. ....

(e) A woman should feel her breasts each month to check for bumps. ....

(f) A woman doesn't need a contraceptive when she has her period. ....

(g) A man produces sperm throughout his life. ....

(h) A woman still needs a contraceptive when she is breast-feeding. ....

5 The following were ways of saying No to sex, that were given by High School students. Tick which of them you think could work for you.

- ☐ I said NO!
- ☐ I'm not sure you're the right person.
- ☐ I can't support a child.
- ☐ Not until we're married.
- ☐ With all these diseases, you must be mad!
- ☐ We won't respect each other later.
- ☐ Sex can be more trouble than it's worth.
- ☐ Have you thought about the consequences?
- ☐ I don't sleep around.
- ☐ I don't want our relationship to be just about sex.
- ☐ It would spoil our friendship.
- ☐ Not everyone is doing it – I'm not.

6 Work with a friend. Discuss which of these statements you agree with.

- ☐ You should only have sex when you're married.
- ☐ Boys can have sex, but girls shouldn't because they'll get a bad name.
- ☐ You should only have sex when you are really committed to each other.
- ☐ It doesn't matter when you have sex as long as you use a contraceptive.
- ☐ You should only have sex when you are able to deal with all the consequences.
- ☐ You should not think of sex as something separate from a loving relationship.

Birth control methods (cont.)

7 Information on the probability of pregnancy using each method of contraception has been collected from various sources. These are average figures using large numbers of couples. Individual figures may vary.

Contraceptive method	Probability of woman's pregnancy in one year		Advantages	Disadvantages
	Method perfect	In actual practice		
No contraceptive	85%	85%		
Withdrawal	9%	40%		
Rhythm method	10%	25%		
Spermicide alone	10%	25%		
Condom alone	10%	15%		
Condom with spermicide	2%	10%		
Diaphragm alone	6%	18%		
Diaphragm and spermicide	4%	15%		
Contraceptive pill	2%	3%		
Contraceptive pill & condom	0%	0.4%		
Hormone implant	0.2%	0.2%		
Depo-Provera	0.2%	0.2%		
IUD	0.6%	0.8%		
Tubal ligation	0.2%	0.4%		
Vasectomy	0.1%	0.15%		

(a) Why are the figures for using each method perfectly, and those found in practice, different?

(b) Complete the table to add the advantages and disadvantages for each method.

(c) Which method would you use, and why?

Checklist

You should know the meanings of these words (check the Glossary and Index in SB9: BCP):

abortion, alcohol, amniotic fluid and sac, artificial birth control, barrier, birth, conception, contraceptives, drug abuse, egg, embryo, fertilisation, foetus, genes, German measles, healthy diet, HIV/AIDS, hormonal, implantation, menstrual cycle, natural birth control, placenta, post-natal, pregnant, premature, prenatal, Rhesus factor, Siameses twins, smoking, sperm, spermicide, surgical, twins, umbilical cord, uterus, zygote

Questions

1 When is the period?
A days 1–5 of the menstrual cycle
B around day 14 of the cycle
C days 17–22 of the cycle
D days 21–28 of the cycle

2 How do chromosomes differ in boys and girls? Boys have
A more chromosomes than girls
B less chromosomes than girls
C a pair that are different: XY
D a pair that are the same: XX

3 Which statement is correct? Identical twins
A are never the same sex
B are always the same sex
C can be one boy and one girl
D can be any combination of sexes

4 Where does fertilisation usually occur? In the
A ovary **B** Fallopian tubes
C cervix **D** vagina

5 Which is the correct order of processes?
A fertilisation, implantation, cell division
B implantation, fertilisation, cell division
C fertilisation, cell division, implantation
D fertilisation, ovulation, implantation

6 Which things travel along the umbilical artery?
A carbon dioxide and other wastes
B oxygen and food to the foetus
C carbon dioxide and oxygen
D food and wastes from the foetus

7 Which of these things usually happens during the second stage of labour?
A the waters break
C the cervix is closed
B the baby settles head down in the uterus
D the afterbirth is passed out

8 Which of these words have similar meanings?
A embryo and foetus
B premature and stillbirth
C stillbirth and cot death
D miscarriage and abortion

9 A premature baby is one that is born
A too early **B** too late
C dead **D** with a twin

10 Which of these things change when a baby is born? How the baby
A gets food **B** gets oxygen
C removes wastes **D** all of the above

11 In vitro fertilisation is also called
A IUD **B** IVF
C HIV **D** none of the above

12 Which problem(s) might a teenage pregnancy cause?
A economic **B** educational
C physical **D** all of the above

13 Which of these things should NOT form a large part of a healthy diet for a pregnant woman?
A fruit **B** vegetables
C saturated fat **D** protein

14 Which of these foods should NOT be increased during pregnancy?
A green vegetables
B liver
C starchy foods
D fruit

15 Care given before birth is called
A postnatal care **B** prenatal care
C perinatal care **D** postbirth care

16 Which of these things might be caused by drinking too much alcohol during pregnancy?
A birth defects
B learning difficulties
C miscarriage
D all of the above

17 When is the greatest risk of damage to the foetus?
A 1st three months **B** 2nd three months
C 3rd three months **D** in the last month

18 Without treatment, what percentage of babies are infected with HIV from their mothers?
A all the babies
B 50% of babies
C 25% of babies
D 10% of babies

19 Which of these are effects of taking cocaine during pregnancy?
A miscarriage **B** brain damage
C death of mother **D** all of the above

20 If a woman is addicted to heroin, what should she do if she becomes pregnant?
A quit quickly **B** quit slowly
C use methadone **D** continue with heroin

21 Babies with limbs that were like flippers were caused by mothers taking
A cocaine **B** thalidomide
C heroine **D** all of the above

22 If a non-immune woman catches German measles, what chance will there be of damage to a foetus?
A 0% **B** 25%
C 50% **D** over 75%

23 There may be problems for the baby with the Rhesus factor if the
A woman is Rhesus –ve and the man is Rhesus +ve
B woman is Rhesus +ve and the man is Rhesus –ve
C both the woman and man are Rhesus +ve
D both the woman and man are Rhesus –ve

24 Natural birth control methods depend on avoiding intercourse on days
A during the period **B** around ovulation
C when non-fertile **D** all of the above

25 A woman with a regular 28-day menstrual cycle will ovulate
A exactly on the 14th day every month
B usually on the 14th day every month
C usually between the 12th and 16th days
D on the first day of the period

26 Which contraceptive method stops sperm entering the uterus?
A diaphragm
B an IUD
C contraceptive pill
D having sex on safe days

27 Which of these is NOT a barrier method?
A male condom **B** female condom
C spermicide cream **D** diaphragm

28 Which of these methods does NOT use chemicals?
A contraceptive pill **B** spermicide cream
C rhythm method **D** Depo-Provera

29 The 'morning-after' pill should be taken within which time after unprotected sexual intercourse?
A 3 days **B** 5 days
C a week **D** two weeks

30 How do IUDs work? By
A the making of mucus to block the cervix
B thinning the uterus wall to stop implantation
C using chemicals
D all of the above

31 What is cut during a tubal ligation?
A vas deferens **B** Fallopian tubes
C uterus **D** vagina

Puzzle

Complete the crossword. The clues are given below.

Across

3 Device or chemical used to stop pregnancy (13)
9 Device put into the uterus for birth control (3)
10 Pre .... is growth inside the uterus (5)
11 The female gamete (3)
14 Number of babies in 4 Down (3)
16 Do not drink this in pregnancy (backwards) (7)
17 Time when the foetus leaves the uterus (5)
18 Name given to the embryo after the 8th week (6)
19 Substances that can be dangerous in pregnancy (backwards) (5)
21 Blood returns to foetus in umbilical .... (4)
22 Joins with egg in fertilisation (5)

Down

1 A barrier contraceptive (6)
2 Process that forms the zygote (13)
4 Two babies born close together (5)
5 Fluid that surrounds the foetus (8)
6 Name of male sterilisation (9)
7 A healthy .... is important in pregnancy (4)
8 Place in the uterus where the foetus gets what it needs and gets rid of wastes (8)
12 What happens in the uterus (6)
13 Dangerous during pregnancy (7)
15 Formed from zygote by cell division (7)
20 Dangerous infection caused by a virus (3)

Unit 19

Chemical bonding, reactions and equations

Chemical bonding: Groups of elements (SB9: BCP, Unit 19 p 112–16)

1 (a) Add the names of each element to the table.

Name	Symbol	Atomic number	Electrons in shells			
			1st	2nd	3rd	4th
	H	1	1			
	He	2	2			
	Li	3	2	1		
	Be	4	2	2		
	B	5	2	3		
	C	6	2	4		
	N	7	2	5		
	O	8	2	6		
	F	9	2	7		
	Ne	10	2	8		
	Na	11	2	8	1	
	Mg	12	2	8	2	
	Al	13	2	8	3	
	Si	14	2	8	4	
	P	15	2	8	5	
	S	16	2	8	6	
	Cl	17	2	8	7	
	Ar	18	2	8	8	
	K	19	2	8	8	1
	Ca	20	2	8	8	2

(b) Pick out and name the Group 0: Noble gases (with complete outer shells of 2 or 8 electrons).

(c) Pick out and name the Group 1: The alkali metals (with 1 electron in their outer shells).

(d) Pick out and name the Group 2: Alkaline earth metals (with 2 electrons in their outer shells).

(e) Pick out and name the Group 6: The oxygen group (with 6 electrons in their outer shells).

(f) Pick out and name the Group 7: The halogens (with 7 electrons in their outer shells).

2 The atoms of metals form ions by losing electrons, to make positive ions.
Show by diagrams of the outer shell how:

(a) a Group 1 metal forms ions.

(b) a Group 2 metal forms ions.

3 The atoms of non-metals form ions by gaining electrons, to make negative ions.
Show by diagrams of the outer shell how:

(a) a Group 6 non-metal forms ions.

(b) a Group 7 non-metal forms ions.

4 Look at the ions you have drawn.

(a) How many electrons are there in the outer shell of positive ions made from Groups 1 and 2?

....

(b) How many electrons are there in the outer shell of negative ions made from Groups 6 and 7?

....

Chemical bonding: Ionic bonding (SB9: BCP, Unit 19 p 117–18, 120–2)

1 Use the words to fill-in the spaces:

outer, positively, negatively, few, gain, lose, lot, electrons, shell, ions

Metals usually have only a (a) .... electrons in their (b) .... shell. In chemical reactions, metals usually (c) .... electrons to become (d) .... charged (e) .... Non-metals usually have a (f) .... of (g) .... in their outer (h) .... Non-metals usually gain (i) .... to become (j) .... charged.

2 (a) Choose a Group 1 metal ion and show how it will form an ionic compound with a Group 6 non-metal ion.

(b) Choose a Group 2 metal ion and show how it will form an ionic compound with a Group 7 non-metal ion.

3 Complete the table.

Metal/ non-metal	Group	Number electrons in outer shell	Combining power
	1		
	2		
	6		
	7		

4 Use the words to fill-in the spaces:

ion(s), negative, charges, attract, ionic, two

An (a) .... compound is formed when positive and (b) .... ions (c) .... each other. The numbers of (d) .... will depend on their (e) .... For example, one magnesium (f) .... will attract (g) .... chloride ions.

5 The table shows the combining power of elements and, in brackets, of radicals.

Combining power	Examples
1+	H, Li, Na, K, (NH_4)
2+	Be, Mg, Ca, Cu, Zn
3+	Al
3–	N, P
2–	O, S, (CO_3), (SO_4)
1–	F, Cl, (NO_3), (OH), (HCO_3)

Write the chemical formulae for:

(a) Lithium chloride ....

(b) Beryllium suphate ....

(c) Aluminium chloride ....

(d) Calcium sulphate ....

(e) Potassium nitrate ....

(f) Potassium sulphate ....

(g) Zinc nitrate ....

(h) Copper hydroxide ....

(i) Ammonium hydrogencarbonate

....

(j) Ammonium sulphate ....

(k) Ammonium carbonate ....

(l) Magnesium hydrogencarbonate

....

(m) Aluminium sulphate ....

(n) Zinc chloride ....

(o) Aluminium hydroxide ....

(p) Sodium carbonate ....

Chemical bonding: Covalent bonding (SB9: BCP, Unit 19 p 119–20, 122)

1 Use the words to fill in the spaces:
sharing, electrons, combining, non-metals, outer, 8, gases

Covalent compounds are formed by
(a) .... electrons to fill the
(b) .... shell with 2 or (c) ....
electrons. They form between different
(d) ...., and in (e) ....,
such as chlorine. The number of (f) ....
shared is determined by the (g) ....
power and number of (h) .... in the
(i) .... shell of the elements.

2 (a) Complete the table for the combining power of common non-metals.

Non-metals	Number electrons in outer shell	Combining power
C, Si	4	
N, P	5	
O, S	6	
F, Cl	7	

(b) Add the names and arrangement of electrons in the atoms of these non-metals.

Name	Symbol	Atomic number	Electrons in shells			
			1st	2nd	3rd	4th
	C	6				
	N	7				
	O	8				
	F	9				
	Si	14				
	P	15				
	S	16				
	Cl	17				

(c) How are carbon and silicon
(i) similar? ....
(ii) different? ....

(d) How are oxygen and sulphur
(i) similar? ....
(ii) different? ....

3 Common covalent compounds are often gases
- formed from one non-metal element, e.g. chlorine, oxygen, nitrogen, fluorine; or
- from two non-metal elements, e.g. ammonia, carbon dioxide, sulphur dioxide, water vapour.

The outer shell of hydrogen, carbon, nitrogen, oxygen and chlorine are shown below.

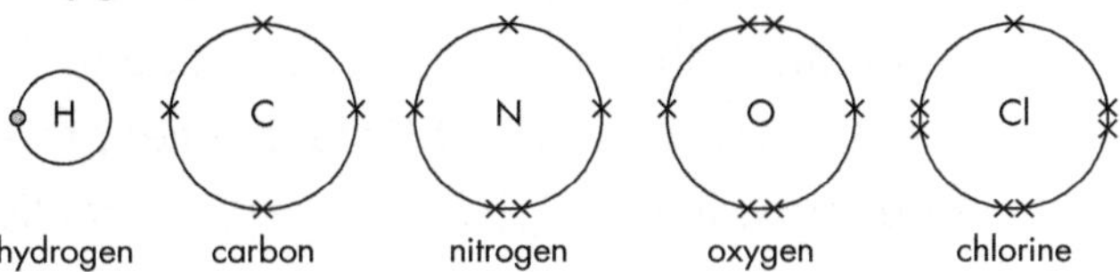

Draw the structures of the following covalent compounds. The first one is done for you.
(a) ammonia (NH_3), (b) oxygen gas (O_2),
(c) chlorine gas (Cl_2),
(d) hydrogen chloride (HCl),
(e) water (H_2O), (f) carbon dioxide (CO_2),
(g) methane (CH_4)

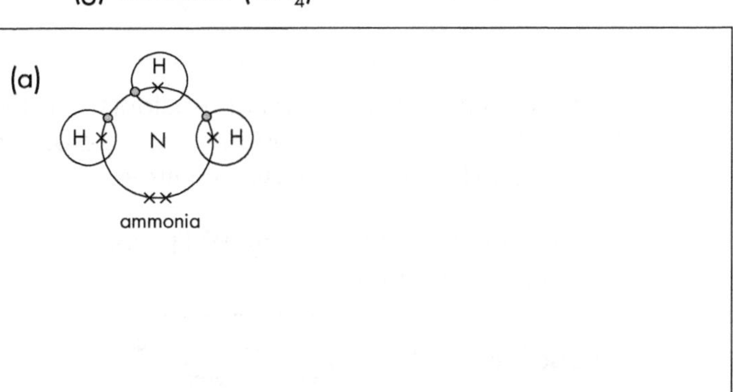

Chemical reactions: Oxidation (SB9: BCP, Unit 19 p 123–6)

1 Use the words to fill-in the spaces:
products, reactants, exothermic, reaction, mass

In a chemical (a) .... the (b) .... interact to form (c) .... According to the law of conservation of (d) ...., the numbers of atoms in the (e) .... equals those of the (f) .... If there is a net production of energy, it is an (g) .... reaction.

2 See SB9: BCP p 123, Activity 19.10. Record your results in the table below.

Mass before mixing	Mass after mixing
Reactants:	Products:
10 cm^3 lead nitrate .... g 10 cm^3 potassium iodide .... g	20 cm^3 of products .... g

You should find that the mass of reactants = mass of the products. Equation: Lead nitrate + potassium iodide = lead iodide + potassium nitrate.

3 See SB9: BCP p 124, Activity 19.11. Record your results in the table below.

Reaction	What happens? Exo- or endothermic?
Sodium + water	
Potassium nitrate + water	
Ammonium chloride + water	

4 See SB9: BCP p 124, Activity 19.12. Record your results in the table below.

Reaction	What happens? Exo- or endothermic?
Sodium chloride + water	
Calcium oxide + water	

5 SB9: BCP p 125, Activity 19.13. Record your results in the table below.

Activity	Result
Heat magnesium in air	
Test the result with damp litmus paper	
Magnesium with water	
Magnesium with dilute hydrochloric acid	
Test the result with a lighted splint	

6 See SB9: BCP p 126, Activity 19.14. Record your results in the table below.

Activity	Result
Heat sulphur in air	
Test the result with damp litmus paper	
Sulphur with water	
Sulphur with dilute hydrochloric acid	
Test the result with a lighted splint	

Synthesis and decomposition (SB9: BCP, Unit 19 p 127–8)

1 Use the words to fill-in the spaces:
simple, elements, combination, larger, exothermic

Synthesis reactions are the (a) .... of (b) .... substances to make (c) .... ones. It is often (d) .... that combine, and the reaction is (e) ....

2 Tables for synthesis reaction of iron and sulphur (see SB9: BCP, p 127, Activity 19.15).

(a) Properties of the reactants: iron and sulphur.

Test	Result
1 Magnet	
2 Water	
3 Acid	
4 Appearance	

(b) Properties of the product: iron sulphide.

Test	Result
5 Magnet	
6 Water	
7 Acid	
8 Appearance	

Write the word equation:

....

Why is it a chemical and not a physical change?

....

3 The following are also exothermic, synthesis reactions. Write word and chemical equations.

(a) Sodium + chlorine =

(b) Hydrogen + oxygen =

(c) Carbon + oxygen =

4 Use the words to fill-in the spaces:
energy, simpler, breaks, endothermic, single, electricity

In a decomposition reaction a (a) .... compound (b) .... down into This part is (c) .... substances. These reactions usually require (d) .... such as heat or (e) .... and so are (f) ....

5 Table for thermal decomposition reaction (see SB9: BCP, p 128, Activity 19.16).

(a) Decomposition of copper carbonate.

Test	Result
1 Colour of $CuCO_3$	
2 Heating	
3 Testing of gas	
4 Final colour of CuO	

Word equation:

(b) Decomposition of calcium carbonate.

Test	Result
1 Colour of $CaCO_3$	
2 Heating	
3 Testing of gas	
4 Final colour of CaO	

Word equation:

Displacement and reactions of metals (SB9: BCP, Unit 19 p 129–30)

1 Use the words to fill in the spaces:

compound, metal, displacement, less, displace, swap

Displacement reactions are when an element (often a (a) ....) will (b) .... a (c) .... reactive one from its (d) .... In a double (e) .... reaction the compounds (f) .... partners.

2 Table for displacement reaction (see SB9: BCP p 129, Activity 19.17).

Magnesium added to copper sulphate solution.

Before	After
Colour of magnesium:	Colour of copper:
Colour of copper sulphate solution:	Colour of magnesium sulphate solution:

Write the word equation:

....

Write the balanced chemical equation:

....

3 Table for double displacement reaction (see SB9: BCP p 129, Activity 19.18). Sodium sulphate solution added to barium chloride solution.

Before	After
Colour of zinc sulphate solution:	Colour of zinc chloride solution:
Colour of barium chloride solution:	Colour of barium sulphate solution:

Write the word equations and chemical equations:

(a) Zinc sulphate + barium chloride →

(b) Sodium sulphate + barium chloride →

4 Use the words to fill-in the spaces:

reactivity, metals, copper, reactive, magnesium

The action of (a) .... depends on how (b) .... they are. We can make a (c) .... series for the (d) ...., e.g. (e) .... is more (f) .... than (g) ....

5 Look at SB9: BCP p 130, Activities 19.19 and 19.20 where you did activities with calcium, iron and magnesium. Based on what you found, which is:

(a) the most reactive of the three?

(b) the least reactive of the three?

6 We can list the metals in a reactivity series as shown in the table. Add the symbols for the metals.

Metal	Symbol	Reactivity
Potassium		Most reactive
Sodium		
Calcium		
Magnesium		
Aluminium		
Zinc		
Iron		
Copper		Least reactive

Discuss these questions in small groups. Remember:

- A very reactive metal may react explosively with other chemicals and may be dangerous.
- A very unreactive metal will not react readily with other chemicals and will not corrode easily.

(a) Why are potassium and sodium stored under oil? Why have we not done experiments with potassium?

(b) If you had samples of calcium and magnesium, which test could you use to find which was more reactive? What would be the result?

(c) Why do you think zinc and aluminium are used for roofing materials?

(d) Which metal would be best for water pipes? Why would you use this and not the other metals?

(e) Why is acid rain a problem?

Balancing chemical equations (SB9: BCP, Unit 19 p 131–5)

1 Enter the symbols of elements, and radicals (in brackets), with the correct combining powers.

H, K, Cu, Zn, O, Li, F, Al, Na, Mg, Ca, N, S, Be, Cl, (CO_3), (HCO_3), (NO_3), (SO_4), (OH), (NH_4)

3–	2–	1–	1+	2+	3+

2 Writing chemical formulae. For each rule on the left, give another example on the right.

Rules for writing chemical formulae	Examples
(a) If the combining power of metal and non-metal is 1, then there are equal numbers in the compound	potassium fluoride: KF
(b) If the combining power of metal and non-metal is 2, then there are equal numbers in the compound	magnesium oxide: MgO
(c) If the combining power of metal is 2, and of non-metal is 1, we use a subscript	magnesium chloride: $MgCl_2$
(d) If the combining power of metal is 1, and of non-metal is 2, we use a subscript	lithium oxide: Li_2O
(e) If the combining power of metal and radical is 1, then there are equal numbers in the compound	sodium nitrate: $NaNO_3$
(f) If the combining power of metal and radical is 2, then there are equal numbers in the compound	copper sulphate: $CuSO_4$
(g) If the combining power of metal is 2, and of radical is 1, we use a subscript with brackets	zinc hydroxide: $Zn(OH)_2$
(h) If the combining power of metal is 1, and of radical is 2, we use a subscript	potassium carbonate: K_2CO_3
(i) In a chemical reaction, hydrogen loses an electron to make an ion with 1 positive charge	sulphuric acid: H_2SO_4
(j) In a chemical reaction, the ammonium ion has 1 positive charge	ammonium chloride: NH_4Cl

For each of the following chemicals, add the letter for the rule used in writing its formula.

1 zinc sulphate: $ZnSO_4$ ....
2 lithium chloride: LiCl ....
3 zinc chloride: $ZnCl_2$ ....
4 calcium oxide: CaO ....
5 copper nitrate: $Cu(NO_3)_2$ ....
6 nitric acid: HNO_3 ....
7 ammonium sulphate: $(NH_4)_2SO_4$ ....
8 sodium sulphide: Na_2S ....
9 sodium hydrogencarbonate: $NaHCO_3$ ....
10 potassium sulphate: K_2SO_4 ....

3 Write the chemical formulae of these compounds.

(a) aluminium chloride	(c) ammonia gas
(b) aluminium nitrate	(d) aluminium sulphate

Balancing chemical equations (cont.)

4 Complete the word equations, add chemical formulae and balance the equations.

(a) magnesium + chlorine →
(b) copper oxide + sulphuric acid →
(c) sodium carbonate + calcium chloride →
(d) sodium + water →
(e) calcium hydroxide + nitric acid →
(f) barium chloride + potassium sulphate →
(g) hydrogen + oxygen →

5 In ionic equations, we identify the ions that produce a new compound, such as a precipitate; we ignore the 'spectator' ions that are present in both the reactants and the products.
We use (aq) for in water and (s) for a solid precipitate.

(a)	barium chloride	+	sodium sulphate	→	barium sulphate	+	sodium chloride
	$BaCl_2$	+	Na_2SO_4	→	$BaSO_4$	+	$2NaCl$
Ions	$Ba^{2+}(aq) + 2Cl^-(aq)$	+	$2Na^+(aq) + SO_4^{2-}(aq)$	→	$BaSO_4(s)$	+	$2Na^+(aq) + 2Cl^-(aq)$

Which are the spectator ions? (present in both reactants and products): ....

Which ions combine to make the solid precipitate? ....

We can write the ionic equation as:

$Ba^{2+}(aq) + SO_4^{2-}(aq) = BaSO_4(s)$ (check the positive and negative charges are equal; yes, 2+ and 2-)

Write ionic equations for these reactions.

(b)	iron nitrate	+	sodium hydroxide	→	iron hydroxide	+	sodium nitrate
	$Fe(NO_3)_3(aq)$	+	$3NaOH(aq)$	→	$Fe(OH)_3(s)$	+	$3NaNO_3(aq)$
(c)	copper chloride	+	sodium hydroxide	→	copper hydroxide	+	sodium chloride
	$CuCl_2(aq)$	+	$2NaOH(aq)$	→	$Cu(OH)_2(s)$	+	$2NaCl(aq)$

Checklist

You should know the meanings of these words (check the Glossary and Index in SB9: BCP):

atom, atomic number, balancing equations, charge, chemical change, chemical equation, formulae, combining power, compound, covalent bonding, decomposition, displacement, endothermic, electron, element, exothermic, group, ion, ionic bonding, law of conservation of mass, mass number, metal, mixture, molecule, negative charge, non-metal, nucleus, neutron, orbit, oxidation, periodic table, physical change, positive charge, products, proton, radicals, reactants, reactivity series, sharing electrons, shell, symbol, synthesis, valency, word equation

Questions

1 Elements can made of
A atoms only
B molecules only
C atoms or molecules
D atoms or compounds

2 Hydrogen gas is
A an element **B** a mixture
C a compound **D** an atom

3 The nucleus of an atom contains
A protons only **B** protons and neutrons
C electrons only **D** protons and electrons

4 In an atom the numbers of
A protons and neutrons are the same
B neutrons and electrons are the same
C protons and electrons are the same
D protons and neutrons are never the same

5 The electrons have a
A positive charge and are found in the nucleus
B negative charge and are found in the nucleus
C positive charge and orbit the nucleus in shells
D negative charge and orbit the nucleus in shells

6 The atomic number is the same as the number of
A neutrons **B** neutrons plus protons
C protons **D** neutrons plus electrons

7 An atom has 9 protons. There will be
A 9 neutrons **B** 9 electrons
C 18 neutrons **D** 18 electrons

8 The mass number is 27, and atomic number is 13. How many electrons will there be in the atom?
A 13 **B** 14 **C** 27 **D** 13 or 14

9 How many electrons are in the outside shell of halogens?
A 0 **B** 1 **C** 2 **D** 7

10 When a halogen becomes an ion, how many electrons are in its outer shell?
A 1 **B** 2 **C** 7 **D** 8

11 What kind of ion does a halogen make? Ions with
A one positive charge **B** two positive charges
C one negative charge **D** two negative charges

12 Which of these is a metal?
A sodium **B** chlorine
C oxygen **D** argon

13 How many electrons do metal atoms have in their outside shells?
A 0 **B** 1 **C** 2 **D** 1–3

14 What is the combining power of sodium?
A 0 **B** 1 **C** 2 **D** 1–3

15 What is the chemical formula of common salt?
A $NaCl$ **B** Na_2Cl
C $NaCl_2$ **D** $NaHCl$

16 How many atoms of oxygen in $Ca(NO_3)_2$?
A 1 **B** 2 **C** 3 **D** 6

17 How many atoms of oxygen in $2Al(NO_3)_3$?
A 6 **B** 9 **C** 18 **D** 20

18 What is the NO_3 group called?
A a metal **B** a non-metal
C a radical **D** a sulphate

19 Combining power of copper is 2, and of chlorine is 1. What is the formula of copper chloride?
A $CuCl$ **B** Cu_2Cl
C $CuCl_2$ **D** $CuHCl$

20 What is the compound of iron and sulphur called?
A iron oxide **B** sulphur oxide
C iron chloride **D** iron sulphide

21 What is formed when magnesium is burned in air?
A oxygen **B** a basic oxide
C a salt **D** an acidic oxide

22 The heating of which of these is likely to produce carbon dioxide?
A copper oxide
B copper carbonate
C sodium chloride
D sodium sulphate

23 Carbon dioxide bubbled into limewater is an example of which kind of change?
A chemical
B physical
C chemical and physical
D sometimes chemical and sometimes physical

24 Which reaction is likely to produce hydrogen?
A acid + base **B** acid + basic oxide
C acid + metal **D** acid + alkali

25 Hydrogen gas does what with a burning splint?
A puts it out **B** has no effect
C makes it burn **D** makes a 'pop'

26 Give an example of each of the following:

(a) An element ....

(b) A compound ....

(c) A metal ....

(d) A non-metal ....

27 (a) What are atomic number and mass number?

....

....

....

(b) When ions are formed, which part(s) of the atom change in number? ....

28 (a) How are Group 1 and Group 2 elements

(i) similar? ....

(ii) different? ....

29 (a) How are Group 6 and Group 7 elements

(i) similar? ....

(ii) different? ....

Puzzle

Complete the crossword. The clues are given in the next column.

		1			2					3		4		
5				6			7							
												8		
						9			10					11
	12											13		
14						15					16			
17														
						18				19		20		21
22		23												
					24			25						
												26		
27			28									29		
							30			31				
	32				33				34			35	36	

Across

4 Gas formed from burning sulphur (3)
5 Particle containing two or more atoms (8)
8 Chemical symbol for beryllium (2)
9 Chemical symbol for iron (2)
10 Is made in the reaction between an acid and a metal (backwards) (4)
12 Loses electron(s) when forming ions (5)
13 Turns limewater milky (3)
15 Made of a nucleus and electrons (4)
16 Chemical symbol for a noble gas (2)
17 Are electrons in or out of the nucleus? (3)
18 Compound formed by transfer of electrons (5)
20 Abbreviation for a solid made in a reaction (3)
22 Charged particle formed from an atom (3)
24 The .... of reactants and products is the same (4)
27 Related to the combining power of elements (7)
29 Chemical symbol for the hydroxide ion (2)
31 Negatively charged ions are formed from .... metals (3)
32 A group of atoms that stays together in chemical reactions and has an overall charge (7)
34 Chemical symbol for a noble gas (2)
35 A .... placement reaction: a more reactive metal pushes out another one from its compound (3)

Down

1 Simplest chemical existing on its own (7)
2 Chemical symbol for copper (2)
3 Orbit in which electrons are found (5)
4 Small number in chemical formulae to show how many of particular atoms are present (9)
5 Chemical symbol for a Group 2 metal (2)
6 Compound formed by sharing electrons (8)
7 Negative particles that orbit the nucleus (9)
11 Chemical formula for water (3)
14 Charge on ions formed in 12 Across (8)
19 Elements .... in synthesis reactions (7)
21 For finding out: 13 Across is an example (4)
23 Chemical symbol for a Group 1 metal (2)
25 In a .... thesis reaction simple substances combine (3)
26 Forms to hold compounds together (4)
28 Energy is taken in during an .... thermic reaction (4)
30 Chemical formula for chlorine gas (3)
33 Chemical symbol for a Group 2 metal (2)
34 Chemical formula for hydrogen gas (2)
36 Are neutrons in or out of the nucleus? (2)

Unit 20

Acids and alkalis

Acids, alkalis and indicators (SB9: BCP, Unit 20 p 140–3)

1 See SB9: BCP p 140–2, Activities 20.1–20.5. Record all the results of your tests in the table below. You could also make a class chart of results.

Name of substance	Appearance	Activity with water	List chemicals present	pH: acid or base	Use

2 See SB9: BCP p 143, Activity 20.7.

(a) What colour was your extract when you made it?

....

(b) Why were you able to make an extract?

....

(c) Name two things present in your extract.

....

(d) What colour did your indicator turn

(i) in acids? ....

(ii) in alkalis? ....

(f) Is this what you expected? ....

(g) Did other groups get the same results?

....

3 Find out how concentrated acids and alkalis should be stored and handled safely.

....

....

....

....

Projects

- Make a long coloured strip showing the different colours for different pH values (see SB9: BCP p 141 for an idea). Cut out pictures, or draw your own, of household and laboratory chemicals. Stick these into position on your pH strip.
- Identify acids and alkalis in foods that we eat and drink.

Acids and bases; reactions of acids (SB9: BCP, Unit 20 p 144–7)

1 Compare acids and bases. See SB9: BCP p 146–7 and fill in the table.

Characteristic	Acids	Bases
Range of pH values		
Colour with litmus paper		
Corrosive or not		
Ions produced in solution		
Reaction with each other		
Reaction with metals		
Reaction with carbonates		
Reaction with metal salts		
Reaction with ammonium salts		
Examples in the laboratory		
Examples in nature		

2 Reactions of acids. See SB9: BCP p 144–6. Activity 20.10 Reacting acids with metals.

(a) Record your observations for each metal as you add hydrochloric acid, and test for hydrogen

Metal	Observations	Test gas
Calcium		
Magnesium		
Aluminium		
Zinc		
Copper		

(b) What is the test for hydrogen gas?

....

(c) Which metals release hydrogen gas from hydrochloric acid?

....

....

(d) Write a word equation and balanced chemical equation for the most reactive metal.

3 Activity 20.11 Reacting acids with carbonates and hydrogencarbonates.

(a) Record your observations as you add acid to the carbonates and test for carbon dioxide

Carbonate / hydrogen-carbonate	Observations	Test gas
Na_2CO_3		
$NaHCO_3$		
$CaCO_3$		

(b) What is the test for carbon dioxide gas?

....

Write a balanced chemical equation.

....

(c) Which carbonates/hydrogencarbonates produce carbon dioxide gas with hydrochloric acid?

....

....

(d) Write a word equation and balanced chemical equation for the most reactive carbonate.

Reactions of alkalis (SB9: BCP, Unit 20 p 147–9)

1 Explain what is meant by the following, what is the likely pH range, and give an example.

(a) Weak alkali

(b) Strong alkali

2 (a) See SB9: BCP p 148. Summarise the action of carbonates and hydrogencarbonates with alkalis.

(b) How does this compare with the reaction of carbonates and hydrogencarbonates with acids? (see SB9: BCP p 144–5)?

3 Reactions of alkalis. See SB9: BCP p 149. Activity 20.13: Reacting alkalis with ammonium salts.

(a) Record your observations as you add ammonium chloride solution to sodium hydroxide solution. Also test for ammonia.

Ammonium salt	Observations	Test gas
Ammonium chloride		

(b) What is the test for ammonia gas?

....

(c) Is ammonia gas acidic or basic?

....

(d) Write a word equation and balanced chemical equation for the reaction between ammonium chloride and sodium hydroxide.

4 Reactions of alkalis. See SB9: BCP p 149. Activity 20.13: Reacting alkalis with metal salts.

(a) Record your observations in the table below, such as colour changes and formation of precipitates, as you add metal salt solutions to sodium hydroxide solution.

Metal salt	Observations
Iron chloride	
Copper sulphate	

(b) Write a word equation and balanced chemical equation for

(i) iron chloride + sodium hydroxide.

(ii) copper sulphate + sodium hydroxide

5 In Unit 19, SB9: BCP p 134–5, you learned how to write ionic equations that showed which ions came together to form a precipitate (leaving out the spectator ions that were present in the reactants and products).

Based on the reactions in question 4 above, show the steps in writing the ionic equations for the formation of

(i) iron hydroxide

(ii) copper hydroxide

Neutralisation (SB9: BCP, Unit 20 p 150–3)

1 See SB9: BCP p 150, Activity 20.14.
Lime juice and ammonia solution.
Record colour changes and the reasons for them.

Chemicals	Colours	Reasons
Ammonia solution alone		
Lime juice alone		
Ammonia solution with litmus paper		
Lime juice with litmus paper		
Lime juice + ammonia solution and litmus paper		

3 See SB9: BCP p 151, Activity 20.15.
Dilute hydrochloric and sodium hydroxide solutions. Record colour changes and the reasons for them.

Chemicals	Colours	Reasons
Hydrochloric acid alone		
Sodium hydroxide alone		
Hydrochloric acid with litmus paper		
Sodium hydroxide with litmus paper		
Hydrochloric acid + sodium hydroxide and litmus paper		

2 Neutralisation reactions. In each case, add the chemical formulae and write balanced chemical equations. Identify that each reaction is an acid + base = salt + water only.

(a) hydrochloric acid + sodium hydroxide → sodium chloride + water
(b) nitric acid + ammonium hydroxide → ammonium nitrate + water
(c) carbonic acid + sodium hydroxide → sodium carbonate + water
(d) sulphuric acid + magnesium hydroxide → magnesium sulphate + water
(e) hydrochloric acid + copper oxide → copper chloride + water
(f) nitric acid + potassium hydroxide → potassium nitrate + water
(g) sulphuric acid + iron oxide → iron sulphate + water
(h) carbonic acid + copper hydroxide → copper carbonate + water

Neutralisation (cont.)

4 See SB9: BCP p 152, Activities 20.16 to 20.18 on uses of neutralisation.

Choose one of the activities and decide how you are going to set it up, and what observations you will make. Carry out your activity and record your results and conclusions.

6 (a) What is neutralisation? ....

....

(b) Write a general equation for neutralisation.

....

(c) What is an acid? ....

(d) What is a base? ....

(e) What is an alkali? ....

(f) What is a salt? ....

(g) How are hydrogen and hydroxide ions involved in neutralisation? ....

....

(h) Which kind of indicator would you use? Give an example.

....

(i) How do you know when the neutralisation reaction is complete? ....

....

5 Explain how neutralisation can be used in each of these situations. Where possible name the exact chemical that is used.

(a) Treating indigestion.
(b) Treating acid insect stings.
(c) Treating alkaline insect stings.
(d) Avoiding tooth decay.
(e) Removing acid stains.
(f) Removing alkaline stains.
(g) Improving alkaline soils.
(h) Improving acid soils.

Making salts (SB9: BCP, Unit 20 p 154–7)

1 Making salts. In each case, complete the word equations, add the chemical formulae and write balanced chemical equations. Then add three more examples of your own.

(a) hydrochloric acid + magnesium oxide →
(b) nitric acid + ammonium hydroxide →
(c) sulphuric acid + sodium carbonate →
(d) sulphuric acid + zinc →
(e) sodium + chlorine →
(f)
(g)
(h)

2 Complete the table for chemical names and formulae, and uses of salts.

Common name	Chemical name and formula	Use
Table or common salt		
Baking soda		
Washing soda		
Epsom salts		
Chalk and limestone		
Fertiliser		

(a) Choose one example of a salt from the table and write a balanced equation of how it can be made.

(b) What is the difference between baking soda and washing soda?

Checklist

You should know the meanings of these words (check the Glossary and Index in SB9: BCP):

acid, acid-base indicator, alkali, ammonia, atom, balancing equations, base, carbonate, carbon dioxide, chemical equations, combining power, concentrated, dilute, formulae, element, hydrogen, hydrogencarbonate, indicator, litmus, ionic equation, ions, metal, methyl orange, neutral, neutralisation, pH, phenolphthalein, precipitate, reaction, salts, state symbols, strong, test, water, weak, word equation

Questions

1 Which of these can be found in the home?
A acids **B** alkalis
C bases **D** all of the above

2 Which of these is an acid?
A toothpaste **B** bleach
C vinegar **D** soap

3 Which of these is alkaline?
A vinegar **B** distilled water
C bleach **D** lemon juice

4 The pH scale is used to identify
A acids **B** neutral substances
C bases **D** all of the above

5 Litmus and hibiscus indicators are different in the colour they give with which substances?
A bases **B** acids
C neutral solutions **D** all of the above

6 Acids ionising to make a lot of hydrogen ions are
A strong acids **B** weak acids
C dilute acids **D** dilute alkalis

7 Which of these is NOT an acid-base indicator?
A litmus **B** universal
C methyl orange **D** phenolphthalein

8 What colour does litmus paper go in lime juice?
A blue **B** purple
C red **D** white

9 What is produced when an acid reacts with a carbonate?
A carbon dioxide only
B a hydrogencarbonate
C a salt and water only
D a salt, carbon dioxide and water

10 When carbon dioxide is bubbled into limewater,
A nothing happens **B** it goes milky
C it goes 'pop' **D** it turns red

11 The reaction in Question 10 is which kind of change?
A chemical
B physical
C chemical and physical
D sometimes chemical and sometimes physical

12 Acids react with some metals to make
A water **B** carbon dioxide
C hydrogen **D** oxygen

13 The reaction in Question **12** depends on how reactive is the
A acid **B** metal
C hydrogen **D** water

14 What is produced when an alkali reacts with a metal salt in solution?
A water **B** carbon dioxide
C hydroxide **D** hydrogen

15 What is produced when an alkali reacts with an ammonium salt in solution?
A ammonia **B** carbon dioxide
C hydroxide **D** hydrogen

16 What is produced when an acid reacts with a base?
A a salt only **B** a salt and water only
C water only **D** carbon dioxide only

17 What is the reaction in Question **16** called?
A neutralisation **B** solution formation
C dissolving **D** emulsification

18 What are the salts formed by nitric acid called?
A nitrates **B** sulphates
C chlorides **D** ammonium salts

19 Acids react with which substances to make salts?
A metals **B** metal oxides
C metal carbonate **D** all of the above

20 What could be used to treat acid soils?
A slaked lime **B** fertiliser
C dilute vinegar **D** dilute sulphuric acid

21 Baking soda is
A sodium chloride
B sodium carbonate
C sodium hydrogencarbonate
D sodium hydroxide

22 Limestone is
A calcium carbonate
B calcium hydroxide
C calcium hydrogencarbonate
D calcium oxide

23 Give an example of the following:

(a) An acid ....

(b) A base ....

(c) How they react together ....

....

(d) The balanced chemical equation ....

....

....

24 (a) Name a salt and its chemical formula

....

(b) Write a word equation of how it may have been formed ....

....

(c) Write the balanced chemical equation

....

....

(d) Describe how your salt is used

....

....

....

Puzzle

Complete the crossword. The clues are given in the next column.

	1		2						3					
4					5						6		7	
8														
				9										
			10											
11			12										13	
	14	15			16		17							
18													19	
							20							21
				22									23	
						24								
									25				26	
27														
							28							

Across

4 Reaction between an acid and base (14)
8 Chemical symbol for calcium (2)
9 An oxide or hydroxide that reacts with an acid to make salt and water only (4)
12 Make hydrogen with many metals (5)
13 Abbreviation for 'aqueous' (in solution) (2)
14 Formed when an acid and base interact (5)
17 With 24 Across this gas is released from carbonates by 12 Across (6)
20 Shows the reactants and products (8)
23 Are all bases alkalis? (2)
24 Part of a gas, it means two oxygen atoms (7)
27 Descriptions of the kind of matter, e.g. (s) and (g), present in a reaction (5)
28 A common acid-base indicator (6)

Down

1 Combine with non-metals and radicals (6)
2 Building block of matter (4)
3 Nitrate and sulphate are example of this (7)
5 A base that dissolves in water (6)
6 A substance that changes colour at different pH values (9)
7 A substance with a pH value of 7 (7)
10 Made of a metal or ammonium group together with a non-metal or radical (4)
11 A scale that describes how many hydrogen ions are present (2)
15 Made when alkalis react with ammonium salts (7)
16 Colour that 12 Across makes with litmus (3)
17 The kind of change when carbon dioxide combines with limewater (8)
18 Describes a fully ionised acid or alkali (backwards) (6)
19 H^+ and OH^- are examples of this (3)
21 Chemical symbol for nitrate radical (3)
22 Colour that 5 Down turns litmus (4)
25 Abbreviation for precipitate (3)
26 The pH value of the strongest alkali (2)

Projects

Make your own crossword puzzle. Draw yourself a square that has 10 small squares across and 10 small squares down. Collect words from this Unit and place them in your Crossword. Then number your words, colour the squares you have not used, and write your clues. Make an incomplete puzzle for a friend and see if they can solve it.

Unit 21

Electricity and magnetism

Static electricity (SB9: BCP, Unit 21 p 170–2)

1 See SB9: BCP p 170–1, Activities 21.1 and 21.2). Complete the table to record your results.

Activity	Before rubbing	After rubbing	Explanation
Activity 21.1: (a) Plastic pen, woollen cloth, hair			
(b) Plastic pen, woollen cloth, small pieces of paper			
(c) Balloon, woollen cloth, wall			
Activity 21.2: (a) Plastic pen, woollen cloth, flow of water			
(b) Plastic spoon, cotton cloth, small pieces of paper			
(c) Metal spoon, cotton cloth, small pieces of paper			

2 Try your own combinations. You will need two non-metal materials. (Metals would conduct the charges away.)

- Choose a material, e.g. plastic, wood, rubber
- Choose a cloth, e.g. of wool, cotton, nylon.

(a) Do your activity on a very dry day. (Moisture or water will conduct away the charges, so static electricity does not build up.)

(b) Rub the material with the cloth. Try picking up small pieces of paper. What happens?

....

....

3 (a) Which combination of material and cloth worked best?

....

(b) Repeat the activity on a damp day. Explain what you notice.

....

....

3 Checklist for activities. Tick which things you can do. You should be able to give an example.

- ☐ I work safely when handling hot materials.
- ☐ I take the necessary precautions to be safe in the laboratory.
- ☐ I take my fair share of responsibility for group work.
- ☐ I help to collect the materials we need.
- ☐ I help the group without taking over.
- ☐ I contribute an idea to group discussion.
- ☐ I work co-operatively with other team members.
- ☐ I help to clear up after an activity.

Projects

As a class, collect information and research online for the uses and dangers of static electricity. Discuss your findings and prepare an illustrated display. Another group could produce a PowerPoint© presentation of their findings.

Electrical circuits (SB9: BCP, Unit 21 p 173–5)

1 You can make your own circuit board.

Materials: 4 cm square blocks of expanded polystyrene (from packing material) or heavy cardboard or bagasse board, ruler, screw-in type bulbs (1.25V, 0.25A), insulated wire, scissors, knife, pencil, masking tape, paperclips, thumbtacks, dry cell, rubber band

Method

(a) Use the knife, and then the pencil, to make a hole of about 5 mm diameter in the middle of a block of polystyrene or other material.

(b) Use the scissors to cut three lengths of about 15 cm of wire. Carefully cut away the end insulation to expose 3 cm lengths of bare wire. Twist the small strands of wire together if necessary.

(c) Wrap one exposed end of wire around the neck of a bulb, secure it with tape, and push it gently into the hole that you have made.

(d) Put a paperclip in contact with the protruding underside of the bulb. Secure it on each side with a thumbtack. Make sure all the metal-metal contacts are tight (i).

(e) Make a switch as shown in (ii). Underneath the thumbtacks will be bared ends of the wires, which are part of the circuit. The paperclip is moved to open and close the circuit.

(f) Use the rubber band to hold the bare end of one wire to the top (+) part of the dry cell, and another wire to the bottom (-) part as in (iii).

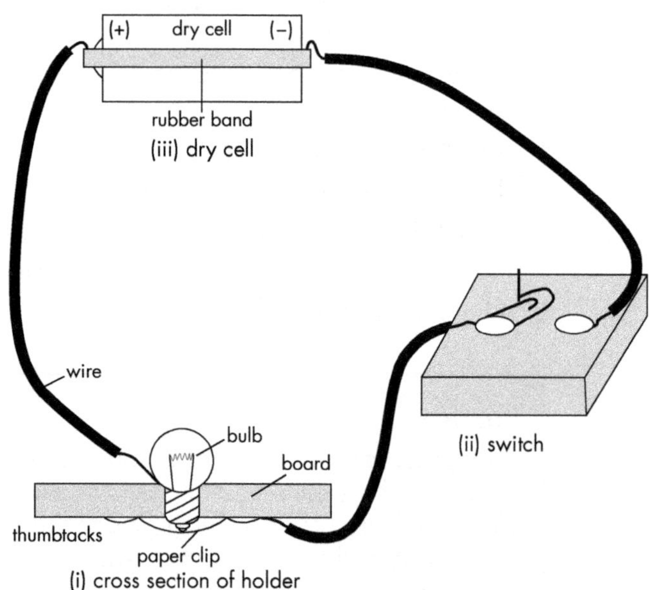

2 Conductors and insulators (see SB9: BCP, p 174 Activity 21.5). Record the conductors and insulators of electricity in the table below.

Conductors	Insulators

(a) What do you notice about the conductors?

....

(b) How could they be used?

....

(c) What do you notice about the insulators?

....

(d) How could they be used?

....

(e) What is unusual about graphite (a non-metal)?

....

(f) Is air a conductor or an insulator? How do you know? ....

....

3 (a) Draw the symbol for each part of a circuit.

+ 1.5 V – dry cell	bulb	connecting wire
+ 9V – battery	switch open	switch closed

(b) Use the symbols to draw the circuit diagram for the circuit in column 1.

Comparing series and parallel circuits (SB9: BCP, Unit 21 p 175–9)

1 (a) Cross out the incorrect words for a series circuit.
(b) Then write similar *correct* statements to describe a parallel circuit.

	Series circuit	Parallel circuit
Arrangement	Bulbs are arranged (one after each other/on separate paths).	
Bulbs	If one bulb breaks this (doesn't/does) affect the others. (All/None) of the other bulbs stay lit.	
Current	The current (is not/is) the same all around the circuit.	
Voltage	The voltage across the cell (is not/is) the same as that across similar bulbs.	
Use	Where it is important to have all the lights (on at once/able to be turned on or off one at a time). An example is (house lights/Christmas tree decorations).	

2 Make a quiz board.

Materials: cardboard 35cm × 20cm, bulb in holder, rubber band, dry cell, wires, scissors, two nails, paper, thumbtacks, paper fasteners

Method

(a) Connect wires to the bottom and top of the dry cell using the rubber band. Connect the wire to the bulb and to the board. Attach the ends to nails. Push in paper fasteners in two rows down the board.

(b) On the underside of the board connect the paper fasteners in any pattern that you like. (Only the ends of the wires should be bare. Why?)

(c) Make up a sheet of questions, 1–7, with the answers written on the paper in the same way as the wiring you did underneath. Make holes in the paper so that the heads of the paper fasteners show through.

(d) Use the nails in contact with the paper fasteners to select a question and an answer. If you are right, then the bulb should light up.

(e) You can make other sheets of paper with other questions and answers and put them on your board.

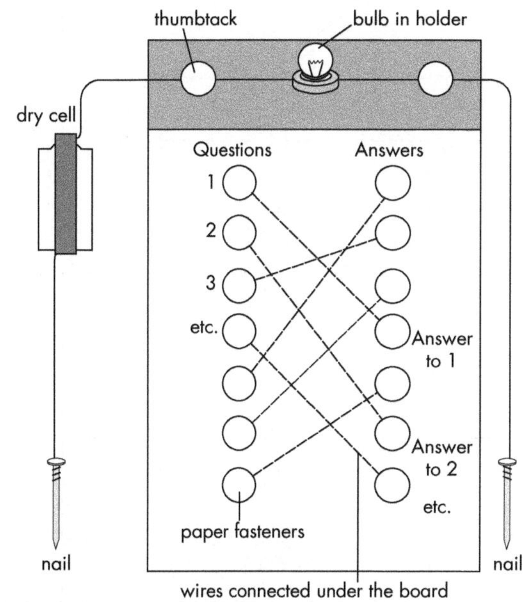

Projects

- Design and make a two-way switch controlling red and green stop and go bulbs.
- Design and make a model three-bulb traffic light.

Series circuits (SB9: BCP, Unit 21 p 176–7)

1 Draw the circuit diagrams below each of these circuits.

(a) What would happen if bulb **X** in each circuit is unscrewed? ....

(b) With which circuits below is each one most similar? **A** is like ...., **B** is like ....

2 Set up these circuits and use them to fill in the table.

Series circuits	Number of cells	Total valts	Number of bulbs	Volts used by each bulb	Bulbs: *Bright or Normal or Dim*
S (a)	1	1.5 V	1	1.5 V	
S (b)			2	0.75 V	
S (c)					
S (d)	2	3.0 V	1	3 V	
S (e)					
S (f)					

3 How does increasing the number of cells affect the brightness of the bulbs?

4 How does increasing the number of bulbs affect the brightness of the bulbs?

Parallel circuits (SB9: BCP, Unit 21 p 178–9)

1 Draw the circuit diagrams below each of these circuits.

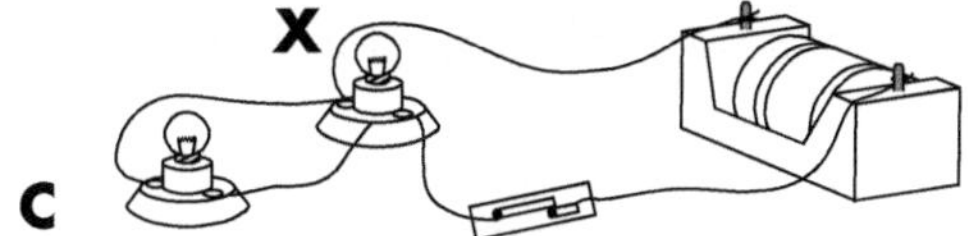

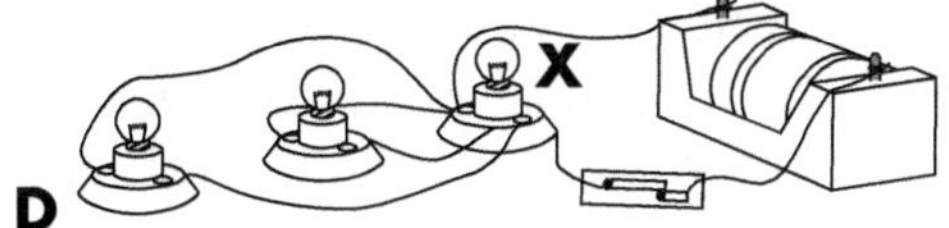

(a) What would happen if bulb **X** in each circuit is unscrewed? ....

(b) With which circuits below is each one most similar? **C** is like ...., **D** is like ....

2 Set up these circuits and use them to fill in the table.

Parallel circuits	Number of cells	Total valts	Number of bulbs	Volts used by each bulb	Bulbs: Bright or Normal or Dim
P (a) 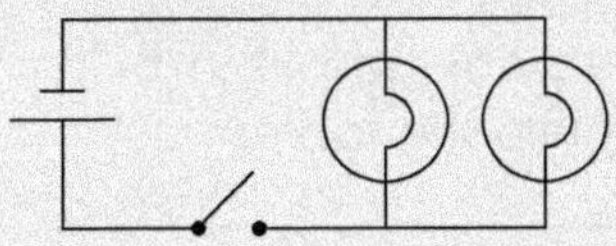	1	1.5 V	2	1.5 V	
P (b) 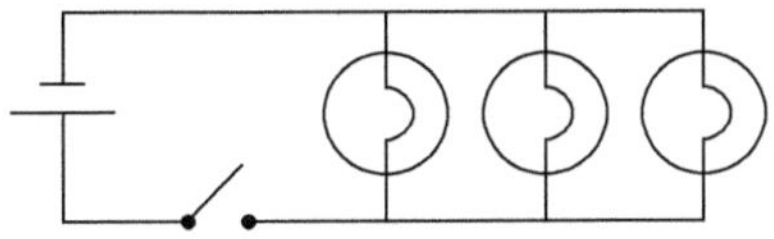		1.5 V			
P (c) 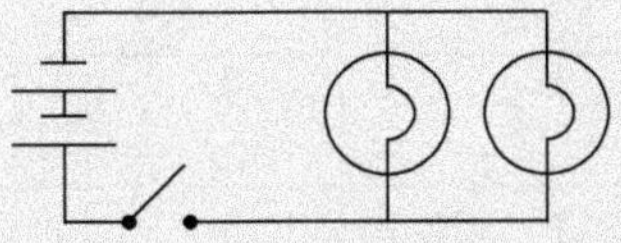	2	3.0 V			
P (d) 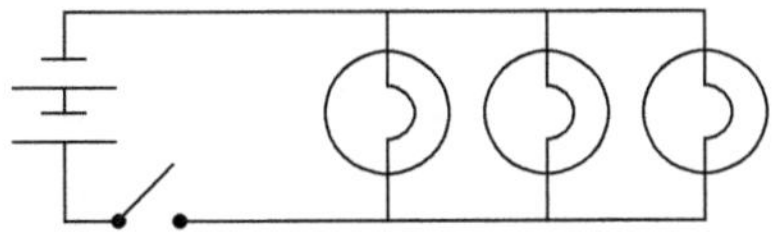					
P (e) 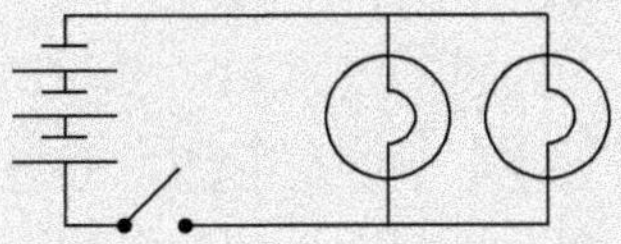	3				
P (f) 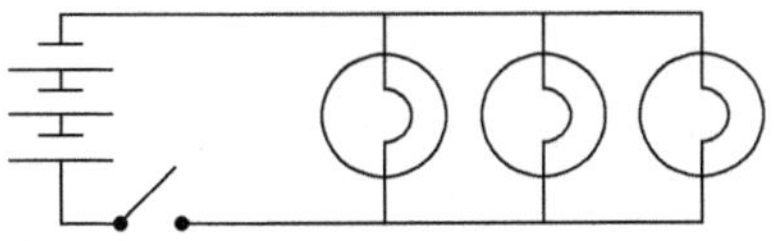					

3 How does increasing the number of cells in series affect the brightness of the bulbs?

4 How does increasing the number of bulbs in parallel affect the brightness of the bulbs?

Electrical circuits (SB9: BCP, Unit 21 p 180–2, 184–7)

1 Make your own cell.

(a) Choose a fruit such as a lemon, lime or orange, and two different conducting materials. For example: paperclip (steel), drawing pin (brass), 'lead' from inside a pencil (graphite), bare wire (copper).

(b) Stick the materials into the fruit: close but not touching each other. Connect the materials by wires to a bulb or a voltmeter. Try different combinations.

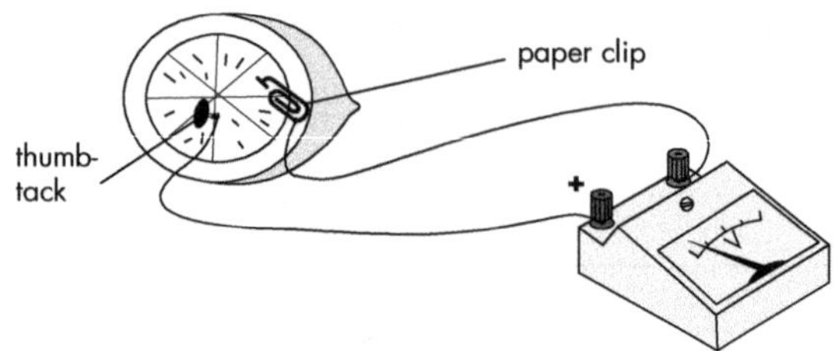

(c) Record your results.

Fruit	Metal A	Metal B	Result

2 Make a flashlight.

Materials: two cells, connecting wire, scissors, paper tape, aluminium foil, coloured card, paper clips

Method

(a) Tape the dry cells together and enclose them in a roll of cardboard that you also tape together.

(b) Tape the bulb to the +ve terminal of the top cell. Make a curved 'reflector' from aluminium foil to surround the bulb and attach it.

(c) Make a wire connection from the side of the bulb and another from the base of the lower cell. Attach these to paper clips to serve as your 'switch'.

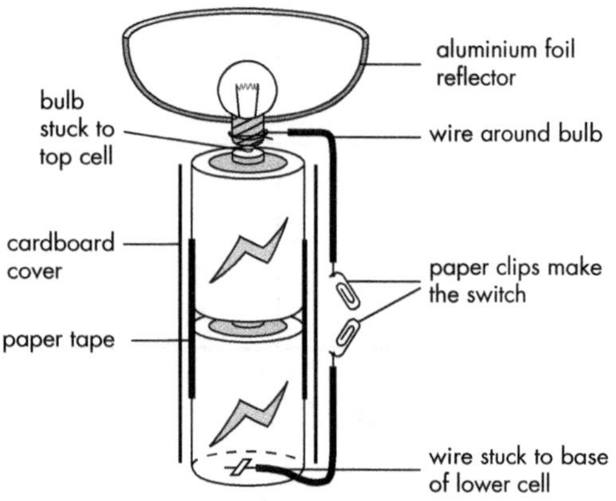

3 Resistance. See SB9: BCP p 180–1 Activities 21.13 and 21.14.

(a) How does a variable resistor work?

....

(b) How could it be used?

....

(c) What happens when current passes through a very narrow wire? ....

....

(d) How could this effect be

(i) useful? ....

(ii) not useful? ....

(e) How do we find the resistance of a wire?

....

....

4 Energy conversions (see SB9: BCP p 182 Activity 21.15). Complete the table.

Appliance	Energy change

4 Record the readings on these dial meters.

(a)

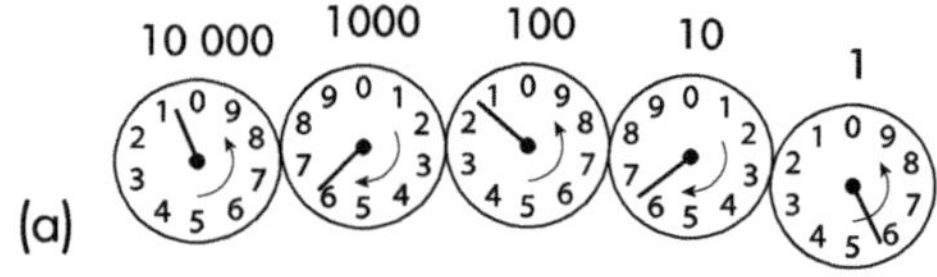

(b)

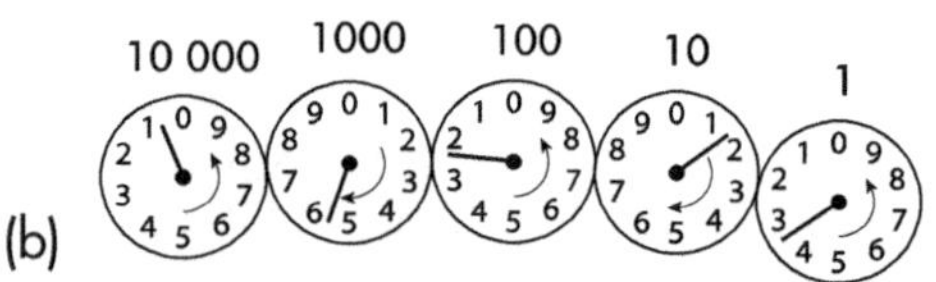

(c) What do we mean when we say 'we use electricity'?

Safe use of heat and electricity (SB9: BCP, Unit 21 p 183, 188–9)

1 Choose three of the safety rules from SB9: BCP p 183 and 188. For each one, give a reason why it is useful and the danger involved.

(a) Rule:

(b) Rule:

(c) Rule:

(d) Combine your ideas with other class members to prepare a chart on 'Safe use of heat and electricity'.

(e) Work in a group to enact some of the safety rules, and what might happen if they were not followed. Be safe at all times.

2 Add labels to the diagram of the iron and add what the materials would be: conductors (C) or insulators (I). Discuss why each one is used in that position.

(a) handle
(b) covering
(c) wire
(i) case
(h) bar
(g) heating element
(f) base of iron
bimetallic strip (d) on top
(e) underneath

3 (a) Which appliances use 2-pin plugs?

(b) Which appliances use 3-pin plugs?

(c) What is the use of the third pin?

(d) What is a fuse?

(e) How do fuses vary, and why?

(f) Why is it important to use the correct fuse?

4 See SB9: BCP p 183 Activity 21.16.

First, one of you follows the instructions and drawings to wire a 3-pin plug for a certain appliance. Then your partner marks what you have done. Your partner will need to take the plug apart to check your work. Then it will be the other person's turn.

This is the marking scheme out of 20. Each part gains 0 (incorrect), 1 (partly correct) or 2 marks (correct). Add up the total.

- ☐ The plug is screwed back together tightly
- ☐ The fuse is correct for the appliance (check with your teacher).
- ☐ The fuse is fitted in the plug properly.
- ☐ The cable clamp is against the outer insulation of the cable.
- ☐ The cable clamp is done up tightly.
- ☐ The live pin has the brown wire connected to it.
- ☐ The neutral pin has the blue wire connected to it.
- ☐ The earth wire has the green-yellow wire connected to it.
- ☐ You cannot get the wires out of the pins without undoing the screws.
- ☐ There are no strands of wire poking out of any of the pins.

Safe use of heat and electricity (cont.)

5 Discuss in your group:

(a) What is dangerous in each of these pictures and why it is a problem?

(b) What should be done to avoid the problem?

(c) Collect the class ideas and make a booklet on 'Safe use of heat and electricity'.

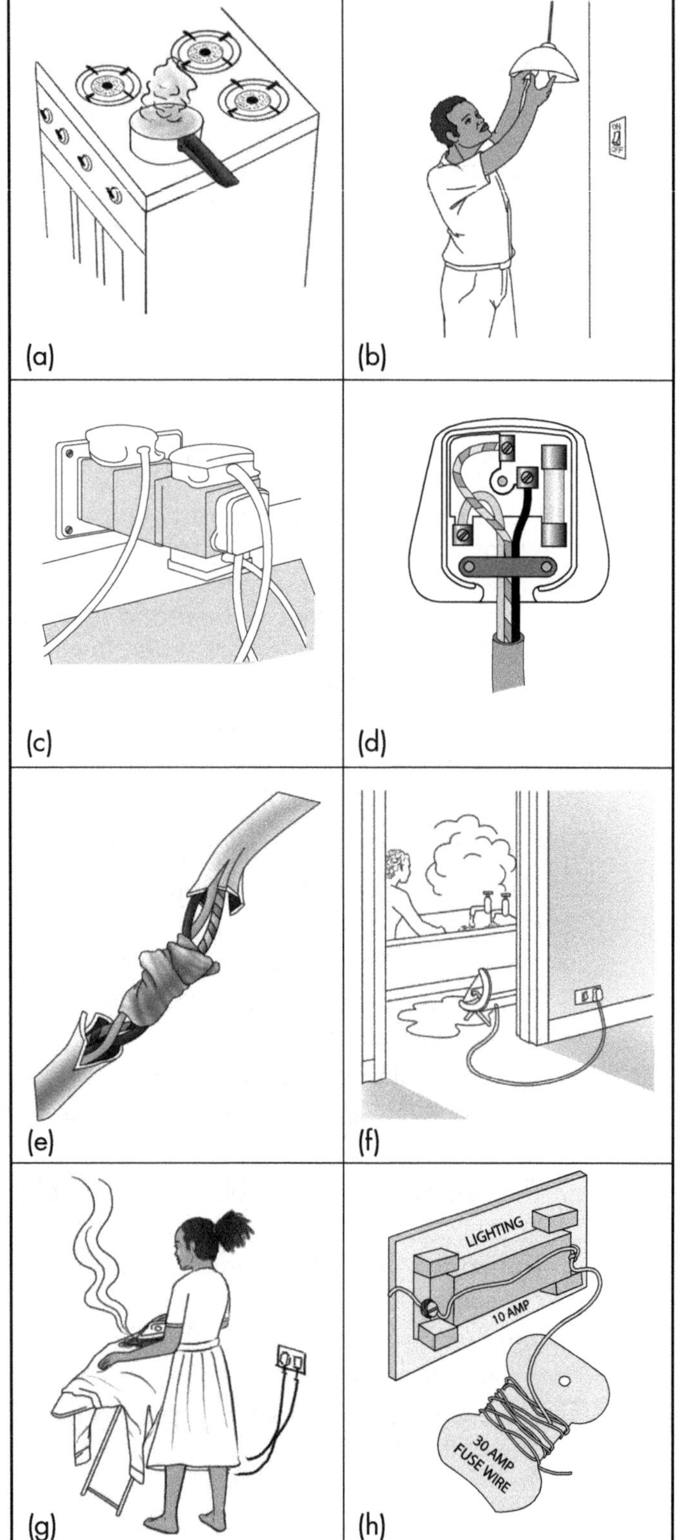

6 The diagram shows a circuit breaker. Use it to write a description of how a circuit breaker works.

reset button
iron bar
current
pivot
spring
contacts
iron
current

7 Checklist for activities. Tick which things you know or can do. You should be able to give an example.

- ☐ I do not touch hot appliances.
- ☐ I do not leave cooking pans with hot water where young children could pull them off.
- ☐ I do not leave cooking unattended.
- ☐ I am careful when ironing not to burn the clothes.
- ☐ I do not put too many plugs in one socket to overload it.
- ☐ I check carefully which cable and fuse should be used for a certain appliance.
- ☐ I know how to wire a plug correctly.
- ☐ If a fuse blows, I make sure the problem is corrected before replacing the fuse.
- ☐ I never use cables where the insulation has been broken.
- ☐ I never use a heater and cable in the bathroom.
- ☐ I make sure my hands are dry before handling electrical appliances.
- ☐ I make sure the mains switch is off when doing any work with electrical appliances.
- ☐ I never put anything except plugs into electrical sockets.
- ☐ I take the necessary precautions to be safe in the laboratory.

Magnetism (SB9: BCP, Unit 21 p 190–1)

1 Use the words to fill in the spaces:

repel, poles, attract, magnetic, north, iron, compass, steel

A magnet attracts objects containing (a) .... and (b) .... The magnetic force is concentrated at the (c) ....

A magnet rests with its N Pole pointing toward the Earth's (d) .... Pole. A (e) .... is an example of a magnet. Like poles of magnets (N – N and S – S) (f) .... each other. Unlike poles of magnets (N – S) (g) .... each other. We can use iron filings to show the invisible (h) .... field around a magnet, where it shows its effect.

2 Make these magnetic games, and describe to a friend how they work. Use the words:

magnet, attract, iron, steel, magnetic field

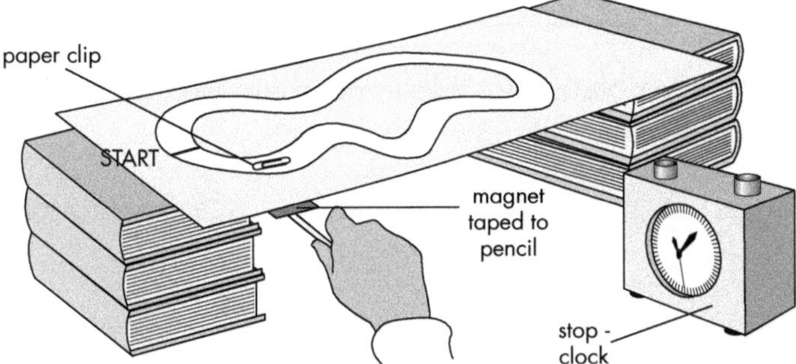

(a) Who can get the paper clip fastest around the track without touching the sides?

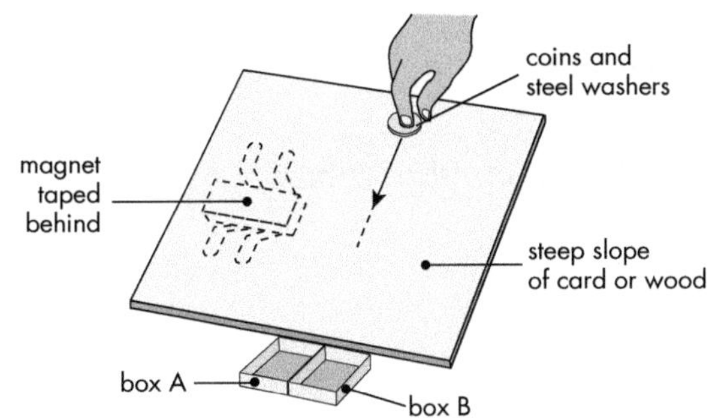

(b) Who can make the most succesful machine to sort steel washers from non-iron coins?

3 Can magnetism work through a barrier? Plan an activity to find out the effect of using thin and thick, and magnetic and non-magnetic barriers. You could use this set-up.

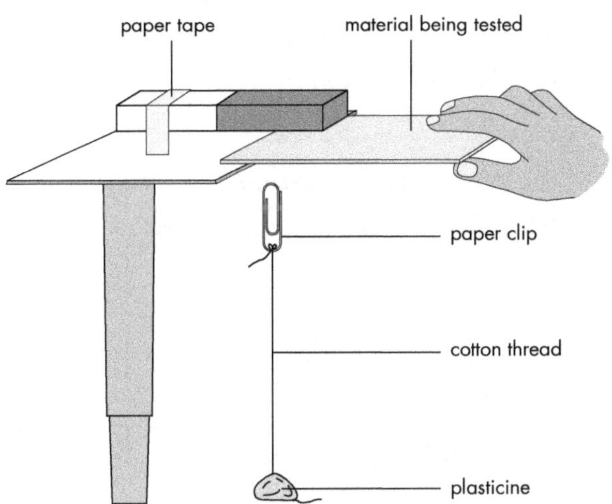

4 Make your own compass.

(a) Make a steel needle into a magnet (see SB9: BCP p 191). Find out which is the N-pole.

(b) Push the needle through a drinking straw and plug each end of the straw with Blu-tack.

(c) Float the needle and straw in a shallow bowl.

(d) The N-pole of the needle will point to the North. You can add the other compass markings to the rim.

(e) Your needle may be magnetised as in the picture, or the opposite way. You have to decide.

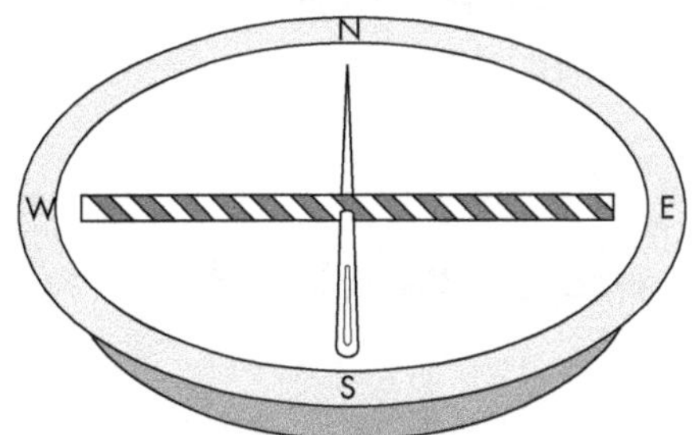

Projects

- Prepare a wall chart, with drawings, to outline some of the uses of magnets in everyday life.
- Make your own design of a machine that could separate magnetic materials (iron and steel) from non-magnetic ones. Where would your machine be useful?
- Do research on the materials used to stop magnetism from getting through. Name some machines that use magnetic shielding.

Magnetism (cont.) Unit 21 p 192–5

5 Making an electromagnet (see SB9: BCP p 192). Report on the part of the activity where you tried to increase the strength of the electromagnet.

(a) Method chosen ....

....

(b) Were you successful? ....

(c) What did other groups find? ....

....

6 Electromagnetic induction (see SB9: BCP p 193, Activity 21.28).

Moving the wire	Result
While moving While still	
Moving the magnet	
While moving Whole still	

SB9: BCP p 193, Activity 21.29. Record the results of your tests.

Moving the magnet more quickly:
Using a stronger magnet:
More loops in the solenoid:

7 (a) How is electricity used to make a magnet?

....

....

....

(b) How can a magnet be used to generate electricity? ....

....

....

8 Look at p 194 in SB9: BCP. Use the picture of the electric bell to help you plan, design and make a similar model.

You will first have to choose the materials. If you don't have the same ones as in the picture, then think of other things you could use to improvise. For example, an iron nail could be used instead of the iron bar to make the electromagnet.

Plans and results:

9 Complete the table to compare permanent magnets and electromagnets.

	Permanent magnets	Electromagnets
How made?		
Materials		
Strength		
Uses		

10 See SB9: BCP p 195. Describe how these work.

(a) A step-up transformer

(b) A step-down transformer

Checklist

You should know the meanings of these words (check the Glossary and Index in SB9: BCP):

ammeter, amps (A), attract, battery, bimetallic strip, charge, circuit, circuit symbols, current, dry cell, dynamo, electricity meter, electromagnet, electromagnetic induction, electrons, energy conversion, energy unit (kWh), fuses, generator, lightning, magnet, mains electricity, ohms(Ω), parallel, pole, power (W, kW), plugs, repel, resistance, rheostat, safety, series, solenoid, static electricity, transformer, voltage, voltmeter, volts (V).

Questions

1 What is transferred when a pen is rubbed?
A atoms **B** electrons
C nuclei **D** protons

2 Which of these uses static electricity?
A photocopying **B** spraying cars
C removing smoke **D** all of the above

3 Which of these materials could be used to complete a circuit?
A paper **B** string
C aluminium foil **D** plastic

4 When comparing the flow of electric current in a circuit with the flow of water in pipes, the dry cell in the circuit is similar to the
A water pipes
B heater and pump
C water
D a radiator

5 The rate of flow of charge is measured in
A amperes with an ammeter
B amperes with a voltmeter
C volts with an ammeter
D volts with a voltmeter

6 The kind of circuit where the removal of one light puts off all the others
A parallel
B series
C two-way switch
D mains circuit

7 A parallel circuit has two similar bulbs, and another similar bulb is added. All the bulbs
A will stay about the same brightness
B will become brighter
C will become dimmer
D may break

8 A series circuit has two similar bulbs, and another dry cell is placed in series. The bulbs
A will stay about the same brightness
B will become brighter
C will become dimmer
D will break

9 Which of these fuels is a liquid?
A charcoal **B** LPG
C kerosene **D** wood

10 Which of these appliances can usually be run both from the mains and with a battery?
A toaster **B** flashlight
C iron **D** laptop

11 Which part of a power station produces electricity?
A generator **B** turbine
C boiler **D** transformer

12 A two-pin plug
A does not have an earth pin
B cannot carry much electricity
C only has live and neutral wires
D cannot be wired as easily as a 3-pin one

13 What are the units used to measure power?
A watts and joules
B kilowatts and amps
C watts and kilowatts
D joules and volts

14 Which of the following appliances uses the most energy units (kWh)?
A 350 W television for 3 hours
B 1 kW air conditioner for 1 and a half hours
C 3 W electric clock for 330 hours
D 100 W light bulb for 10 hours

15 Which of these would things would be attracted by the N-pole of a magnet?
A piece of wood
B aluminium pan
C N-pole of a magnet
D S-pole of a magnet

16 Which of these is the odd-one-out?
A iron filings **B** the Earth
C a magnet **D** a compass needle

17 An electromagnet can be made from
A steel **B** iron
C any metal **D** any non-metal

18 The best explanation for why a bimetallic strip bends is that
A it is made of metal
B it is heated
C it is heated more on one side than the other
D the two metals expand different amounts

19 The function of a fuse is to
A produce electricity
B use up electricity
C protect appliances in the circuit
D conduct electricity to earth

20 (a) How do static and current electricity differ?

....

....

(b) How do series and parallel circuits differ?

....

....

(c) How do magnets and electromagnets differ?

....

....

(d) How do a generator and transformer differ?

....

....

21 (a) In the circuit below, if bulb (a) is unscrewed

what will happen to bulb (b)? ....

what will happen to bulb (c)? ....

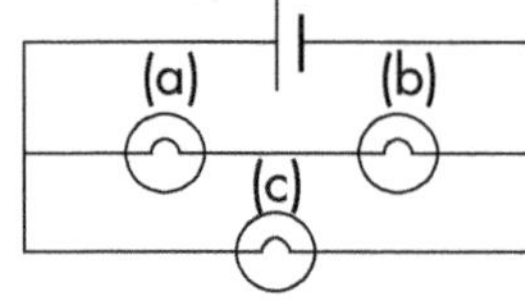

Puzzle

Complete the crossword. The clues are given in the next column.

■	■	■	1	■	■	2	■	■	■	■	3		4	
5		6		7				8		■		■		■
	■		■		■		■		■	■		■		■
	■		■		■		■		■	9	■	■		■
	■		■		■		■	10						■
	■		■		■		■		■		■	■		■
	■		■		■		■		■		■	11	■	■
	■	■	■	■	■	12			■		■		■	13
	■	14			15	■	■	■	16					
■	■	■	■	■	17			■		■	■	■	■	
■	■	18				■	■	■		■	■	19	■	
■	■	■	20	■		■	■	■	■	■	■		■	
21	■	22						■	■	23	■		■	
24		■		■		■	■	25						
	■	■	■	■	■	■	■	■	■		■	■	■	■
26								■	27					■

Across

3 Used to measure 5 Across (4)
5 The force opposing the flow of current (10)
10 Negative property of electrons (6)
12 If a bulb is removed from a parallel circuit, the other bulbs remain .... (3)
14 Contains chemicals to generate electricity (4)
16 Used on a bicycle to generate electricity (6)
17 With 15 Down it is a discharge of charge (6)
18 Connects appliances to the mains (4)
22 Device to open and close a circuit (6)
24 Air is an .... sulator (2)
25 Rate of flow of electrons (7)
26 Negatively charged particle (8)
27 Measured by an electricity meter (5)

Down

1 A word meaning two (2)
2 Each bulb has a circuit to the cell (8)
3 If one bulb in a series circuit is broken, the other bulbs go .... (3)
4 Attracts iron and steel (6)
5 A device, e.g. a bulb, which resists flow of current in a circuit (8)
6 Electricity at rest (6)
7 A circuit where the current is the same all the way around (6)
8 A complete pathway for electricity (7)
9 Important to practise in the laboratory (6)
11 Current is measured in .... (backwards) (3)
13 Metals can .... electricity (7)
15 With 17 Across it is a discharge of charge (6)
16 An example of 14 Across (3)
19 Thin wire used as a safety device (4)
20 Unit of energy on which we are charged (3)
21 The brown wire in a plug (4)
23 A .... sformer is used to increase or decrease the voltage (4)

Which is the correct order (from dimmest to brightest) for bulbs in these circuits? ....

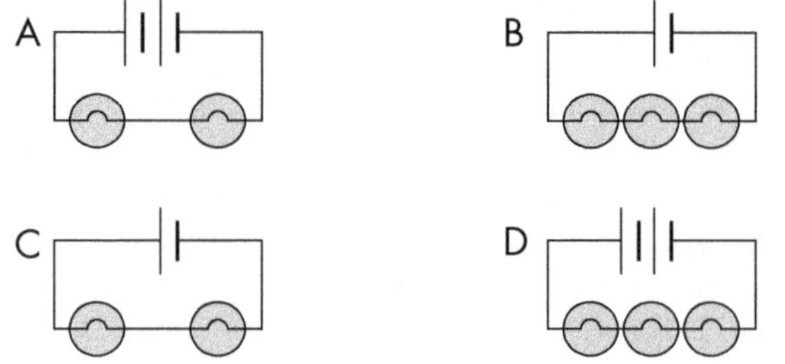

Which kind of circuit is shown ....

Unit 22

Thermal energy

Kinetic energy (SB9: BCP, Unit 22 p 200–1)

1 *Materials*: measuring cylinder, two beakers, heating apparatus, glass rod, thermometer, watch

Method

(a) Measure 50 cm³ of water into one beaker (**A**). Measure 100 cm³ of water into the other (**B**).

(b) Set up the tripod, gauze and Bunsen burner. Adjust the burner to a steady flame.

(c) Heat beaker **A** for *exactly* one minute. Stir with the glass rod and record the highest temperature reached. ....

(d) Do not adjust the burner. Record the time you put beaker **B** on the burner. Heat the water until the *same temperature* is recorded as for **A.** How long did this take? ....

(e) Why did the water in beaker **B** need more heat energy to get to the same temperature?

....

....

2 *Materials*: beaker of boiling water (**X**), beaker of tap water with ice cubes (**Y**), thermometer, watch

Method

(a) Find the temperature of the room. ....

(b) Put beakers **X** and **Y** on the bench. Find the temperature of the water in each one.

(c) At 10-minute intervals, for the next hour, record the two temperatures again.

Time	Water in X	Water in Y
Start		
10 minutes		
20 minutes		
30 minutes		
40 minutes		
50 minutes		
60 minutes		

(d) What happens to the temperature of the

(i) hot water? Why?

....

(ii) cold water? Why?

....

3 What is meant by the following terms?

(a) Kinetic energy ....

....

....

(b) Thermal energy ....

....

....

(c) Temperature ....

....

....

(d) Heat energy ....

....

....

4 Comparing thermal energy in liquids.
SB9: BCP, p 200: Total kinetic energy = thermal energy = temperature × volume

(a) There are two liquids: **A** has a temperature of 30 °C and a volume of 150 cm³. **B** has a temperature of 25 °C and a volume of 200 cm³. Which liquid has the most thermal energy?

Liquid **A**'s thermal energy is 30 × 150 = 4500.

Liquid **B**'s thermal energy is 25 × 200 = 5000.

So liquid **B** has more thermal energy although it is at a lower temperature.

(b) There are two liquids: **C** has a volume of 250 cm³ and a temperature of 30 °C. **D** has a volume of 300 cm³ and a temperature of 20 °C. Which lquid has the most thermal energy?

....

....

(c) There are two liquids: **E** has a temperature of 50 °C and a volume of 100 cm³. **F** has a temperature of 45 °C and a volume of 150 cm³. If the liquids are put in contact, in which direct does heat energy flow?

....

Methods of heat transfer: Conduction (SB9: BCP, Unit 22 p 202–3)

1 *Materials*: beaker of water, thermometer, heating apparatus, metal, plastic and wooden spoons

Method

Warm the water in the beaker to about 40 °C. Put in the metal, plastic and wooden spoons at the same time. Keep a finger on the end of each of the spoons and record what you feel.

Results

Metal spoon: ....

Plastic spoon: ....

Wooden spoon: ....

Questions

(a) Which spoon got hottest the quickest?

....

(b) Only part of the spoon was in hot water, so how did the far end of the spoon get hot?

....

(c) Why did we only heat the water to 40 °C and not to boiling point?

....

(d) What is your conclusion?

....

....

(e) Explain the method of transfer.

....

....

(f) What improvements can you suggest?

....

....

2 Fill in the tables on good conductors and poor conductors (insulators) of heat.

Good conductors	Uses

Insulators	Uses

3 Is water a good conductor of heat?

Materials: test tube, burner, water, small piece of ice, small piece of wire gauze, test tube holder

Method

Put ice in the bottom of the test tube to a depth of 2 cm. Push the gauze down over the ice to keep it in place.

Add water to two-thirds fill the test tube.

Light the burner and hold it so the flame heats the top of the water. Record what happens.

(a) Did the water boil? ....

(b) What happened to the ice? ....

....

(c) Explain your results ....

....

....

4 *Materials*: two similar clean tin cans, cotton wool, hot water, sticky tape, thermometer

Method

Insulate one can (**A**) with cotton wool held on by sticky tape. (The cotton wool contains trapped air.)

Leave the other can (**B**) uncovered.

Put similar amounts of hot water into the cans.

Record the temperature of the water in both cans after 30 minutes.

(a) What happened in can A, and why? ....

....

....

(b) What happened in can B, and why? ....

....

....

(c) Is air a good conductor of heat? ....

....

Convection (SB9: BCP, Unit 22 p 204–5)

1 Convection depends on hot air expanding and rising, and cool air contracting and sinking.

You can show this in the following activity.
Materials: glass bottle with a narrow neck, balloon, string, scissors, two bowls, hot water, ice cubes

Method

Fit the balloon over the neck of the bottle. Tie it on tightly with string.

(a) Put the bottle into the bowl filled with hot water. What happens? Explain why.

....

....

(a) (b)

(b) Now move the bottle to the bowl filled with ice cubes. What happens? Explain why.

....

....

(c) How does this help explain convection currents?

....

....

....

2 How can convection currents help to

(a) heat water in an electric jug? ....

....

....

....

(b) cool a house? ....

....

....

....

3 Make some coloured ice cubes with Cool-Aid, instant coffee or other colouring matter. You are going to put these into some hot water.

(a) Predict what you think will happen.

....

....

....

(b) Carry out the activity and report and explain your observations.

....

....

....

4 (a) Explain, with a diagram when and how a sea breeze occurs.

(b) Explain, with a diagram, when and how a land breeze occurs.

(c) Do they only occur near the sea? Explain.

Radiation (SB9: BCP, Unit 22 p 206–8)

1 Compare heat absorption of black and white cars (see SB9: BCP p 206, Activity 22.9).

(a) Set up a fair test (use page 5 in this book to help you). Fill in the spaces, such as the variables you will keep constant and when you will make readings.

(b) If you cannot find two similar cars outside, then you could use two model cars or some containers. How would you have to adjust your plans?

....

....

(c) Carry out the activity and report your results.

....

....

....

....

2 Make a solar oven (see SB9: BCP p 207, Activity 22.10).

(a) How does heat energy come to the box?

....

....

(b) Why is it useful to paint the box black?

....

....

(c) Why is the aluminium foil used? Does the oven work without having foil?

....

....

....

(d) What use is the sheet of glass? Does the oven work without the glass?

....

....

....

(e) Were you successful in cooking some biscuits?

....

(f) What improvements can you make?

....

....

3 Describe how you could set up a fair test to show that

(a) a dull black surface is a better absorber of radiant energy than a shiny white surface.

....

....

....

(b) a dull black surface is a better emitter of heat energy than a shiny white surface.

....

....

....

(c) colours also vary in how well they absorb and emit heat.

....

....

....

4 Complete the table to compare heat transfer by: (a) Conduction, (b) Convection and (c) Radiation.

Characteristics	Examples of use
(a)	
(b)	
(c)	

Heating and cooling (SB9: BCP, Unit 22 p 209–11)

1 Heating increases the kinetic energy of particles. This can cause expansion and change of state. Describe how we can show this for

(a) a solid ....

(b) a liquid ....

(c) a gas ....

Cooling decreases the kinetic energy of particles. This can cause contraction and change of state. Describe how we can show this for

(d) a solid ....

(e) a liquid ....

(f) a gas ....

2 Name the processes for changes of state.

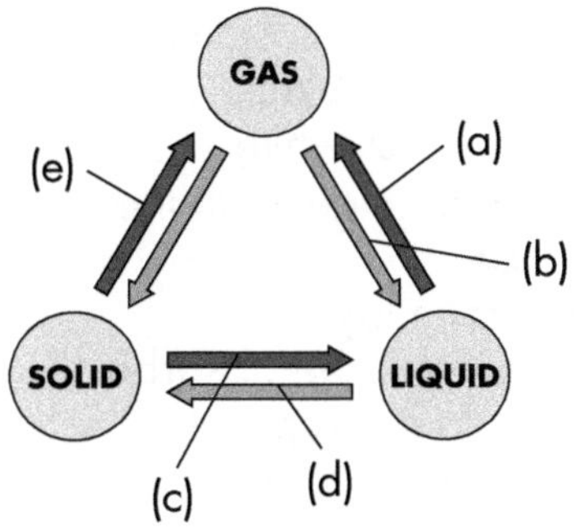

GAS
SOLID
LIQUID
(a)
(b)
(c)
(d)
(e)

(a) ....

(b) ....

(c) ....

(d) ....

(e) ....

3 How does a thermos flask reduce heat transfer?

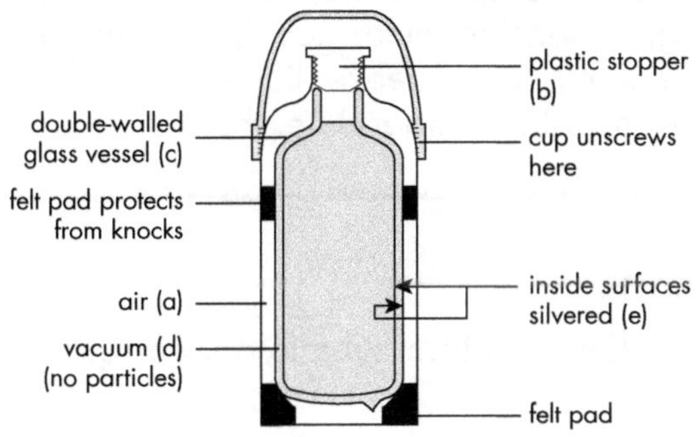

plastic stopper (b)
double-walled glass vessel (c)
cup unscrews here
felt pad protects from knocks
air (a)
inside surfaces silvered (e)
vacuum (d) (no particles)
felt pad

(a) by conduction ....

(b) by convection ....

(c) by radiation ....

4 Explain how each of the following use all three methods of heat transfer.

(a) Using a toaster

....

(b) Cooking food on a gas stove

....

Checklist

You should know the meanings of these words (check the Glossary and Index in SB9: BCP):

absorption, change of state, conduction, conductors, contraction, convection, cooling, current, emission, emitting, expansion, fluid, gas, greenhouse effect, heat, heating, heat transfer, infrared radiation, insulators, kinetic energy, land breeze, liquid, meniscus, microwave oven, particles, radiation, sea breeze, solar energy, solar oven, solid, temperature, thermal energy, thermometer, thermos flask, vacuum

Questions

Use the following information to answer questions 1 and 2.

(i) 100 cm^3 water at 15 °C

(ii) 50 cm^3 water at 30 °C

(iii) 40 cm^3 water at 32 °C

1 Which amounts of water have the highest temperature?
A (i)
B (ii)
C (iii)
D (ii) and (iii) the same

2 Which amounts of water have the most thermal energy?
A (i)
B (ii)
C (iii)
D (i) and (ii) the same

3 Thermal energy is equal to
A total kinetic energy
B average kinetic energy
C half the kinetic energy
D temperature taken with a thermometer

4 Particles in a solid
A do not move at all **B** vibrate in place
C move around a little **D** move around a lot

5 Heat energy is transferred from a higher to a lower
A temperature **B** thermal energy
C kinetic energy **D** concentration

6 Conduction occurs best
A in solids **B** in fluids
C in solids and fluids **D** in a vacuum

7 Which is the best insulator?
A iron **B** copper
C graphite **D** plastic

8 Which of these is the best conductor of heat?
A glass **B** wood
C copper **D** plastic

9 A fluid is a
A solid only **B** gas only
C liquid only **D** liquid or gas

10 Convection occurs in
A solids only **B** liquids only
C gases only **D** liquids and gases

11 A sea breeze occurs
A only during the day
B only during the night
C day and night
D only when it rains

12 In order to make a sea breeze
A the sea is warmer than the land
B the land is warmer than the sea
C the tide needs to be in
D the tide needs to be out

13 When a fluid is heated, the particles
A become more dense
B become less dense
C stop moving
D sink down

14 Heat transfer can occur in a vacuum by
A conduction **B** convection
C radiation **D** all of the above

15 The main source of infrared radiation is
A the Sun
B the Moon
C the atmosphere
D the clouds

16 The surface colour that absorbs most infrared radiation is
A red **B** black
C yellow **D** white

17 The surface colour that emits most heat energy is
A red **B** black
C yellow **D** white

18 The build-up of greenhouse gases in the atmosphere can cause
A damage to the ozone layer
B infrared radiation not to be absorbed
C more heat energy to be trapped
D less heat energy to be trapped

19 The process of changing a gas to a liquid is
A melting **B** condensation
C boiling **D** evaporation

20 A thermos flask cuts down heat transfer by
A conduction **B** convection
C radiation **D** all of the above

21 Which processes are used in cooking food on a gas stove?
A conduction **B** convection
C radiation **D** all of the above

22 (a) How is kinetic energy important?

....

....

....

....

(b) How are liquids and gases

(i) similar? ....

....

(ii) different? ....

....

(c) How are conduction and convection

(i) similar? ....

....

(i) different? ....

....

(d) How is radiation different from other methods of heat transfer?

....

....

(e) How does a mercury thermometer work?

....

....

....

23 Give and explain an example from your everyday life of how you use

(i) conduction ....

....

....

....

(i) convection ....

....

....

....

(i) radiation ....

....

....

....

Puzzle

Complete the crossword. The clues are given below.

Across

3 Heat transfer between particles (10)
7 At .... time land breeze can form (5)
9 When a fluid is heated, it rises .... (2)
10 A good insulator (3)
11 A .... breeze forms when the land is warmer than the sea (3)
14 Heat transfer through a vacuum (9)
16 State with definite volume but changing shape where particles can move from place to place (6)
18 Clue 8 Down is an example of this (6)
20 Nature of a substance at room temperature (5)
21 Name given to liquids and gases (5)
22 Protective gases around Earth (10)

Down

1 Absorb is to take .... (2)
2 State with definite volume and shape where the particles just vibrate (5)
3 Currents formed in fluids (10)
4 The average kinetic energy of a substance (11)
5 This is a good conductor of heat (5)
6 A convection .... can be set up in a liquid or gas (7)
8 The form in which energy is transferred (4)
12 Total energy of movement of particles (7)
13 To emit energy means to give it .... (3)
15 Total kinetic energy in a substance (7)
17 When a fluid is cooled, it sinks .... (4)
19 State with changing volume and shape, its particles move very quickly (3)

Worksheet 1 The scientific method (SB9: BCP, Introduction p 2–4, 7–9)

Scientists are organised. They work in a step-wise (systematic) way to solve problems about living things, materials or forms of energy. We call this the scientific method. It makes use of fair tests, where only one thing, or variable, is changed at a time – so we can find out what its effect is.

1 Put the steps of the scientific method in order.

(a) Make a scientific guess (prediction) based on the hypothesis, e.g. if I leave seeds without water, they will not germinate.	(d) Do your results support your prediction and hypothesis? Do you need to do any other experiments?
(b) Carry out the experiment. Keep all the other variables constant and record your results.	(e) Make a general statement (hypothesis), e.g. water affects the germination of seeds.
(c) Set up a fair test with a control. Change only one variable, e.g. leave some seeds dry and some damp.	(f) Interpret your results and report your findings. Write your conclusion on what you found out.

Order: 1 (e), 2 , 3 , 4 , 5 , 6 .

2 The diagram shows seeds in a test tube. Answer questions (a) and (b).

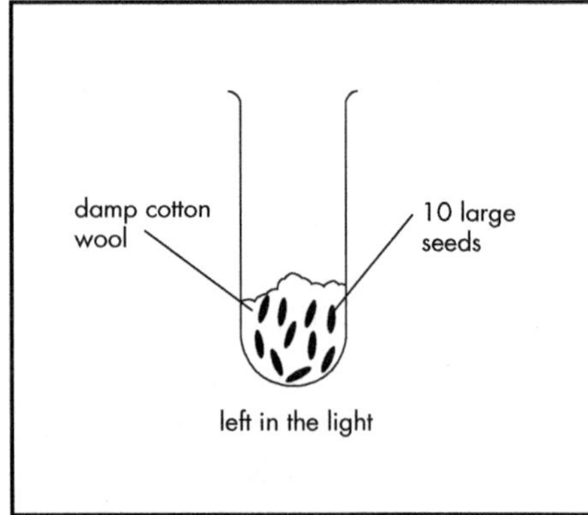

What other set-up is needed to test the prediction that:

(a) Only damp seeds germinate

(b) Seeds need light to germinate

3 Write or record where these words should fit.

y- independent control variable(s) prediction hypothesis fair dependent x-

When we have a problem we first make a general statement ((a) ....) about the answer. Then we predict what might happen ((b) ....) that we can test. We must set up a ((c) ....) test where we change only one thing ((d) .... (e) ....). We have to keep the same ((f) ....) the other things ((g) ....). We carry out our investigation and collect our results ((h) .... (i) ....). We find out if our ideas ((j) .... and ((k) ....) were correct.

If we want to make a line graph showing our results, we put the values of the variable we changed ((l) .... (m) ....) on the horizontal ((n) ....) axis of the graph and the results ((o) .... (p) ....) on the vertical ((q) ....) axis.

Worksheet 2 Engineering design process (SB9: BCP, Introduction p 2–4, 7, 10–11)

Technologists, particularly engineers, make new things to solve special problems. The process is called the engineering design process (EDP) and it includes art and design. Steps include brainstorming, sketching, drawing, choosing a design, and making; then improving and testing it several more times.

1 Put the steps of the engineering design process in order.

(a) I ask about the problem and find the requirements and constraints. I think about what materials I need to make a model.

(b) I follow my plan, write about any problems, make labelled, annotated drawings to scale and see how my model works.

(c) I imagine some solutions, make sketches, and research and brainstorm ideas. I compare and then select the best two designs.

(d) When I have my final model I evaluate what I have done and see if I have solved my original problem.

(e) I check my design and improve it, e.g. make it attractive. I report to others, and if necessary improve the model again.

(f) I choose the design likely to be best for my purpose. I make detailed drawings and gather materials. I make my action plan.

Order: 1 (a), 2 , 3 , 4 , 5 , 6 .

2 The diagram shows the steps in the engineering design process on the left. Write descriptions of what you do in each step, on the right.

Engage	
Explore	
Elaborate	
Execute	
Explain	
Evaluate	

Worksheet 3 Measuring physical quantities (SB9: BCP, Introduction p 14–17, 108–9, 165)

Physical quantities are characteristics we can measure, such as length, mass and volume. We use measuring instruments marked with scales and numbers. For example, we measure length, using a ruler or metre rule. We read the scale and the units, e.g. centimetres. We record the amount of the measurement, e.g. 3 and the abbreviation of the unit, e.g. cm.

The values of the small divisions on different measuring instruments can be different (see below).

1

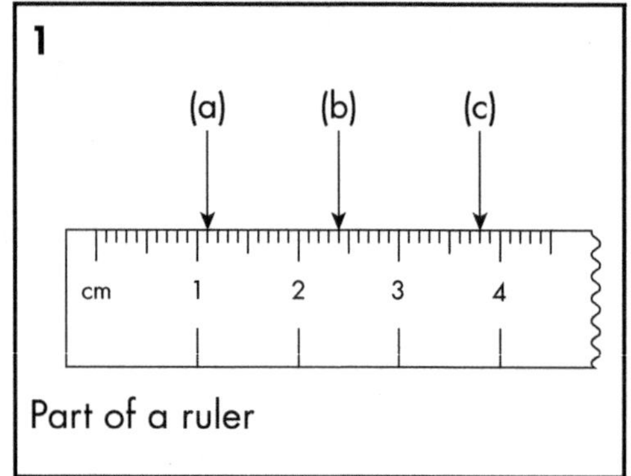

Part of a ruler

What are the readings shown at (a), (b) and (c)?

(a) ....

(b) ....

(c) ....

(d) What is being measured? ....

(e) What is the value of each small division? ....

2

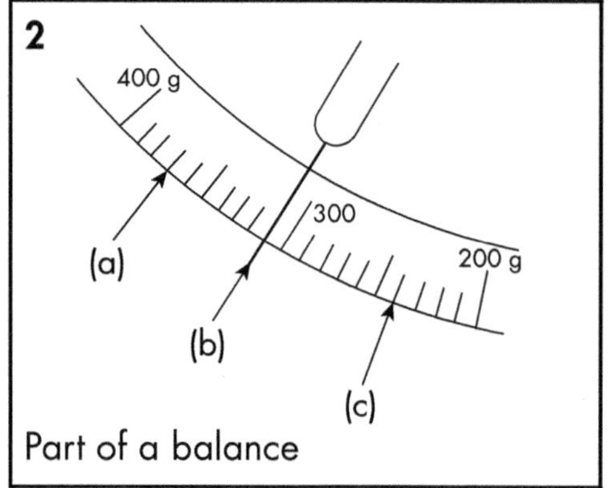

Part of a balance

What are the readings shown at (a), (b) and (c)?

(a) ....

(b) ....

(c) ....

(d) What is being measured? ....

(e) What is the value of each small division? ....

3

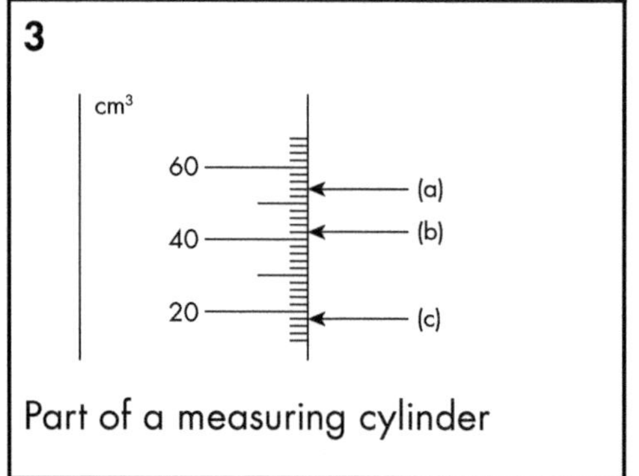

Part of a measuring cylinder

What are the readings shown at (a), (b) and (c)?

(a) ....

(b) ....

(c) ....

(d) What is being measured? ....

(e) What is the value of each small division? ....

4

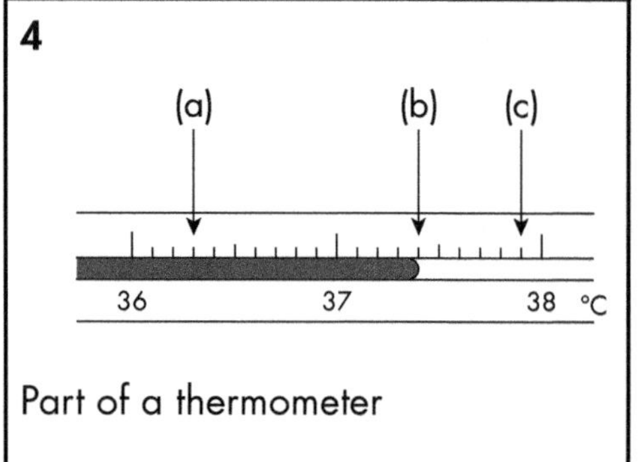

Part of a thermometer

What are the readings shown at (a), (b) and (c)?

(a) ....

(b) ....

(c) ....

(d) What is being measured? ....

(e) What is the value of each small division? ....

Worksheet 4 Working with numbers (SB9: BCP, Introduction p 14–19, 163)

Prefixes

Prefixes come before a unit to show powers of ten: make units larger (e.g. kilo) or smaller (e.g. centi)

1 What fraction of a litre is a
(a) centilitre .... (b) decilitre ....
(c) millilitre ....

2 The mass of a stone is 50 g. What is this in
(a) kilograms .... (b) milligrams ....

3 I walk 1000 metres. What is this in
(a) kilometres .... (b) decimetres ....

4 How far do I move the digits relative to the decimal point so as to:
(a) multiply by 10 ....
(b) divide by 100 ....
(c) divide by 1000 ....

5 Give the values, in powers of 10, for:
(a) deci .... (b) mega ....
(c) milli .... (d) kilo ....
(e) giga .... (f) centi ....

Significant figures

Significant figures are digits that carry meaning for the precision of a number.

1 Which measurement is most precise?
(a) 8, (b) 8.1, (c) 7.9, (d) 7.90 ....
(e) 14.7, (f) 14, (g) 14.6, (h) 14.57 ....

2 How many significant figures?
(a) 6 cm .... (b) 71 m ....
(c) 8.2 km .... (d) 0.500 ....
(e) 6.0 cm .... (f) 0.037 ....

3 Round these figures to 3 significant figures:
(a) 7.654 .... (b) 0.02378 ....
(c) 0.1369 .... (d) 23.98 ....

4 Add and give the answer to 3 significant figures
(a) 145 + 27.36 ....
(b) 0.569 + 31.6 ....

5 Multiply and give the answer to 3 significant figures
(a) 23.98 × 28 ....
(b) 67.05 × 0.6 ....

Area and volume

Area: how much surface, e.g. in m^2 or cm^2
Volume: how much space is taken up, e.g. in m^3 or cm^3

1 Match the formula for area for each shape.

Circle	a^2
Square	$a \times b$
Right-angled triangle	$\frac{1}{2}\pi r^2$
Rectangle	πr^2
Semicircle	$\frac{1}{2} a \times b$

2 What is the area of each shape?
(a) Square of sides 6 cm ....
(b) Rectangle of sides 2 m and 4 m ....
(c) Right-angled triangle sides 3 × 4 cm ....

3 Match the formula for volume for each shape.

Cube	$\frac{4}{3}\pi r^3$
Cuboid	a^3
Sphere	$\pi r^2 \times b$
Cylinder	$a \times b \times c$

4 What is the volume of each shape?
(a) Cube of side 5 cm ....
(b) Sphere of radius 5 cm ....
(c) Cuboid of sides 3, 6 and 7 cm ....

Standard form

This is a numeral between 1 and 10, multiplied by a power of ten, e.g. 4.2×10^2 or 5.67×10^{-3}

1 Change these numerals to standard form
(a) 4500 .... (b) 63700 ....
(c) 0.560 .... (d) 0.078 ....

2 Change these from standard form
(a) 2.34×10^2 ....
(b) 5.7×10^2 ....
(c) 8.3×10^{-2} ....
(d) 6.23×10^{-4} ....

3 Add in standard form
(a) $2.5 \times 10^5 + 7.43 \times 10^6$ ....
(b) $5.6 \times 10^{-3} + 8.1 \times 10^{-5}$ ....

4 Subtract in standard form
(a) $4.32 \times 10^4 - 4.32 \times 10^3$ ....
(b) $9.96 \times 10^{-3} - 7.5 \times 10^{-3}$ ....

5 Multiply in standard form
(a) $(3.54 \times 10^2) \times (5.98 \times 10^{-2})$ ....
(b) $(8.45 \times 10^{-3}) \times (4.7 \times 10^{-2})$ ....

6 Divide in standard form
(a) $(8.7 \times 10^4) \div (5.8 \times 10^3)$ ....
(b) $(9.3 \times 10^{-2}) \div (3.75 \times 10^{-3})$ ....

Worksheet 5 Line graphs and gradients (SB9: BCP, Introduction p 20–3)

Line graphs

These show how two sets of numerical data vary with each other. We plot the values on axes on graph paper.

Independent variable is on the horizontal x-axis

Dependent variable is on the vertical y-axis

Gradient

The gradient of a line graph describes the slope =

$$\frac{\text{numerical change on the y-axis}}{\text{numerical change on the x-axis}}$$

1 Distance–time graph

(a) Plot the graph.

Use these readings of distance (m) and time (s)

m	0	25	50	50	50	100
s	0	5	10	15	20	25

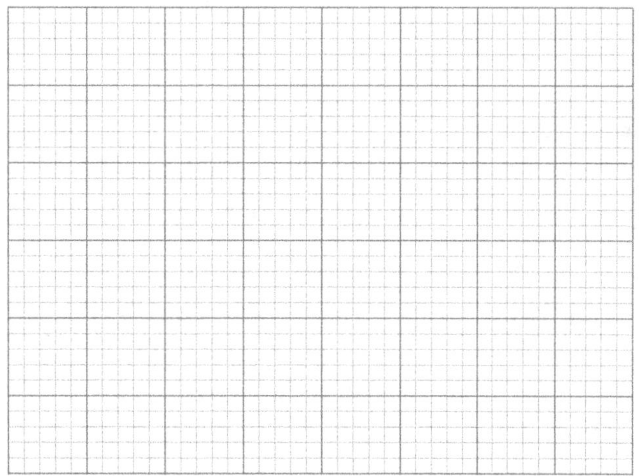

(b) What is the gradient (speed in ms^{-1})?

(i) Between 0 and 10 s

(ii) Between 10 and 20 s

(iii) Between 20 and 25 s

(iv) Describe how the speed varies.

2 Velocity–time graph

(a) Plot the graph.

Use these readings of velocity (ms^{-1}) and time (s)

ms^{-1}	0	5	10	10	10	20
s	0	5	10	15	20	25

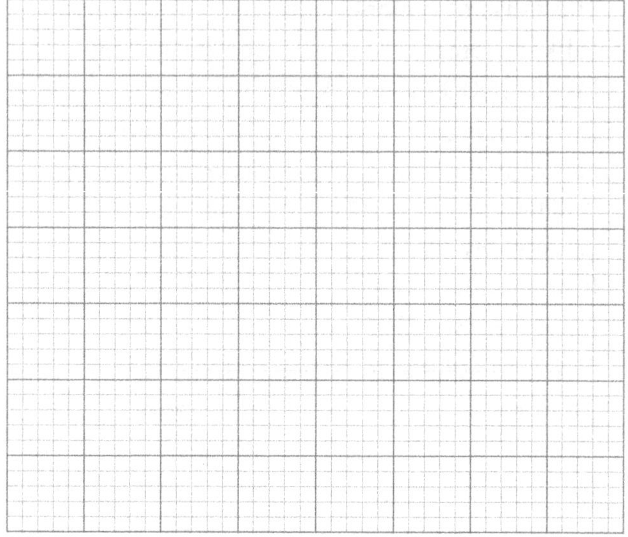

(b) What is the gradient (acceleration in ms^{-2})?

(i) Between 0 and 10 s

(ii) Between 10 and 20 s

(iii) Between 20 and 25 s

(iv) Describe how the acceleration varies.

3 What is the meaning of the flat part of the line you have plotted on a

(a) distance–time graph?

(b) velocity–time graph?

Worksheet 6 Diffusion and osmosis (SB9: BCP, Unit 16 p 30–3)

Matter is made up of very small particles. In a solid, these vibrate but do not move around. In liquids and gases, the particles can move (diffuse) from place to place to become evenly spread out. If one of the substances is water and there is a partially (selectively) permeable membrane to stop movement of the other substance, then the water passes through the membrane by osmosis. The cell membrane in cells is partially (selectively) permeable, so water enters and leaves the cells by osmosis.

1 Match the descriptions with the explanations.

Descriptions	Explanations
(a) Liquid A volume 30 cm^3 and liquid B volume 10 cm^3 when mixed have a final volume of 38 cm^3.	1 Cells have a cell membrane that lets small water particles pass through by osmosis, while preventing larger particles.
(b) The smell of an air freshener spreads out into a room.	2 Crystals dissolve and diffuse in water and water particles take their place.
(c) The colour of crystals gradually spreads through a glass of water.	3 There are spaces between particles of liquid A into which particles of liquid B can fit.
(d) A raisin or dry seed left in water swells up and gets bigger.	4 Air freshener particles move from areas of higher to lower concentration.

2 Match the names to the descriptions.

Names	Descriptions
(a) Diffusion	1 The change of state of water from liquid to vapour
(b) Osmosis	2 Movement of particles from a region of higher to a lower concentration
(c) Evaporation	3 Water moving from higher to lower concentration through a partially (selectively) permeable membrane

3 Add words from below to fill in the spaces.

(i) **vibrate liquids move concentration diffuse gradient lower solvent**

Particles in solids only (a) .... Their particles can only (b) .... around when they are heated to become (c) ...., or when they dissolve in a (d) .... In liquids and gases, the particles move (e) ....) from a region where they are in high (f) .... to an area of (g) .... concentration along a (h) .... (i) ....

(ii) **small osmosis larger membrane gradient enter diffusion higher**

Water moves by osmosis. (j) .... is a special case of (k) .... (water moves from a place of (l) .... concentration to a lower one) along a concentration (m) .... Water particles are (n) .... enough to pass through the spaces in the cell (o) .... (p) .... particles cannot pass through, so water can (q) .... or leave the cell.

Worksheet 7 Transport in plants (SB9: BCP, Unit 16 p 34–41)

Water (by osmosis) and mineral salts (by diffusion) enter the plant by the root hairs. The plant transports water and salts (up in xylem) to the leaves, and food (up and down in the phloem) to all parts of the plant. Water evaporates from the leaves (by transpiration) and this cools the plant.

1 Match the things that are transported to how they are transported.

(a) water and salts	1 up the plant from the roots to the leaves	A in the phloem
(b) food	2 out of leaves during respiration; and into leaves during photosynthesis	B by diffusion
(c) oxygen	3 up and down from the leaves to the plant parts	C in the xylem
(d) carbon dioxide	4 out of leaves during photosynthesis; and into leaves during respiration	

2 Match the movement of water to the processes.

(a) water enters the root by the root hairs	
(b) mineral salts enter the root by the root hairs	1 Transpiration
(c) water passes across the root cells	2 Diffusion
(d) water and mineral salts rise in the xylem	3 Osmosis
(e) water evaporates and passes out of the leaves	4 Transpiration pull and root push

3 Answer the questions and label the plant.

Label the lines and the arrows shown in the diagram on the right. Use these words.

phloem, carbon dioxide, water and salts, water and salts, food, xylem, sunlight energy, transpiration pull, root push

How is the entry of water and mineral salts different?

Why?

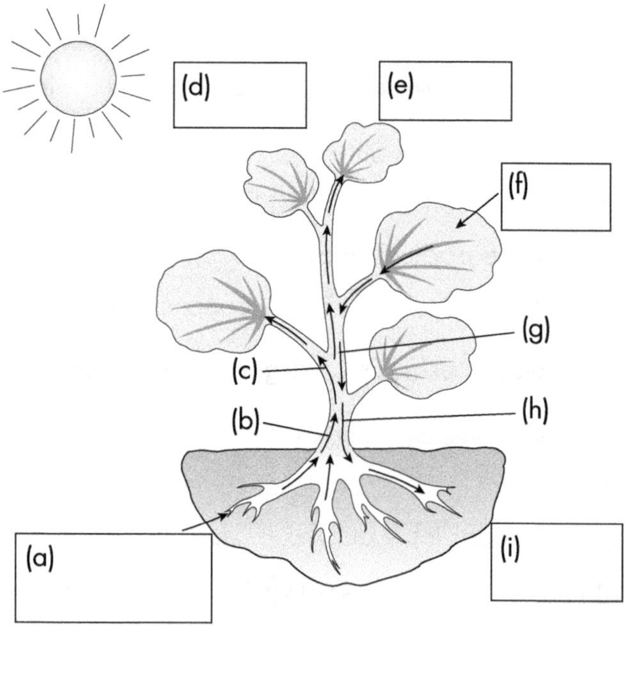

(d)
(e)
(f)
(g)
(c)
(b)
(h)
(a)
(i)

Worksheet 8 Blood and the heart (SB9: BCP, Unit 16 p 42–3, 46)

The blood transports gases, food, hormones and wastes, mends wounds and helps to fight disease. Arteries take blood away from the heart and veins return blood to the heart. Blood is either oxygenated (with a lot of oxygen) on the left side of the heart or de-oxygenated (with little oxygen) on the right side of the heart. The chambers of the heart beat to push blood around the body.

1 Match the parts of the blood to their functions.

(a) red cells	1 fight disease organisms by making antibodies and antitoxins
(b) white cells: lymphocytes	2 contain haemoglobin to pick up and carry oxygen
(c) platelets	3 liquid for carrying food, carbon dioxide, wastes, hormones
(d) white cells: phagocytes	4 surround and digest disease organisms
(e) plasma	5 with chemicals in the plasma, they help the blood to clot

2 Label the blood vessels and compartments (a) to (h) and the types of blood shown by arrows (i) to (l) on the diagram of a section of the heart. Then colour the oxygenated blood red and the de-oxygenated blood blue.

venae cava	pulmonary artery	blood to lungs from right ventricle
aorta	pulmonary vein	blood from body to right atrium
right atrium	right ventricle	blood from lungs to left atrium
left atrium	left ventricle	blood to body from left ventricle

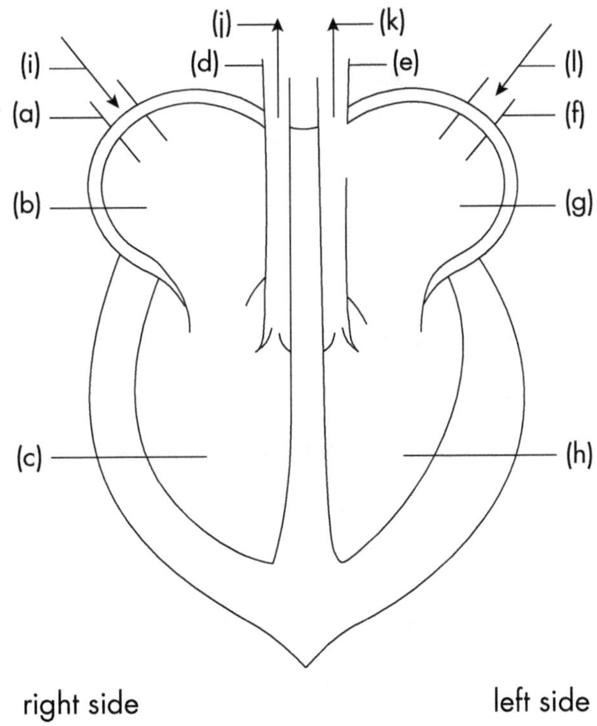

3 Why is it important that the two sides of the heart are separate? ....

....

Worksheet 9 Circulation in humans (SB9: BCP, Unit 16 p 45, 47–9)

There is a double circulation. Most arteries contain oxygenated blood, with food, that is taken to parts of the body to the capillaries that supply oxygen and food to individual body cells. The blood in the capillaries picks up carbon dioxide, heat and other wastes and returns it to veins. The veins return to the heart. The other circulation is of the pulmonary artery (with de-oxygenated blood) going to the lungs where it picks up oxygen, and returns in the pulmonary vein (with oxygenated blood) to the heart.

1 Match the names to the functions and diagrams.

(a) arteries 	1 Walls one-cell thick; provide food and oxygen to cells by diffusion and remove wastes.
(b) capillaries 	2 Thinner walls than arteries; return blood to the heart and have valves in their walls.
(c) veins	3 Thick, muscular walls; take blood away from the heart towards the body organs.

A

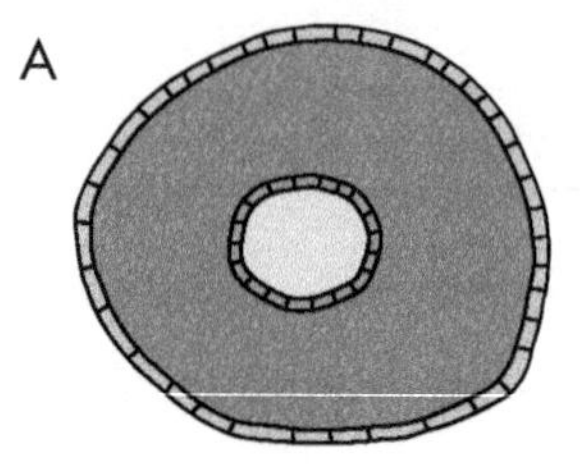

B

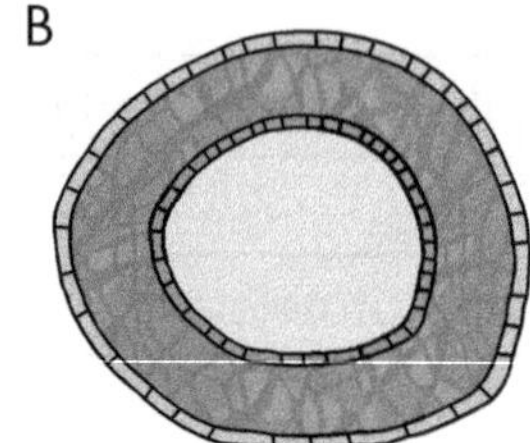

C

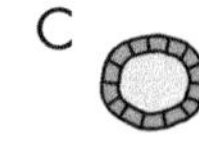

2 Add the labels below to the diagram which shows how the heart sends blood to the body cells.

Add arrows to show the direction of blood flow.

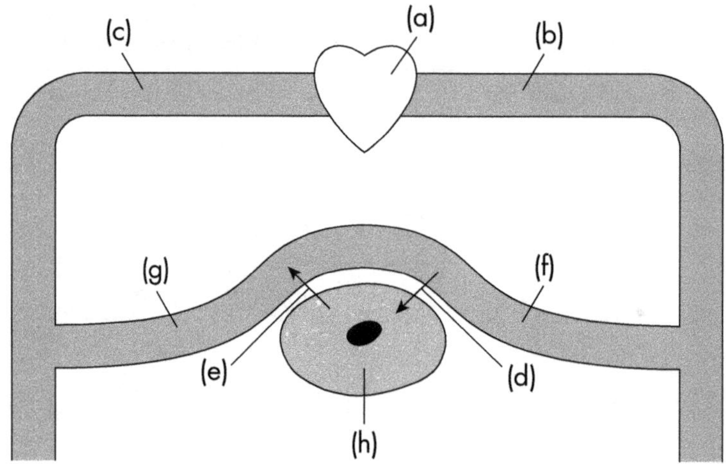

de-oxygenated blood	arteries carry blood from heart to capillaries
oxygenated blood	veins carry blood from capillaries to heart
heart pumps blood	oxygen and food diffuse into the cell
body cell	carbon dioxide, heat and wastes diffuse out of the cell

3 Fill in the spaces using these words.

carbon dioxide **vein** **oxygen** **artery** **alveoli**

Blood is brought to the (a) .... of the lungs in the pulmonary (b) ....

The (c) .... diffuses out of the blood, and (d) .... diffuses into it. The blood returns to the heart in the pulmonary (e) ....

Worksheet 10 Problems with circulation (SB9: BCP, Unit 16 p 50–3)

Problems with circulation have several causes (deficiency, inherited, parasitic and functional). Problems lead to changes in the blood, the vessels (arteries and veins) or the heart and our health is affected. We can avoid some problems by making changes to our diet, exercise and lifestyle.

1 Match the cause of the problem to the reason and an example.

(a) deficiency disease	1 problems with the functioning of the arteries, veins or heart	A HIV/AIDS
(b) inherited disease	2 caused by micro-organisms, e.g. virus causing HIV	B varicose veins, heart attack
(c) parasitic disease	3 insufficient minerals or vitamins in the diet, e.g. iron	C sickle cell anaemia
(d) functional disease	4 faulty genes inherited from one or both parents	D anaemia

2 Match the part of the circulatory system to the problems.

(a) Veins	1 Anaemia, sickle cell anaemia, HIV/AIDS
(b) Arteries	2 High blood pressure, hardening or narrowing of the arteries
(c) Heart	3 Backflow through the valves, aching legs, varicose veins
(d) Blood	4 Problems with damaged heart valves or coronary arteries

3 Identify things you should (√) or shouldn't do (X) to help your circulatory system.

	1 Eat a balanced diet and avoid overweight.
	2 Avoid exercise and enjoy fatty foods.
	3 Avoid saturated fats and check cholesterol levels are low.
	4 Avoid taking medicines to help lower high blood pressure.
	5 Smoke cigarettes and eat pizza and chips.
	6 Lead a healthy lifestyle with exercise and adequate sleep.

4 Fill in the table to describe the cause and possible precautions or treatment.

Problem	Cause	Precautions or treatment
Anaemia		
Varicose veins		
High blood pressure		
Angina		
Heart attack		

Worksheet 11 Sense organs: Skin, tongue and nose (SB9: BCP, Unit 17 p 58–62)

We have special sense organs that contain sensory cells or nerve endings sensitive to various stimuli. For example, chemicals in our food are sensed as tastes by our tongue, and smells by our nose. When the sensitive cells are stimulated, they send messages along nerves to the brain for interpretation.

1 Match the senses to the organs and stimuli.

Senses	(a) Touch	(b) Taste	(c) Smell	(d) Sight	(e) Hearing

Sense organs	1 Nose	2 Skin	3 Ear	4 Tongue	5 Eye

Stimuli	A Light	B Sound	C Temperature	D Chemicals	E Touch

2 Match the senses to the sensitive cells.

(a) Touch

(b) Taste

(c) Smell

1 Sensitive cells in taste buds: sensitive to dissolved chemicals:

- Bitter, e.g. sensitive to coffee
- Sour, e.g. sensitive to lime
- Salt, e.g. sensitive to common salt
- Sweet, e.g. sensitive to sugar

2 Sensitive cells in the skin:

- Heat and cold sensors: sense differences in temperature
- Pain sensors: in the top layer of the skin, very sensitive
- Light touch sensors: common in the fingertips, used to respond to textures
- Pressure sensors: deeper in the skin, stimulated by continuous pressure

3 Sensitive cells in the nasal cavity sensitive to chemicals in the air and from our food, e.g.

- Pleasant and unpleasant smells
- Familiar and unfamiliar smells

3 Did you know? When we have a cold, our nasal passages become blocked. So the odours from our food cannot stimulate the sensory cells sensitive to smells – so our food seems less tasty.

4 Match each sense organ to the sensitive cells or sensitive nerve endings that respond to stimuli.

(a) Skin

(b) Tongue

(c) Nose

(d) Eye

(e) Ear

1 Sensory cells are rods (sensitive to light and dark) and three kinds of cones (sensitive to red, green and blue). Impulses are sent along the optic nerve.

2 Sensory cells have hairs and different cells respond to different vibrations and set up impulses sent to the brain along the auditory nerve.

3 Sensory cells with sensitive hairs at one end and a sensory nerve fibre at the other end sending impulses to the brain. Arranged inside taste buds.

4 Simple nerve endings: pain sensors (no covering), heat and cold sensors (simple coverings) and touch and pressure sensors (several covering layers).

5 Sensory cells with sensitive hairs at one end and a sensory nerve fibre at the other end sending impulses to the brain. Found in the nasal cavity.

Worksheet 12 Sense organs: Eye and ear (SB9: BCP, Unit 17 p 63–71)

The sensory cells in the eye are the rods and cones in the retina. Rods are sensitive to dark and light. Different cones are sensitive to red, blue or green light. The lens focuses the light rays to form an image on the retina. All the colours we see depend on the numbers of red, blue or green sensitive cones that are stimulated. Impulses are then sent in to the brain along the optic nerve and we see.

1 Match the parts of the eye to their functions.

Part
(a) aqueous humour
(b) blind spot
(c) choroid
(d) ciliary muscle
(e) conjunctiva
(f) cornea
(g) eye muscle
(h) iris
(i) lens
(j) optic nerve
(k) pupil
(l) retina
(m) sclera
(n) suspensory ligament
(o) vitreous humour

Function
1 transparent protective covering of the eye
2 transparent front of the eye
3 hole to let light into the eye
4 watery material in front of the lens
5 coloured part: controls the size of the pupil
6 can make the lens change its shape
7 curved transparent part to focus the light
8 holds the lens in place
9 contracts or relaxes to move the eye
10 protective outer layer
11 middle layer: contains blood vessels
12 sensitive layer containing rods and cones
13 jelly that keeps the eyeball in a round shape
14 place where the optic nerve leaves the eye
15 nerve that takes messages to the brain

Sounds are set up as objects vibrate and in turn make particles of nearby solids, liquids or gases vibrate to make sound waves. There are no sounds in a vacuum. Our ears collect the sound waves and vibrations are passed along through the parts of the ear and finally stimulate the sensory cells in the cochlea. Here nervous impulses are set up and sent in to the brain along the auditory nerve which produces 'hearing'.

2 Match the parts of the ear to their functions.

Part
(a) anvil
(b) auditory nerve
(c) cochlea
(d) ear bones
(e) ear canal
(f) eardrum
(g) ear flap
(h) Eustachian tube
(i) hammer
(j) oval window
(k) round window
(l) semi-circular canals
(m) stirrup

Function
1 part that collects sound waves
2 canal that directs sounds to the eardrum
3 at the end of the ear canal; it vibrates
4 first of the ear bones, nearest to the eardrum
5 middle ear bone
6 third ear bone, connects to the oval window
7 three ear bones pass on vibrations
8 vibrates when moved by the stirrup
9 organ concerned with balance
10 contains sensitive cells and sets up messages
11 nerve that takes messages to the brain
12 releases pressure in the middle ear
13 moves in an opposite way to the oval window

Worksheet 13 CNS and reflex actions (SB9: BCP, Unit 17 p 72–6)

The central nervous system is made up of the brain and spinal cord. The other part of the nervous system is the peripheral nervous system. This is made up of sensory nerves that bring in messages from the sense organs, and motor nerves that take messages out to the muscles and glands. If the messages go to the forebrain, we think about them (voluntary). But if messages only go to the spinal cord or lower part of the brain, there is quick, rapid action of a reflex action (arc) without thought (involuntary).

1 Match the systems to their parts and examples.

Systems	Parts	Examples
	1 Nerves	A optic nerve
(a) Peripheral nervous system	2 Spinal cord	B eye
		C hindbrain
(b) Central nervous system	3 Endocrine glands	D pancreas
		E forebrain
(c) Endocrine system	4 Brain	F thyroid
		G skin
	5 Sense organs	H auditory nerve

2 Match the parts of the brain to their functions.

Part	Function
(a) Forebrain (cerebrum)	1 Co-ordinates movement and balance; involuntary and voluntary
(b) Midbrain (cerebellum)	2 Automatic responses for heart rate, breathing and temperature.
(c) Hindbrain (medulla oblongata)	3 Largest part; allows us to think, plan and remember. It receives and interprets nervous impulses from the sense organs.

3 Fill in the spaces using these words.

voluntary **hindbrain** **forebrain** **involuntary** **reflex** **sensory**

The sense organs pass in impulses along (a) .... nerves. In a (b) .... action, messages go to the spinal cord or (c) .... and there is an immediate (d) .... response. But if the messages go to the (e) ...., there can be a (f) .... response.

4 Match the parts of a reflex arc to their functions.

Part	Function
(a) effector	1 a change in the surroundings, e.g. heat
(b) motor nerve fibre	2 sensitive cells in a sense organ
(c) receptor	3 nerve taking impulses in to the spinal cord
(d) relay fibre	4 linking nerve fibre in the spinal cord
(e) response	5 nerve taking impulses away from spinal cord
(f) sensory nerve fibre	6 muscle that receives impulses and contracts
(g) stimulus	7 resulting action to prevent damage

Worksheet 14 Nervous and endocrine systems (SB9: BCP, Unit 17 p 72–9)

In the nervous system, messages are sent very quickly along nerves using electrical impulses. One nerve then passes on its message to another one using chemicals. In the endocrine system, special chemicals, hormones, are passed into the blood and can affect the growth or action of other organs over a long period of time. The different hormones have different actions and the body responds to over- or under-production in various ways.

1 Fill in the table comparing the nervous and endocrine systems.

Characteristics	Nervous system	Endocrine system
How it works		
How messages are transported		
Speed of action		
Importance		
Effect		
Effects of not working well		

2 Match the endocrine organs to their hormones and their importance.

Organ	Hormone	Importance
(a) pituitary	1 testosterone	A fight or flight hormone
(b) thyroid	2 growth hormone	B rate of body reactions
(c) pancreas	3 insulin	C female sex hormone
(d) adrenals	4 oestrogen	D controls rate of growth
(e) ovary	5 thyroxine	E male sex hormone
(f) testes	6 adrenaline	F controls blood sugar

3 Fill in the spaces using these words.

(i) **nervous endocrine long-lasting electrical short hormones**

The (a) .... system depends on (b) .... impulses passed along nerves and having a (c) .... -term effect. The (d) .... system depends on (e) .... passed straight into the blood that have a (f) .... effect.

(ii) **quick oxygen insulin adrenaline diabetes fight muscles**

The adrenal glands produce the hormone, (g) .... This is unusual in because its action is very (h) .... It prepares the body for flight or (i) .... The heart and breathing rates are increased, so that more (j) .... and food are sent to the (k) .... The pancreas produces (l) .... that helps to control how much glucose is in the blood. A person without enough of the hormone, suffers from (m) .... and may need to take daily injections.

Worksheet 15 Before and after birth (SB9: BCP, Unit 18 p 86–9)

Growth from a fertilised egg to eight weeks is called the embryo; from then until birth is called the foetus. The foetus receives oxygen and food from the mother via the placenta and umbilical cord and gets rid of carbon dioxide and other wastes back to the placenta. After birth the baby has to breathe, receive and digest food, and get rid of wastes for itself.

1 Match the stages to the descriptions.

(a) unfertilised egg
(b) fertilised egg
(c) ball of cells
(d) embryo
(e) foetus: 2 months
(f) foetus: 6 months
(g) foetus: 9 months

1 buds grow out to become arms and legs
2 made by division of the zygote and imbeds in the uterus
3 zygote produced when sperm fertilises the egg
4 full term; born as a baby
5 released from the ovary in middle of menstrual cycle
6 can hear, suck its thumb and hiccup
7 stage from imbedding to 8 weeks; has brain and heart

2 Label the blood vessels and the things transferred in the blood. Labels may be used more than once.

umbilical vein **food** **carbon dioxide** **other wastes** **oxygen** **umbilical artery**

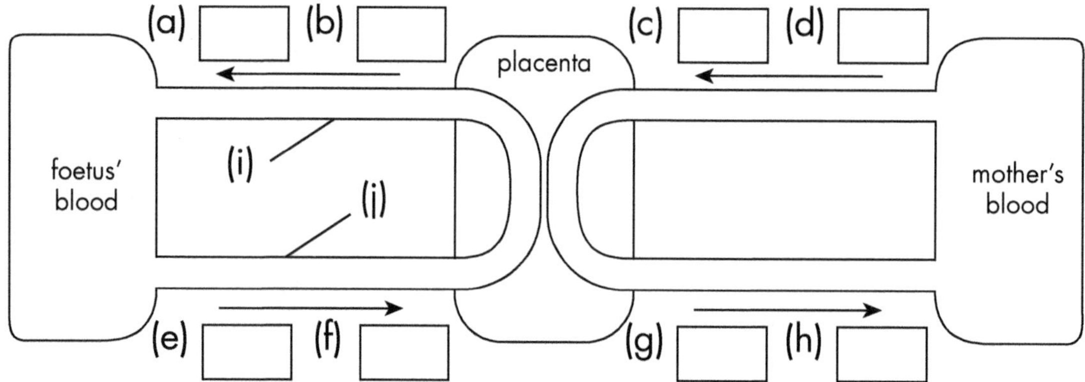

3 Match what happens before and after birth.

(a) Oxygenated blood from the placenta.
(b) Wastes, e.g. urea are taken away to the placenta.
(c) Food is supplied from the placenta.
(d) De-oxygenated blood goes from the foetus to the placenta.
(e) Foetus does not digest its food.
(f) Amniotic fluid keeps the foetus at a steady temperature.

1 Baby needs to be wrapped up to keep warm.
2 Blood returns from the lungs to the left atrium.
3 Urea is excreted by the kidneys.
4 Blood is sent from the right ventricle to the lungs.
5 Food is given as mother's milk.
6 Digestion in the gut produces wastes passed out as faeces.

Worksheet 16 A healthy pregnancy (SB9: BCP, Unit 18 p 91–6)

Unplanned teenage pregnancies can cause problems for the mother, father and the child. A pregnant woman should try to plan her pregnancy and have a healthy diet, avoid alcohol, smoking and illegal drugs. She should be careful with prescription drugs and avoid catching STIs, especially HIV. She should have vaccinations against German measles. Regular prenatal check-ups are also important.

1 Match the likely problems of teenage pregnancies to their possible results.

(a) Unplanned	1 Unlikely that the mother or father-to-be will have the money to support the new family.
(b) Physical problems	2 Pregnancy upsets the education of the mother-to-be, making it less likely to get a good job later on.
(c) Emotional problems	3 A young teenager still has to grow and develop her own body, and this can cause problems in the pregnancy and at birth.
(d) Financial problems	4 Unlikely that the mother or father-to-be have been following guidelines for a healthy pregnancy.
(e) Educational problems	5 Adolescence is a time of hormonal changes; pregnancy will add an additional strain.

2 Match the actions to the possible results.

(a) Being exposed to picking up STIs, e.g. HIV	1 Possible birth defects, miscarriage and learning difficulties can occur.
(b) Having a healthy diet	2 For example, thalidomide, caused babies with brain damage and flipper-like limbs.
(c) Drinking excess alcohol	3 Diet contains additional nutrients needed by foetus, which is likely to be healthy.
(d) Having an illegal abortion	4 Deficiencies may cause spina bifida, anaemia or poor development of bones.
(e) Taking illegal drugs: drug abuse	5 In early pregnancy, if the mother has not been vaccinated, can cause eye and ear defects.
(f) Avoiding prenatal care	6 Can also cause damage to the mother e.g. infections and becoming unable to have other children later.
(g) Having a lack of folic acid, iron or calcium	7 Without treatment, both mother and baby may be infected with HIV/AIDS.
(h) Taking certain prescription drugs	8 Affects the mother and can cause slow growth of foetus, low birth rate or miscarriage.
(i) Smoking too much	9 For example, heroin, can cause addiction and damage for both mother and baby.
(j) Catching German measles while pregnant	10 Makes it more likely that possible problems with STIs and Rhesus factor will be missed.

Worksheet 17 Birth control methods (SB9: BCP, Unit 18 p 97–101)

Birth control methods reduce the chance of sperm meeting an egg to fertilise it. The methods can be

- natural: by calculating and then avoiding having intercourse on 'fertile' days, or
- artificial: by using a barrier or chemicals, or by having a surgical operation.

1 Match the questions on the left with the likely times on the right.

Questions	Likely times
(a) Roughly, when is an egg released from the ovary?	1 During and each side of her period
(b) Roughly, how long can an unfertilised egg survive?	2 The middle of the menstrual cycle
(c) Roughly, how long can sperm live?	3 About 24 hours
(d) Roughly, when is a woman least likely to conceive?	4 About 5–7 days

2 Match the methods of birth control to the examples.

(a) Natural

(b) Barrier

(c) Chemical

(d) Surgical

1 Diaphragm: rubber cap fitted around the cervix.

2 Withdrawal: removal of penis before ejaculating.

3 Contraceptive pills: chemicals stop eggs being released.

4 Methods without chemicals or artificial devices.

5 Rhythm method: avoiding sex on fertile days.

6 Condom: rubber used over the penis to collect sperm.

7 Billings method: uses temperature and mucus changes.

8 A barrier prevents eggs and sperm from meeting.

9 Female condom: put into the vagina to collect sperm.

10 Need a doctor for surgery or implanting a device.

11 Vasectomy: cutting of sperm ducts.

12 Contraceptive patches or injections: work in a similar way to contraceptive pills.

13 Tubal ligation: cutting the Fallopian tubes.

14 Spermicide cream: kills sperm.

15 IUD: put into the uterus to stop implantation.

16 'Morning-after' pills: taken after intercourse, they stop the fertilised egg from implanting.

Worksheet 18 The periodic table (SB9: BCP, Unit 19 p 112–16)

We describe each element by its mass number (= number of protons + number of neutrons), chemical symbol (e.g. S), name (e.g. sulphur) and atomic number (= number of protons). Atoms are neutral (number of protons = number of electrons). Elements are arranged in the periodic table into family groups based on their similar arrangements of electrons, how they form ions, and their properties.

1 Complete the information in the table. Then use it to fill in a square for each element.

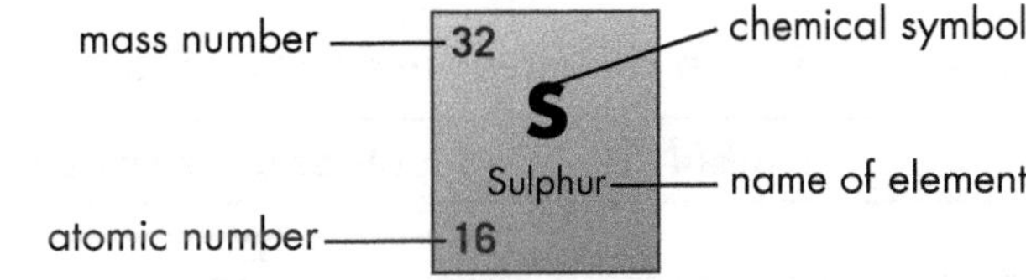

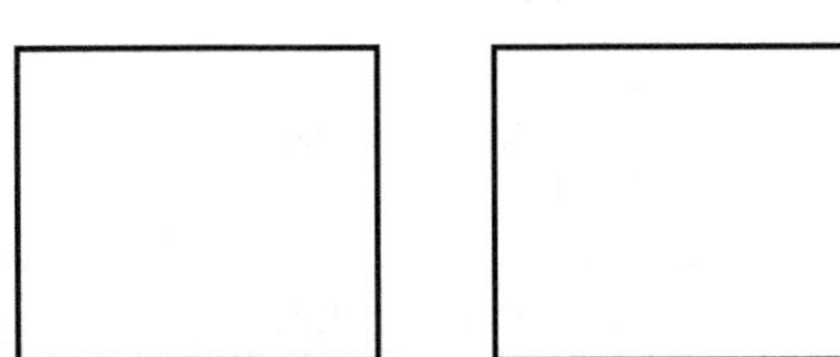
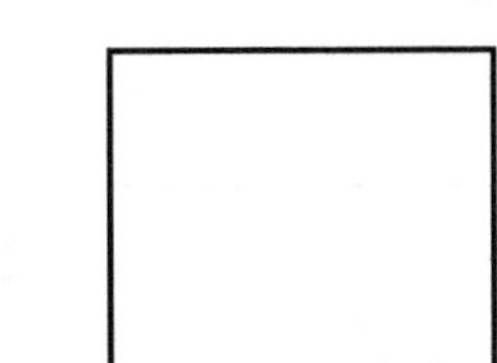
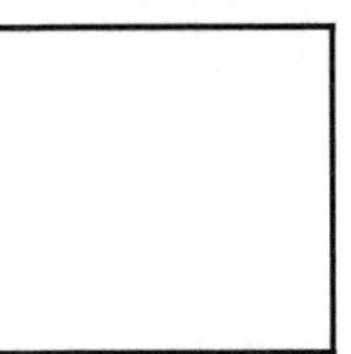
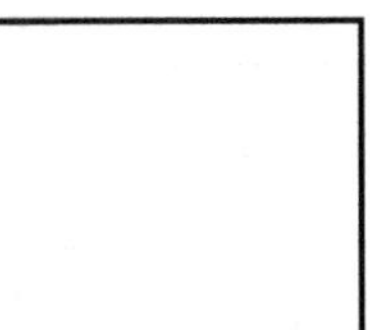

Element	Symbol	Number of protons	Number of neutrons	Mass number
Lithium	Li	3	4	
Potassium			20	39
	He	2		4
Argon			22	40
	F	9		19
Oxygen		8	8	

2 Complete the information in the table for the atoms of these elements.

Element	Symbol	Number of protons	Number of electrons	Atomic number
Sodium	Na		11	11
Neon		10		
	Be	4		
Fluorine				9
	S	16		
Magnesium			12	

3 Match the elements to their groups and their characteristics.

Elements
(a) Helium
(b) Potassium
(c) Argon
(d) Fluorine
(e) Lithium
(f) Neon
(g) Chlorine
(h) Sodium

1 Noble gases

2 Alkali metals

3 Halogens

A All very reactive metals. They lose their outer electron to become +ve ions.

B All very reactive non-metals. They gain an outer electron to become –ve ions.

C All very unreactive. Their outer shell of electrons is full.

Worksheet 19 Ionic and covalent bonding (SB9: BCP, Unit 19 p 116–22)

Ionic bonding occurs between metals and non-metals. Electrons are transferred. The metal atom loses electron(s) to become a positively charged ion, while the non-metal atom gains electron(s) to become a negatively charged ion, e.g. Na^+Cl^-. Covalent bonding occurs between the same or different non-metals. Electrons are shared. Molecules are formed where the outer shells share 2 or 8 electrons, e.g. NH_3, O_2.

1 Complete the table and add if the particles are atoms, or ions (together with their charge).

Element	Symbol	Number of protons	Number of electrons	Atom or ion?
Magnesium		12		Ion Charge 2^+
	Na	11	10	
Chlorine			17	Atom Neutral
Chlorine		17		Ion Charge 1^-
	K		18	Ion Charge 1^+
	F	9	10	

2 Draw the structure of calcium and chloride ions.

Calcium atom	Calcium ion	Chlorine atom	Chloride ion
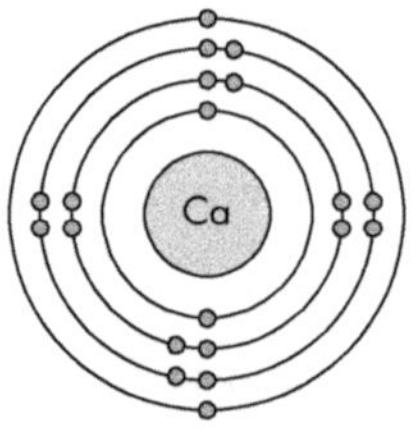 Ca		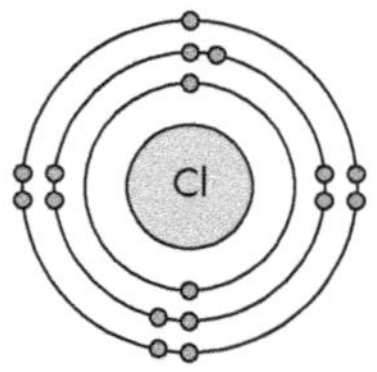 Cl	

3 If calcium and chloride ions combine, what is the compound and formula? ....

4 Draw the structure of an oxygen molecule (O_2) formed by covalent bonding.

Two oxygen atoms	One molecule of oxygen gas
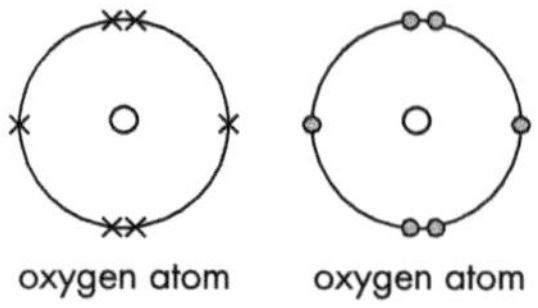 O O oxygen atom oxygen atom	

5 Draw the structure of a molecule of ammonia gas (NH_3) formed by covalent bonding.

Hydrogen and nitrogen atoms	One molecule of ammonia gas
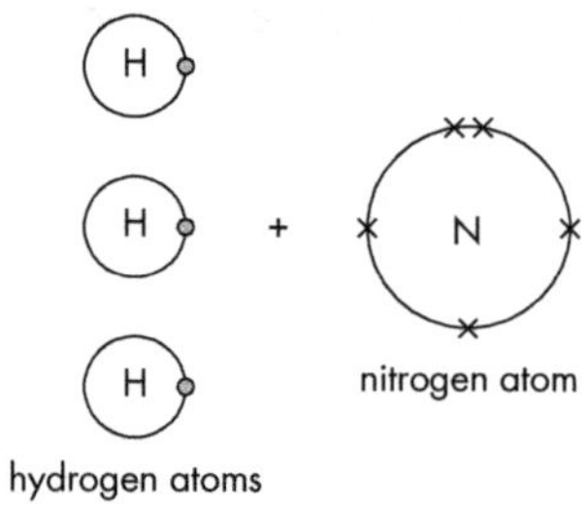 H H H + N hydrogen atoms nitrogen atom	

Worksheet 20 Chemical reactions and equations (SB9: BCP, Unit 19 p 123–30, 133)

Chemical substances (reactants) react to form new substances (products). The numbers of atoms in the products equal the same kinds of atoms in the reactants (law of conservation of mass). Overall, energy is either taken in (endothermic) or produced (exothermic). There are different types of chemical reactions. We write chemical formulae for the reactants and products and then balance the equations.

Oxidation: combining with oxygen

Metals, e.g. magnesium burn in oxygen to form magnesium oxide (a basic oxide).

Non-metals, e.g. sulphur and carbon, burn in oxygen to form sulphur oxide, carbon dioxide and carbon monoxide (acidic oxides).

Complete and then balance the equations.

1 magnesium + oxygen → magnesium oxide

2 sulphur + oxygen → sulphur oxide

3 carbon + oxygen → carbon dioxide

4 carbon + oxygen → carbon monoxide

Synthesis: combination of simple substances

Metals, e.g. iron can combine with a non-metal, e.g. sulphur to make iron sulphide.

Also, sodium can burn in chlorine gas to combine to make sodium chloride.

Photosynthesis is also a combination of simple substances, carbon dioxide and water, to make glucose ($C_6H_{12}O_6$) and oxygen.

Complete and then balance the equations.

1 iron + sulphur → iron sulphide

2 sodium + chlorine → sodium chloride

3 carbon dioxide + water → glucose + oxygen

Decomposition: breaking down

Many carbonates and hydrogencarbonates can be broken down into smaller molecules by heating. The original molecule is decomposed.

Copper and calcium carbonates decompose to make copper and calcium oxide and carbon dioxide.

Sodium hydrogencarbonate decomposes to sodium carbonate, carbon dioxide and water.

Complete and then balance the equations.

1 copper carbonate → copper oxide + carbon dioxide

2 calcium carbonate → calcium oxide + carbon dioxide

3 sodium hydrogencarbonate → sodium carbonate + carbon dioxide + water

Displacement: replacing other elements

A reactive metal, e.g. magnesium, can displace a less reactive one, e.g. copper from its salt.

Double displacement reactions occur where the parts of the molecules swap partners.

Reactive metals can also push hydrogen out of water, and many metals replace the hydrogen in acids.

Complete and then balance the equations.

1 magnesium + copper sulphate → magnesium sulphate + copper

2 barium chloride + zinc sulphate → barium sulphate + zinc chloride

3 calcium + water → calcium hydroxide + hydrogen

Worksheet 21 Balancing chemical equations (SB9: BCP, Unit 19 p 131–5)

The stages in writing a balanced chemical equation are: (a) write the word equation (based on your activity, or you may be given it), (b) write the chemical formulae (based on the combining power and so that each compound is neutral and gases are in the form of molecules), and (c) balance the equation (so that there are as many of each kind of atom in the products as in the reactants).

1 Match the names to the examples and descriptions.

(a) radicals	1 NO_3 and SO_4	A describing the charges on ions
(b) subscript	2 the 2 in Na_2O and Cl_2	B writing chemical formulae
(c) superscript	3 the 2 in 2MgO	C balancing chemical equations
(d) coefficient	4 Cu^{2+} and F^-	D describing combining power
(e) brackets	5 $Ca(NO_3)_2$ and $(NH_4)_2SO_4$	

2 Enter the symbols of elements, and radicals (in brackets), with the correct combining powers.
H, K, Cu, Zn, O, F, Al, Na, Mg, Ca, N, S, Cl, (CO_3), (HCO_3), (NO_3), (SO_4), (OH), (NH_4)

3–	2–	1–	1+	2+	3+

3 How many oxygen atoms in: (a) $2Ca(NO_3)_2$ .... (b) $3Zn(HCO_3)_2$ ....

How many hydrogen atoms in (c) $2C_6H_{12}O_6$ .... (d) $2(NH_4)_2SO_4$ ....

4 For the following word equations: write the chemical formulae and then balance the equations.
(a) magnesium + fluorine → magnesium fluoride

(b) ammonium chloride + sodium sulphate → ammonium sulphate + sodium chloride

(c) calcium + hydrochloric acid → calcium chloride + hydrogen

(d) sodium + water → sodium hydroxide + hydrogen

(e) sodium hydrogencarbonate + hydrochloric acid → sodium chloride + carbon dioxide + water

(f) copper sulphate + sodium hydroxide → copper hydroxide + sodium sulphate

Worksheet 22 Acids, alkalis and indicators (SB9: BCP, Unit 20 p 140–3)

Acids produce hydrogen ions, and alkalis (soluble bases) produce hydroxide ions. Acids turn blue litmus red; bases and alkalis turn damp red litmus blue. Other acid-base indicators are methyl orange and phenolphthalein. An indicator that changes different colours from pH 1 to 14 is called universal indicator. A pH lower than 7 shows an acid with a lot of hydrogen ions; a pH higher than 7 shows a base or alkali. Substances with a pH of 7 are called neutral, e.g. distilled water and many salts.

1 Match the names to acidic or basic and the likely pH.

(a) apple juice	1 Acidic	A pH 3
(b) window cleaner		B pH 4
(c) vinegar	2 Basic or alkaline	C pH 12
(d) oven cleaner		D pH 13

2 Match the names to characteristics and examples

(a) weak acid	1 Produces few hydrogen ions	A Hydrochloric acid
(b) concentrated acid	2 Has a lot of water and little acid	B Citric acid
(c) strong acid	3 Has a lot of acid and little water	C Dilute sulphuric acid
(d) dilute acid	4 Produces a lot of hydrogen ions	D Concentrated sulphuric acid

3 (a) Fill in the colours of the indicators when put into these solutions.

Indicator	Colour in acid	Colour in alkali
Litmus paper or solution		
Methyl orange		
Phenolphthalein		
Universal indicator		
Hibiscus		
Red cabbage		

(b) How is universal indicator different from the others? ....

4 Use the words to fill in the spaces.

hydroxide alkalis 7 hydrogen 12–14 neutral 1–2 acids skin pH ions strong

The (a) .... value describes the number of hydrogen (b) .... in solution. A (c) .... acid will have a lot of (d) .... (e) .... and a (f) .... value of (g) .... A (h) .... alkali will have a lot of (i) .... (j) .... and a (k) .... value of (l) ....

Both strong (m) .... and (n) .... are corrosive and dangerous to eat or have on our (o) .... Most of our food and drink is (p) .... with a pH around (q) ....

Worksheet 23 Reactions of acids and alkalis (SB9: BCP, Unit 20 p 144–9)

Acids, e.g. hydrochloric and sulphuric acids, contain hydrogen atoms and can produce hydrogen ions. Bases are oxides and hydroxides of metals and they can produce hydroxide ions. Alkalis are bases that dissolve in water. Acids and bases have different properties and react in different ways.

1 List the numbers of the characteristics in the correct parts of the table.

1 turns blue litmus red	13 e.g. calcium oxide
2 are metal oxides and hydroxides	14 may dissolve to form an alkali
3 e.g. bee stings	15 make hydrogen ions in solution
4 e.g. ammonium hydroxide	16 releases hydrogen with metals
5 neutralised by acids	17 have a pH over 7
6 have a pH below 7	18 e.g. vitamin C
7 can be corrosive	19 neutralised by bases and alkalis
8 make hydroxide ions in solution	20 e.g. carbonic acid
9 turns red litmus blue	21 change the colour of an indicator
10 e.g. caustic soda (sodium hydroxide)	22 react with carbonates to make carbon dioxide
11 when neutralised, make a salt and water	23 e.g. wasp stings
12 e.g. ethanoic acid in vinegar	24 can be used as antacids

Acids	Bases
1,	

2 Acids react with metals to release hydrogen. Write balanced chemical equations.

(a) calcium + hydrochloric acid = calcium chloride + hydrogen

(b) magnesium + hydrochloric acid = magnesium chloride + hydrogen

(c) aluminium + hydrochloric acid = aluminium chloride + hydrogen

3 Acids react with carbonates and hydrogencarbonates to release carbon dioxide. Write the equations.

(a) sodium carbonate + hydrochloric acid = sodium chloride + carbon dioxide + water

(b) calcium carbonate + hydrochloric acid = calcium chloride + carbon dioxide + water

(c) sodium hydrogencarbonate + hydrochloric acid = sodium chloride + carbon dioxide + water

4 Alkalis react with metal and ammonium salt solutions. Write the equations.

(a) copper sulphate + sodium hydroxide = copper hydroxide + sodium sulphate

(b) iron chloride + sodium hydroxide = iron hydroxide + sodium chloride

(c) barium nitrate + sodium hydroxide = barium hydroxide + sodium nitrate

(d) ammonium chloride + sodium hydroxide = sodium chloride + ammonia + water

Worksheet 24 Neutralisation and making salts (SB9: BCP, Unit 20 p 150–7)

Acids react with bases to produce a salt and water only. This is called neutralisation. The salt produced has the radical from the acid (e.g. chloride, sulphate, nitrate) and the metal or ammonium part from the base (e.g. sodium, calcium, ammonium). Salts can be made in several ways and they have important uses.

1 Use the words to fill in the spaces.

hydroxide metal base neutralise salt hydrogen radical concentration

An acid and a (a) .... in the same amount and (b) .... will (c) .... each other. The (d) .... ions from the acid combine with the (e) .... ions from the base, to form water. The (f) .... from the acid combines with the (g) .... or ammonium group from the base, to form a (h) ....

2 Match the salts to the reactions that make them and to their uses.

(a) Hydrochloric acid and sodium hydroxide	1 Ammonium nitrate	A Laxative
(b) Nitric acid and ammonium hydroxide	2 Sodium chloride	B Common salt
(c) Sulphuric acid and magnesium hydroxide	3 Magnesium sulphate	C Fertiliser

3 Write balanced chemical equations for these neutralisation reactions.

(a) hydrochloric acid + sodium hydroxide →

(b) nitric acid + calcium hydroxide →

(c) nitric acid +ammonium hydroxide →

(d) sulphuric acid + magnesium hydroxide →

4 Explain two ways in which neutralisation is useful in everyday life.

(a) ....

(b) ....

5 Write balanced equations for these reactions that make salts.

(a) hydrochloric acid + calcium oxide →

(b) sulphuric acid + ammonium hydroxide →

(c) nitric acid + sodium carbonate →

(d) hydrochloric acid + magnesium →

(e) iron + sulphur →

Worksheet 25 Static electricity (SB9: BCP, Unit 21 p 170–2)

Atoms contain neutral nuclei surrounded by negatively charged electrons. If a non-metal material, e.g. plastic, is rubbed with a woollen cloth, some of the electrons are removed from the cloth and make the plastic negatively charged. This can then induce the opposite charge in small pieces of paper, which are attracted. Static electricity, and the attraction that follows it, has several uses. It is also responsible for the discharge of charge that occurs during an electric shock and a flash of lightning.

1 Use the words to fill in the spaces.

negative **metals** **paper** **neutral** **plastic** **positive** **electrons** **charges**

An atom has a (a) .... nucleus surrounded by negatively charged (b) .... If a (c) .... pen is rubbed with a woollen cloth (d) .... can be rubbed onto the pen. The pen gets a (e) .... charge. When the pen is brought close to small pieces of (f) ...., (g) .... charges are repelled so its surface becomes (h) .... and it is attracted to the pen. (i) .... cannot be charged like plastic, as they conduct any (j) .... away from the surface.

2 Match the useful and harmful effects of static electricity to their examples.

		A Removing smoke particles in a factory
	1 Useful effects	B Electric shock
(a) Static electricity		C Spraying of crops from aircraft
	2 Harmful effects	D Lightning
		E Copying using a photocopier

3 Choose two uses of static electricity and explain how they work.

(a) ....

....

....

(b) ....

....

....

4 (a) How are static and current electricity similar and different? ....

....

....

(b) How do metals behave with static and current electricity? ....

....

....

....

Worksheet 26 Electrical circuits (SB9: BCP, Unit 21 p 173–81)

Electricity can flow around a closed circuit. Current is the rate of flow of electrons: one ampere (amp: A) is the flow of over 6 million, million, million electrons each second. Voltage is the electrical push from the dry cell that energises the electrons and pushes them around the circuit: measured in volts (V). Resistance, e.g. of a bulb, is the force opposing the flow of current: measured in ohms (Ω).

1 Match the names to the circuit symbols.

dry cell **switch** **battery** **wire** **bulbs**

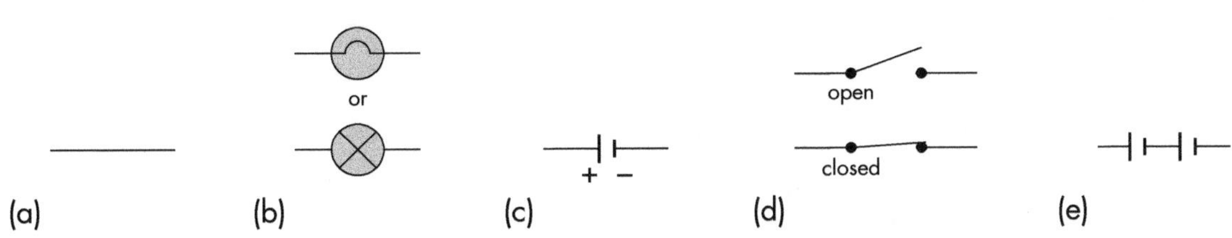

2 In each circuit, name the bulbs that light up when each switch is closed.

(a)

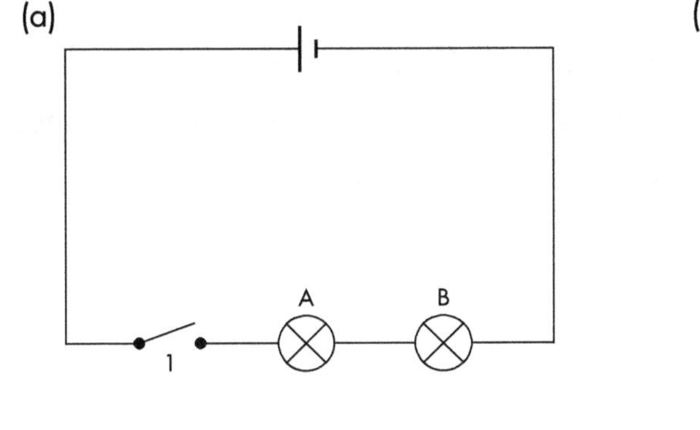

(b)

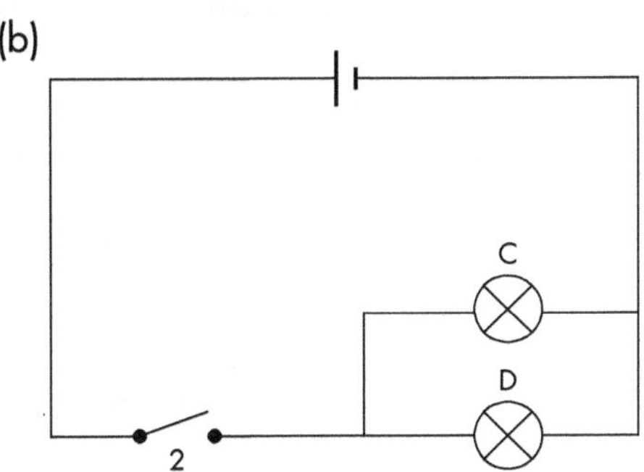

(c)

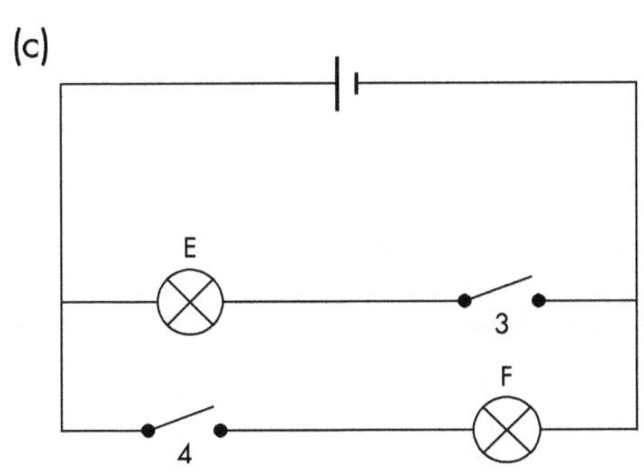

(d)

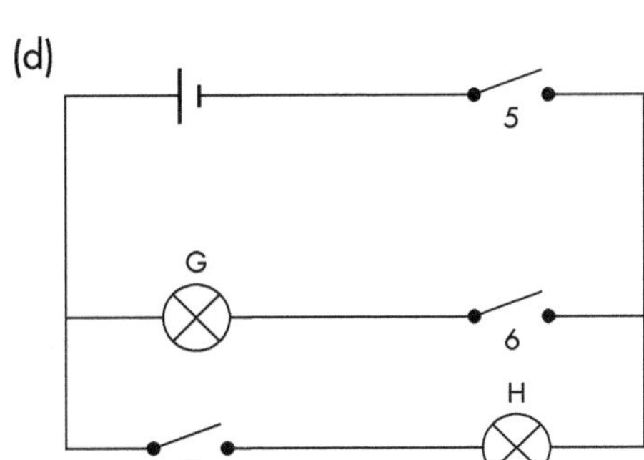

3 Voltage (in volts) = current (I in amps) × resistance (in ohms): $V = IR$

Resistance (in ohms) = voltage (in volts) / current (I in amps): $R = V/I$

Current (I in amps) = voltage (in volts) / resistance (in ohms): $I = V/R$

current **voltage** **resistance** **bulbs** **brighter** **increased**

Flow of current equals (a) .... (of the dry cells) divided by (b) .... (of the (c) ....). In a series circuit, if the number of dry cells is increased, the (d) .... is (e) .... and the (f) .... become (g) .... To find the (h) .... of the bulbs we divide the (i) .... of the dry cells by the (j) ....

Worksheet 27 Series and parallel circuits (SB9: BCP, Unit 21 p 176–9).

In a series circuit, the bulbs are arranged one after another, the current has only one path to take, and the electrical energy (voltage) is shared between the bulbs. In a parallel circuit, the bulbs are on different paths, so the current has a choice of paths, and varies around the circuit but the electrical energy can be used fully by each bulb.

Use the following words to fill in the spaces in Questions 1 and 2.

current bulbs parallel series brighter dimmer unlit unchanged

1 Compare circuits (W) and (X).

(w)

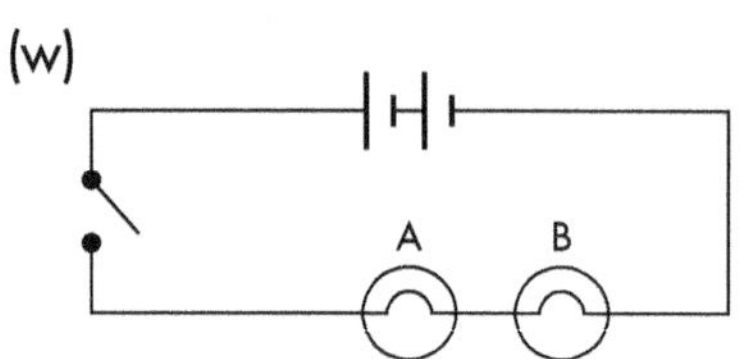

(x)

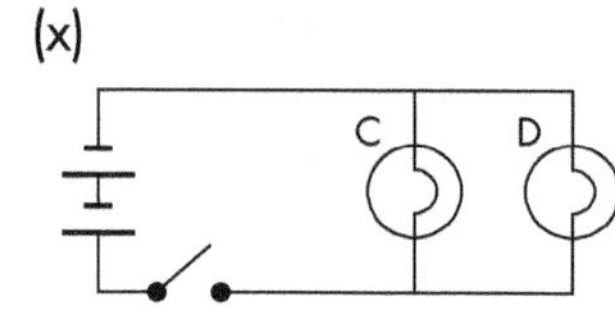

Diagram (W) shows a (a) .... circuit: if bulb A is unscrewed then bulb B is (b) .... because the (c) .... has only one pathway and this has been broken.

Diagram (X) shows a (d) .... circuit: if bulb C is unscrewed then bulb D is (e) .... because it still has a pathway to the battery. Bulbs in circuit (W) are (f) .... than those in circuit (X) because they have to share the electrical energy. For Christmas tree lights we use a (g) .... circuit, but for house lights we use a (h) .... circuit.

2 Compare circuits (Y) and (Z), and the effect of adding a bulb

(y)

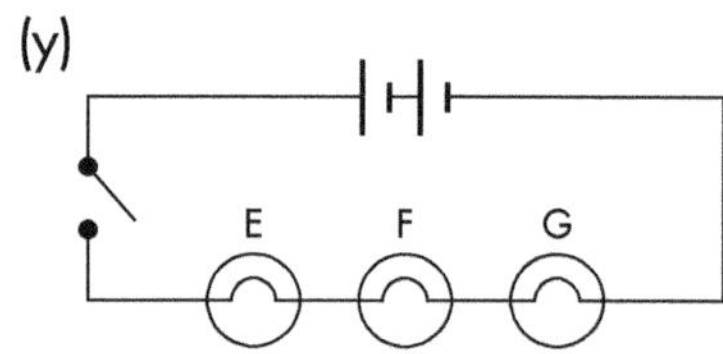

(z)

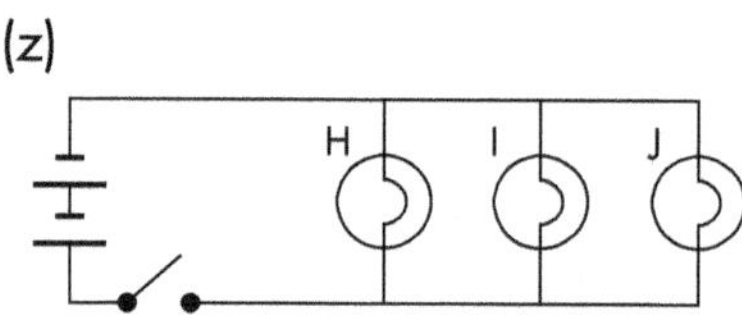

Diagram (Y): in a (i) .... circuit, adding a third bulb will cause all the bulbs to be (j) .... (compare circuits (W) and (Y)), because in circuit (Y) electrical energy is shared between more (k) .... The bulbs in circuit (W) will be (l) .... than those in circuit (Y).

Diagram (Z): in a (m) .... circuit, adding a third bulb will cause all the bulbs to be (n) .... compared to circuit (X) because each bulb has its own connection to the battery.

3 (a) What kind of circuit is used in a flashlight and how does it work? ....

....

....

(b) If your flashlight stopped working, what would you check and how could you get it working again?

....

....

....

....

Worksheet 28 Magnets and electromagnets (SB9: BCP, Unit 21 p 190-5)

Magnets attract iron and steel objects. When left to move freely, the north-seeking (N-pole) of a magnet, e.g. compass, points to the Earth's North pole. Like poles of magnets repel and unlike poles attract. A coil of wire, through which electricity passes, acts like a magnet. It is an electromagnet: its magnetism ceases when the current is stopped. Magnets and electromagnets have several important uses.

1 On each diagram draw arrows to show attraction or repulsion.

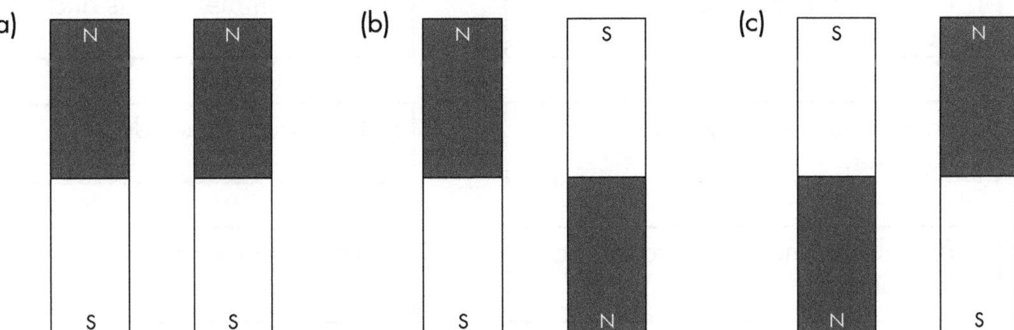

2 Two compasses are brought close together. Label all the poles.

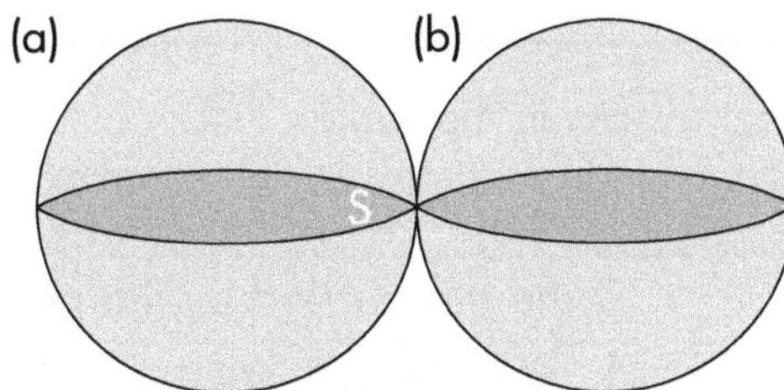

3 Use the words to fill in the spaces. Some words are used more than once.

current **coil** **steel** **electromagnet** **bells** **iron**

Permanent magnets are usually made of (a) ....: they are difficult to make but last a long time. Iron is used to make an (b) .... : the iron is held inside a (c) .... of wire through which an electric (d) .... is passed. The iron becomes an (e) .... for as long as the (f) .... flows. Electromagnets are used in electric (g) ...., some telephones, and attraction of (h) .... and (i) .... waste materials at a recycling centre.

4 Answer the multiple-choice questions.

(a) A magnet will attract
- A iron nails
- B brass screws
- C aluminium foil
- D all of the above

(b) An electromagnet is a
- A true magnet
- B false magnet
- C permanent magnet
- D temporary magnet

5 Describe the use of a magnet or electromagnet of your choice. How is it suited to its use?

....

....

....

....

Worksheet 29 Conduction, convection and radiation (SB9: BCP, Unit 22 p 202–8)

Temperature is the average kinetic energy of the particles and it measures how hot or cold an object feels. Heat energy is transferred from an object at a higher temperature to one at a lower temperature. Transfer of heat can occur in three ways: conduction, convection and radiation.

1 Match the boxes to show the differences between conductors and insulators.

	1 Particles are more loosely packed.	A For example, liquids and gases
(a) Conductors	2 Particles are closely packed together.	B For example, solids
	3 Particles do not move from place to place.	C For example, non-metals such as plastics
(b) Insulators	4 Particles move from place to place.	D For example, metals such as iron

2 List the numbers of the characteristics in the correct places in the table.

1 heat passes between particles	9 e.g. metal pans and wires
2 e.g. through air and a vacuum	10 heat is carried by the particles
3 particles need to be able to move	11 particles are not needed for transfer
4 cannot occur in solids	12 particles have to be closely packed
5 occurs quickest in solids	13 does not warm the space it travels in
6 heat energy travels as waves	14 currents are set up to transfer heat
7 occurs slowest in gases	15 e.g. Sun's energy transferred to Earth
8 e.g. land and sea breezes	16 occurs in liquids and gases

Conduction	Convection	Radiation
1,		

3 Answer the multiple-choice questions.

(a) Which is the best conductor?
A wooden spoon
B metal pan
C glass rod
D rubber tube

(b) Land and sea breezes depend on
A convection
B conduction
C radiation
D evaporation

4 Choose an appliance in the home. How does it work using different methods of heat transfer?

....

....

....

....

Worksheet 30 Kinetic energy, heating and cooling (SB9: BCP, Unit 22 p 200–1, 209–11)

Particles of matter are in constant motion: they have kinetic energy. The thermal energy of a substance is the total kinetic energy of its particles. The temperature is the average kinetic energy, measured with a thermometer. Heat energy is transferred from a substance at a higher temperature to that at a lower temperature; this process is used in many appliances. Heating increases the kinetic energy of particles and causes expansion; it can also cause solids to melt and liquids to boil. Cooling decreases the kinetic energy of particles and causes contraction; it can also cause gases to condense and liquids to solidify.

1 Match the boxes on the left with their descriptions.

(a) Temperature	1 The total energy of motion of particles in a substance.
(b) Kinetic energy	2 The average kinetic energy; degree of hotness or coldness.
(c) Heat energy	3 Equal to the total kinetic energy of a substance.
(d) Thermal energy	4 Form in which heat is transferred from one object to another.

2 Explain each of the following.

(a) Temperature reading × volume of a substance = thermal energy ....

....

(b) My tea goes cold if I don't drink it ....

....

(c) The ice in my lemonade melts ....

....

(d) If a sealed jar is left in the refrigerator, it is very difficult to get off the metal lid ....

....

(e) Hot water run over a metal lid makes it easier to unscrew it ....

....

(f) A hot air balloon can be made to rise and fall in the air ....

....

(g) A piece of chocolate becomes sticky when I hold it ....

....

(h) There are drops of water on the outside of my glass of lemonade ....

....

(i) A thermos can keep hot liquids hot, and cool liquids cool ....

....

(j) A microwave oven heats food more quickly than an electric oven ....

....

....

Selected answers

For SB9: Biology Chemistry Physics (BCP)

Introduction: Working like a scientist (3)

SB9: BCP p 12 Binary numbers in base ten
(a) 10, (b) 28, (c) 45, (d) 22, (e) 41, (f) 38, (g) 69
(On **p 13**, Sonja is saying 'Hello' to Lee)

SB9: BCP p 15 Prefixes and conversions
1 (a) $\frac{1}{10}$, (b) $\frac{1}{100}$, (c) $\frac{1}{1000}$
2 (a) $30 \times 1000 = 30\,000$ mg, (b) $\frac{30}{1000} = 0.03$ kg
3 (a) $\times 10^6$, (b) $\times 10^3$

SB9: BCP p 16 Areas of shapes
(a) Area $= 4 \times 1 + 2 \times 1 = 6\text{cm}^2$
(b) Area $= 3 \times 3 + (\frac{1}{2}\pi r^2) = 9 + (0.5 \times \frac{22}{7} \times 1.5^2) = 9 + 3.54 = 12.5\text{cm}^2$ (to 3 sig figs)
(c) Area $= 3 \times 2 + (\frac{1}{2} \times 3 \times 2) = 6 + 3 = 9\text{cm}^2$
(d) Area $= 2 \times 4 + (\frac{1}{2} \times 2 \times 4) = 8 + 4 = 12\text{cm}^2$

SB9: BCP p 18 Precision and sig figs
1 (c). **2** (a) 1, (b) 2, (c) 3, (d) 2
3 (d). **4** (a) 3, (b) 2, (c) 2, (d) 4
5 Any correct answer, e.g. 457, 62.9, 7.02, 0.0101

SB9: BCP p 19 Rounding up and down
1 (a) 6.17, (b) 3.62, (c) 0.369, (d) 0.0149
2 (a) 4.2, (b) 30, (c) 0.74, (d) 0.037
3 (a) 60, (b) 20, (c) 40

SB9: BCP p 19 Calculations using sig figs
Precision of the answer is to the least precise number.
1 (a) 123.71 = 123.7, (b) 8.37 = 8.4
2 (a) 42.93, (b) 34.18 = 43.2
3 (a) 3.36 = 3.4, (b) 0.045 = 0.05
4 (a) 14.3 = 10, (b) 266.956 = 270

SB9: BCP p 19 Using standard form
1 (a) 5.7×10^4, (b) 6.346×10^7, (c) 4.39×10^{-1}, (d) 7.36×10^{-6}
2 (a) 590 000, (b) 48 000 000, (c) 0.0000027, (d) 0.0000000018

SB9: BCP p 19 Calculations using sig figs
1 (a) $550\,000 + 73\,000\,000 = 73\,550\,000 = 7.355 \times 10^7$
(b) $6\,800\,000\,000\,000 + 1500 = 6\,800\,000\,001\,500 = 6.8000000015 \times 10^{12}$
2 (a) $940\,000 - 580\,000 = 8\,820\,000 = 8.82 \times 10^6$
(b) $710\,000\,000 - 9\,200\,000 = 700\,800\,000 \times 10^8$
3 (a) $(4.0 \times 10^4) \times (8.2 \times 10^8) = 32.8 \times 10^{4+8} = 32.8 \times 10^{12} = 3.28 \times 10^{13}$
(b) $(1.7 \times 10^6) \times (5.9 \times 10^7) = 10.03 \times 10^{6+7} = 10.03 \times 10^{13} = 1.003 \times 10^{14}$
4 (a) $(8.2 \times 10^4) \div (4.1 \times 10^2) = 2 \times 10^{4-2} = 2 \times 10^2$
(b) $(9.0 \times 10^8) \div (1.2 \times 10^5) = 7.5 \times 10^{8-5} = 7.5 \times 10^3$

SB9: BCP p 21 Activity 0.9
2 They both increase together, it is a positive relationship
3 Gradient = 25 – 7.5 divided by 7 – 4 = $\frac{17.5}{3} = 5.83$
4 Units are mm/day or mm day^{-1}

SB9: BCP p 22 Calculations with density
1 (a) Sink: 19.3 gcm^{-3} is larger than water 1 gcm^{-3}
(b) Float: 0.92 gcm^{-3} is smaller than water 1 gcm^{-3}
2 Density $= \frac{\text{mass}}{\text{volume}} = \frac{10}{2} = 5\text{gcm}^{-3}$
3 Smaller mass (silver 10.5 gcm^{-3}, gold 19.3 gcm^{-3})
4 Volume $= \frac{\text{mass}}{\text{density}} = \frac{1000\text{ g}}{7.9\text{ gcm}^{-3}} = 126.6\text{cm}^3$

SB9: BCP p 22 Calculations with speed
1 Speed $= \frac{\text{distance}}{\text{time}} = \frac{2}{5} = 0.4$ m/s or 0.4 ms^{-1}
2 Distance = speed × time $= 50 \times \frac{30}{60} = 25$ km
3 Time $= \frac{\text{distance}}{\text{speed}} = \frac{250}{50} = 5$ hours

SB9: BCP p 23 Calculations with acceleration
1 Velocity = acceleration × time = 20 × 20 = 400 ms^{-1}
2 Acceleration $= \frac{\text{velocity}}{\text{time}} = \frac{10\text{ ms}^{-1}}{5\text{ s}} = 2\text{ms}^{-2}$
3 (a) steady speed, (b) stationary
4 (a) constant acceleration, (b) constant velocity

SB9: BCP p 24 Answers to multiple-choice items
1 **C** 2 **D** 3 **A** 4 **A** 5 **C** 6 **B** 7 **C** 8 **A** 9 **C**
10 **C** 11 **B** 12 **C** 13 **A** 14 **D** 15 **B** 16 **D** 17 **A**
18 **C** 19 **C** 20 **D** 21 **C** 22 **B** 23 **A** 24 **B** 25 **C**
26 **B** 27 **D** 28 **C** 29 **D** 30 **B** 31 **D** 32 **C** 33 **D**
34 **A** 35 **A** 36 **A** 37 **B** 38 **D** 39 **C** 40 **C**

Unit 16 Transport in living things

SB9: BCP p 30 Activity 16.2 Questions
1 Bigger crystals (small SA) take longer to diffuse.
2 Smaller ones (large SA) take a shorter time to diffuse.
3 At a higher temperature, particles move more quickly: diffusion and mixing is quicker.
4 At a lower temperature, there is slower movement of particles: so diffusion and mixing is slower.

SB9: BCP p 31 Activity 16.4 Questions
Cubes: (a) SA = (1.5 cm × 1.5 cm) × 6 sides = 13.5 cm^2,
V = 1.5 cm × 1.5 cm × 1.5 cm = 3.375 cm^3,
ratio SA:V = 4:1
(b) SA = (1 cm × 1 cm) × 6 sides = 6 cm^2,
V = 1 cm × 1 cm × 1 cm = 1 cm^3, ratio SA:V = 6:1.
(c) SA = (0.5 cm × 0.5 cm) × 6 sides = 1.5 cm^2,
V = 0.5 cm × 0.5 cm × 0.5 cm = 0.125 cm^3,
ratio SA:V = 12:1

SB9: BCP p 31 (cont.)

1 Diffusion is quickest in the smallest cube, with the greatest SA:V ratio.

2 (a) Yes: unicellular organisms are very small with very large SA:V ratios and not very active.
(b) No, they are too active. But diffusion and osmosis occur over short distances through thin membranes.

SB9: BCP p 34 Activity 16.9 Questions

1 Coloured lines will be seen in the stem (in xylem).

4 To produce flowers of unusual colour for selling.

SB9: BCP p 54 Answers to multiple-choice items

1 **C** 2 **A** 3 **D** 4 **D** 5 **D** 6 **B** 7 **C** 8 **C** 9 **B** 10 **C** 11 **B** 12 **C** 13 **A** 14 **B** 15 **B** 16 **D** 17 **A** 18 **A** 19 **D** 20 **B** 21 **D** 22 **C** 23 **C** 24 **A** 25 **B** 26 **B** 27 **A** 28 **C** 29 **A** 30 **B** 31 **C** 32 **D** 33 **A** 34 **B** 35 **D**

Unit 17 Sensitivity and co-ordination

SB9: BCP p 58 Questions on touch

1 We cannot judge actual temperatures, only comparisons. If actual temperature is important, use a thermometer.

2 With a blindfolded partner, you can touch the skin with an ice cube inside a plastic bag and record where it was felt.

3 (a) Heat sensors allow us to move quickly away from danger, (b) pain sensors alert us to dangerous chemicals or sharp objects, (c) light touch sensors allow us to feel textures and to read Braille.

4 The answer is: both. The brain needs to receive the impulses from the skin, but the impulses cannot be interpreted without them going to the brain.

SB9: BCP p 64 Activity 17.11

The change in size of the pupil with bright light (small pupil) and dim light (wide pupil) is called the pupil reflex. It is a reflex action not under our conscious control.

SB9: BCP p 65 Questions on sight

1 If a large amount of bright light is shone onto the retina, it could burn it. So never look at the Sun.

2 The eye needs a blood supply as it is made up of living cells that need oxygen and food and to get rid of wastes.

3 Magenta is seen when red and blue cones are both stimulated.

SB9: BCP p 67 Questions on eye test

5 (a) Optician: can be a person who just fits contact lenses or spectacles. Often they are also qualified to do eye tests and prescribe spectacles.
(b) Optometrist: has been trained to carry out measurements and tests and to prescribe contact lenses and spectacles.
(c) Ophthalmologist: is usually medically qualified and able to perform operations on the eye.

SB9: BCP p 74 Activity 17.19 Measuring reaction times

6 Students' reaction times will vary. Practice should increase reaction time as we learn to anticipate what is going to happen, and prepare for it.

SB9: BCP p 74 (cont.)

Tiredness and alcohol will slow reaction time. This is why they should be avoided when driving. Coffee causes a temporary increase in reaction time, but it may not be accurate.

7 As the pencil is shorter, it may be more difficult to catch. Practice and anticipation do help.

SB9: BCP p 80 Answers to multiple-choice items

1 **C** 2 **B** 3 **D** 4 **C** 5 **A** 6 **D** 7 **A** 8 **B** 9 **C** 10 **B** 11 **B** 12 **D** 13 **C** 14 **B** 15 **A** 16 **A** 17 **C** 18 **C** 19 **A** 20 **D** 21 **B** 22 **C** 23 **B** 24 **D** 25 **C** 26 **B** 27 **A** 28 **D** 29 **A** 30 **A**

Unit 18 Embryo development and birth control

SB9: BCP p 85 Questions

1 (a) Identical twins are always the same sex,
(b) Non-identical twins are both girls, both boys, or one of each.

2 Triplets are all identical (if formed from one fertilised egg). Or two are identical (from the same fertilised egg), and the other non-identical (from a different egg). (Siamese twins are identical and joined at birth.)

SB9: BCP p 86 Questions

2 After fertilisation the egg needs to divide properly, become implanted in the uterus wall, and the placenta set up: then the woman is pregnant.

3 If fertilisation occurs low in the uterus there is not time for the zygote to divide and implant in the uterus.

SB9: BCP p 95 Questions

3 Thalidomide especially damaged the limbs as these are formed early in pregnancy: the most rapid growth is in the first three months.

SB9: BCP p 102 Answers to multiple-choice items

1 **A** 2 **D** 3 **C** 4 **A** 5 **A** 6 **D** 7 **B** 8 **A** 9 **C** 10 **D** 11 **C** 12 **B** 13 **A** 14 **C** 15 **D** 16 **B** 17 **C** 18 **D** 19 **C** 20 **D** 21 **B** 22 **B** 23 **D** 24 **A** 25 **D** 26 **D** 27 **C** 28 **B** 29 **D** 30 **B** 31 **C** 32 **A** 33 **B**

Unit 19 Chemical bonding, reactions and equations

SB9: BCP p 113 Activity 19.1

5 Match the cards for each individual element. You can also pick out the names and arrangements of electrons for each of the groups 0, 1, 2, 6 and 7.

SB9: BCP p 116 Activity 19.3

2 Use the Periodic table on p 115. The mass number (number of protons + neutrons) minus the atomic number (number of protons) = number of neutrons for each element.

SB9: BCP p 117 Activity 19.4

4 Calcium fluoride. **6** NaCl, BeO, K_2S.

SB9: BCP p 123 Activity 19.10

7 Lead nitrate + potassium iodide = lead iodide + potassium nitrate

SB9: BCP p 124 Questions

1 No change in temperature for salt in water. Physical reaction as water can be evaporated to leave the salt.

SB9: BCP p 124 (cont.)

2 Quicklime combines with water in an exothermic reaction to form a new compound, calcium hydroxide.

3 $CaO + H_2O = Ca(OH)_2$

SB9: BCP p 127 Activity 19.15

1 Iron + sulphur = iron sulphide: Fe + S = FeS

SB9: BCP p 127 (cont.)

2 In a mixture, elements keep their own properties (e.g. iron is attracted to a magnet), and these are different from those of the compound.

3 Chemical: heat needed and a new compound is formed.

4 Exothermic: reactants glow red and very hot.

Information on the elements.

Element	Symbol	Atomic number	Mass number	Number of protons	Number of electrons	Number of neutrons
Hydrogen	H	1	1	1	1	None
Helium	He	2	4	2	2	2
Lithium	Li	3	7	3	3	4
Beryllium	Be	4	9	4	4	5
Boron	B	5	11	5	5	6
Carbon	C	6	12	6	6	6
Nitrogen	N	7	14	7	7	7
Oxygen	O	8	16	8	8	8
Fluorine	F	9	19	9	9	10
Neon	Ne	10	20	10	10	10
Sodium	Na	11	23	11	11	12
Magnesium	Mg	12	24	12	12	12
Aluminium	Al	13	27	13	13	14
Silicon	Si	14	28	14	14	14
Phosphorus	P	15	31	15	15	16
Sulphur	S	16	32	16	16	16
Chlorine	Cl	17	35.5	17	17	18 and 20
Argon	Ar	18	40	18	18	22
Potassium	K	19	39	19	19	20
Calcium	Ca	20	40	20	20	20

SB9: BCP p 128 Activity 19.16

1 Copper carbonate is easier than calcium carbonate.

2 Decomposition of copper carbonate is easier to see, as copper carbonate is green and copper oxide is black.

3 (a) Iron carbonate → iron oxide + carbon dioxide
(b) Zinc carbonate → zinc oxide + carbon dioxide

4 Sodium hydrogencarbonate can decompose when heated in the lab to sodium carbonate, carbon dioxide and water.

SB9: BCP p 129 Activity 19.17

2 Copper is less reactive than magnesium, so it cannot replace magnesium. There would be no reaction.

SB9: BCP p 129 Activity 19.18

1 Two displacements occur to make two new compounds.

2 Silver chloride + sodium nitrate.

SB9: BCP p 130 Activity 19.19

1 Calcium is more reactive than iron.

2 A burning splint goes 'pop' with hydrogen.

3 Potassium and sodium are extremely reactive.

SB9: BCP p 130 Activity 19.20

1 Magnesium is more reactive than iron.

2 and **3** Both. Magnesium + hydrochloric acid = magnesium chloride + hydrogen. Iron + hydrochloric acid = iron chloride + hydrogen.

4 Calcium will be more reactive than magnesium, and aluminium less reactive.

5 Predict similar results with dilute acids.

SB9: BCP p 136 Answers to multiple-choice items

1 **A** 2 **B** 3 **A** 4 **C** 5 **D** 6 **B** 7 **D** 8 **A** 9 **A**
10 **C** 11 **D** 12 **A** 13 **A** 14 **D** 15 **C** 16 **B**
17 **B** 18 **A** 19 **B** 20 **C** 21 **C** 22 **B** 23 **D**

SB9: BCP p 137 Balancing equations

40 (a) $Fe + S = FeS$; (b) $NaOH + HCl = NaCl + H_2O$;
(c) $MgO + H_2O = Mg(OH)_2$; (d) $S + O_2 = SO_2$;
(e) $MgO + H_2SO_4 = MgSO_4 + H_2O$;
(f) $CaSO_4 + Na_2CO_3 = CaCO_3 + Na_2SO4$;
(g) $Mg + ZnCl_2 = MgCl_2 + Zn$;
(h) $Fe + CuSO_4 = FeSO_4 + Cu$;
(i) $2Na + 2H_2O = 2NaOH + H_2$

SB9: BCP p 137 (cont.)

41 (a) $Ca(OH)_2 + 2HCl = CaCl_2 + 2H_2O$;
(b) $CaCO_3 + 2HCl = CaCl_2 + H_2O + CO_2$;
(c) $CuO + 2HNO_3 = Cu(NO_3)_2 + H_2O$;
(d) $MgO + 2HCl = MgCl_2 + H_2O$;
(e) $2KHCO_3 + H_2SO_4 = K_2SO_4 + 2CO_2 + 2H_2O$;
(f) $ZnCO_3 + 2HNO_3 = Zn(NO_3)_2 + CO_2 + H_2O$

Unit 20 Acids and alkalis

SB9: BCP p 141 Activity 20.3

3 Litmus is an acid-base indicator and only distinguishes between them. Universal indicator changes colour in all different pH values.

SB9: BCP p 142 Questions

1 and **2** Indicators contain dyes sensitive to pH.
3 Chemical change: the indicator is changed by the surroundings – making different coloured products.

SB9: BCP p 143 Activity 20.7

4 With acids hibiscus indicator is red; in alkalis it is dark green to almost black. Red cabbage contains anthocyanin indicator that turns red in acid and purple-blue in alkalis.

SB9: BCP p 144 Questions on Activity 20.9

1 Calcium carbonate (a) slightly soluble, (b) alkaline: about pH 10, (c) bubbles with lime juice: carbon dioxide.
2 Washing soda (a) soluble, (b) alkaline: pH 10.5, (c) bubbles with lime juice: carbon dioxide.
3 Baking soda (a) soluble, (b) weak alkaline: about pH 8, (c) bubbles with lime juice: carbon dioxide.
4 Baking powder (a) soluble and bubbles carbon dioxide, (b) about neutral (contains a base and an acid), (c) bubbles with lime juice: carbon dioxide.
5 With acid (lime juice), they all produce carbon dioxide.

SB9: BCP p 145 Activity 20.10

1 No, **2** (a) calcium, (b) copper (no reaction);
4 See Worksheet 23, and. $Zn + 2HCl = ZnCl_2 + H_2$

Activity 20.11

2 Carbon dioxide. **4** See Worksheet 23 and Answers.

SB9: BCP p 146 Questions on pie chart.

1 Agricultural chemicals = 109° = 30.28 (30%), Chemicals and plastics, and Paints and pigments both = 53° = 14.7 (15%),
Detergents and soaps = 44° = 12.2 (12%).
2 (c) $CaCO_3 + H_2SO_4 = CaSO_4 + CO_2 + H_2O$

SB9: BCP p 148 Questions on Activity 20.12

1 Bleach and window cleaner turn litmus blue.
2 to **5** Reactions with water as for Activity 20.9 above.
6 Bleach and window cleaner react as water, but do not release any other gases.

SB9: BCP p 149 Activity 20.13

1 Iron and copper salts both give insoluble hydroxides: iron hydroxide (brown), copper hydroxide (blue).
2 Ammonia, sodium chloride and water.
3 See Worksheet 23 and Answers.

SB9: BCP p 151 Questions

1 Answers vary, e.g. (a) sodium hydroxide + hydrochloric acid, (b) magnesium hydroxide + sulphuric acid, (c) copper oxide + hydrochloric acid, (d) potassium hydroxide + nitric acid, (e) iron oxide + sulphuric acid, (f) copper oxide + carbonic acid.
2 Answers vary. Check with your teacher.
3 $HCl + NH_4OH = NH_4Cl + H_2O$

SB9: BCP p 152 Questions

1 A wasp sting is alkaline. For an acidic bee sting you would use an alkali, e.g. sodium hydrogencarbonate.
2 Cheese is an alkali, and therefore better for your teeth than fruit containing citric acid.
3 To remove bits of food and stop it decaying.

SB9: BCP p 154 Activity 20.21

1 Sodium chloride and water.
2 Water is driven off; sodium chloride remains.
3 $NaOH + HCl = NaCl + H_2O$

SB9: BCP p 154 Questions

1 See Worksheet 24 and Answers.
2 Answers vary, e.g.
(a) $Mg + H_2SO_4 = MgSO_4 + H_2$,
(b) $NH_4OH + HNO_3 = NH_4NO_3 + H_2O$

SB9: BCP p 158 Answers to multiple-choice items

1 **B** 2 **A** 3 **C** 4 **B** 5 **D** 6 **D** 7 **C** 8 **A** 9 **A**
10 **C** 11 **C** 12 **B** 13 **B** 14 **B** 15 **C** 16 **B**
17 **D** 18 **B** 19 **B** 20 **A** 21 **A** 22 **C** 23 **D**
24 **A** 25 **D** 26 **D** 27 **A** 28 **C** 29 **D** 30 **C**
31 **D** 32 **C** 33 **B** 34 **B**

Unit 21 Electricity and magnetism

SB9: BCP p 170–1 Activities 21.1 and 21.2.

Non-metals can build up a charge on their surface when rubbed. Then can induce a charge in other non-metals, so that attraction occurs (also see Workbook answers).

SB9: BCP p 171 Questions

Charge can build up on a surface and then be suddenly discharged, to cause an explosion (**1**) or tingle (**2**).

SB9: BCP p 172 Questions

1 Metals conduct charge away from their surfaces, so charges cannot build up as they can on a non-metal.
2 (a) For example, a charged –ve rod attracts bits of paper. (b) The charges on the rod repel –ve charges on the paper, so the surface of the paper becomes +vely charged and is attracted.
4 Electric eel has organs that can produce electricity that kills its prey, and can shock people.

SB9: BCP p 173 Activity 21.3

7 Flashlight: Check (a) the bulb is well screwed in and the wire is complete (not broken or 'blown)'; there is the right number of dry cells, that they are facing the right way, and have nothing non-conducting between them, and that the base is screwed on tight. (b) and (c) Make adjustments and write your report.

SB9: BCP p 176 Activities 21.7 and 21.8
In a series circuit the ammeters all give the same reading: the current is the same all the way around.
In a series circuit, the bulbs share the 'push' of the electrons (voltage). If two bulbs are the same, the voltage reading across each bulb will each be half that across the cell. (With 3 bulbs, a third, etc.)

SB9: BCP p 177 Activity 21.9
In a series circuit: (a) bulbs get brighter when more cells are added (there is more 'push (voltage) to share).
(b) bulbs get dimmer when more bulbs are added (more bulbs are sharing the voltage).

SB9: BCP p 178 Activities 21.10 and 21.11
In a parallel circuit, the ammeters will give different readings, as the current is divided as it goes into a junction, and recombined after a junction.
In a parallel circuit, the bulbs do not have to share the 'push' of the electrons (voltage), as each one is connected to the cell. If the bulbs are the same, the voltage reading across each bulb will be the same as that across the cell.

SB9: BCP p 179 Activity 21.12 In a parallel circuit:
(a) bulbs get brighter when more cells are added (there is more voltage for each of them).
(b) bulbs do not change in brightness when more bulbs are added (as each gets its own new circuit to the cell).

SB9: BCP p 179
1 Bedroom 2 will be lit, as its circuit (S) is complete.
2 If bedroom 1's bulb is broken, the other bulbs can work because they are on parallel circuits: they each have their own connection to the mains. When (C) is in contact with (B), the light is switched off by moving the switch (Z) from (Y) to (X).

SB9: BCP p 180 Activity 21.13
The current goes through the green part on the left. When the slider is moved to the right, more wire is made part of the circuit: increasing the resistance. This decreases the current to the bulb, which goes dim. When the slide is moved left, less wire is part of the circuit: decreasing the resistance. This increases the current to the bulb, which is brighter.

SB9: BCP p 180 Questions
Current (I in amps) = voltage (V)/resistance (R); voltage = current/resistance (V = I/R); resistance = voltage/current (R = V/I).

SB9: BCP p 181 Activity 21.14
The graph using constantan wire is a straight line: the resistance does not vary (R =V/I = 10 ohms). The graph with a bulb shows a curve for the resistance: it increases with temperature.

SB9: BCP p 184 Questions
The flashlight is a series circuit with two dry cells. The switch completes the circuit and the bulb lights.
2 (a) Button cell (small, portable), (b) dry cell (cheap, portable), (c) battery or mains (flexibility), (d) battery (portable), (e) car battery (portable).

SB9: BCP p 186 Questions
1 An energy unit is a kilowatt-hour (kWh).
2 Power ratings are 4kW (cooker) and 650W/1000 = 0.65kW (microwave), so the microwave is cheaper to run. For a fair test: run them for the same time, or use them to cook the same meal.
3 Power (W) = volts × current. Iron is 110V × 7A = 770W. So for the same amount of time, the toaster (1000W) is more expensive to run.

SB9: BCP p 190 Activities 21.24 and 21.25
Magnets attract iron and steel objects.
Similar poles of magnets repel, opposite poles attract. (This is shown in Activity 21.25 with iron filings.)

SB9: BCP p 191 Activity 21.26
7 Iron things are attracted; only magnets can repel.

SB9: BCP p 192 Questions
1 Iron is best for making electromagnets.
2 Magnets are made of steel and keep their magnetism: they are permanent rather than temporary magnets.

SB9: BCP p 193 Questions
8 (a) No reading on the ammeter when the magnet is stationary, (b) when moving, a current is induced – first one way and then the other – as the magnet is moved.

SB9: BCP p 196 Answers to multiple-choice items
1 **C** 2 **D** 3 **D** 4 **B** 5 **B** 6 **A** 7 **C** 8 **C** 9 **A**
10 **B** 11 **A** 12 **C** 13 **D** 14 **B** 15 **C** 16 **D** 17 **A**
18 **B** 19 **B** 20 **D** 21 **D** 22 **C** 23 **A** 24 **A** 25 **B**
26 **A** 27 **C** 28 **B** 29 **D** 30 **C** 31 **C** 32 **B**

Unit 22 Thermal energy

SB9: BCP p 203 Questions (final set)
2 These would allow sweat to evaporate and cool you.
3 and **4** Depend on air being a poor conductor of heat.

SB9: BCP p 204 Questions
1 By convection: hot water rises and more is heated.
2 Gas, as the particles move more quickly.

SB9: BCP p 205 Questions
1 At the top of a wall to take away hot air, so creating a current to pull in cooler air from below.
2 So the water can be heated and rise.

SB9: BCP p 206–7 Questions
Black absorbs more infrared rays than white, and even though it also emits more, the white feels cooler. White also reflects most light.

SB9: BCP p 209 Questions
1 Heating increases the kinetic energy of particles, which then take up more space: the substance expands.
2 Cooling decreases the kinetic energy of the particles, which then take up less space: the substance contracts.

SB9: BCP p 212 Answers to multiple-choice items
1 **A** 2 **B** 3 **A** 4 **C** 5 **D** 6 **B** 7 **A** 8 **A** 9 **B**
10 **D** 11 **C** 12 **D** 13 **C** 14 **B** 15 **B** 16 **A**
17 **C** 18 **B** 19 **D** 20 **C** 21 **D** 22 **C** 23 **A** 24 **D**
25 **D** 26 **B** 27 **C** 28 **A** 29 **B** 30 **D**

For Workbook 9: Biology Chemistry Physics (BCP)

Introduction: Working like a scientist (3)

Workbook 9: BCP p 4 STEAM

1 For example, Science: matter, predicting, fair tests: Tech/EDP: design, model making, testing, use of materials;
Art: choice of materials, design, colour, drawings;
Maths: measuring, calculations, recording, graphs;
Plus ICT: research, making graphs, sharing results;

2 (a) 1, (b) 3, (c) 4, (d) 6, (e) 2, (f) 5

Tables: Working like a scientist p 5–10
Students use these pages for reference and checklists.

p 5 The scientific method
p 6 Engineering design process
p 7 Using art in STEAM
p 8 Writing a report
p 9 Problem-based and Inquiry-based group work.
p 10 Oral presentations and using ICT.

Workbook 9: BCP p 11 Using the binary code

1 Capital letters start with 010 and lower case with 011 (with the same difference of 32 between corresponding letters). In the table check Z is 90 and z is 122.

2 Space (00100000), dollar sign (00100100), comma (00101100), full stop (00101110), question mark (00111111).

4 CPU (central processing unit), ROM (read only memory), RAM (random access memory), VDU (visual display unit), OS (operating system), CD (compact disc), DVD (digital versatile disc), ISP (internet service provider), 'hit' (information found using a search engine), 'spam' (unwanted emails, e.g. advertising).

Workbook 9: BCP p 12 Units and physical quantities

1 Set up the activity as in **SB9: BCP p 15.** Students record their measurements, and the teacher checks.

2 Mass, kg, kilogram, g, mg; Length, m, metre, km, cm, mm; Time, s, second, min, hr, day;
Temperature, K, kelvin, °C

Workbook 9: BCP p 13 Measuring area and volume

1 (a) $9\,cm^2$, (b) $28.3\,cm^2$, (c) $18\,cm^2$, (d) $9\,cm^2$

2 (a) $8\,cm^2$, (b) $22.3\,cm^2$, (c) $18\,cm^2$, (d) $16\,cm^2$

3 (a) $8\,cm^3$, (b) $33.5\,cm^3$, (c) $8\,cm^3$, (d) $50.3\,cm^3$

4 Volumes: A $5\,cm^3$, B $15\,cm^3$, C $25\,cm^3$, D $30\,cm^3$

Workbook 9: BCP p 14 Line graphs and gradients
Line graphs: Teacher checks students' graphs and their assessments on how well they have drawn them.

Workbook 9: BCP p 15 Gradients
Using the graphs produced on p 14:

4 Speed = m/s = gradient on distance-time graph;

$$\text{Gradient} = \frac{\text{change on y-axis}}{\text{change on x-axis}} = \frac{8\text{ m}}{4\text{ s}} = 2\,\text{m/s}$$

or $2\,ms^{-1}$

Workbook 9: BCP p 15 (cont.)

5 Acceleration = ms^{-2} = gradient on velocity–time graph;

$$\text{Gradient} = \frac{\text{change on y-axis}}{\text{change on x-axis}} = \frac{5\,ms^{-1}}{5\,s} =$$

1 m/s/s or 1 ms^{-2}

6 (a) 0–4 s, $\frac{\text{change on y-axis}}{\text{change on x-axis}} = \frac{36\,ms^{-1}}{4\,s} = 9\,ms^{-2}$

(b) 4–6 s, $\frac{\text{change on y-axis}}{\text{change on x-axis}} = \frac{12\,ms^{-1}}{2\,s} = 6\,ms^{-2}$

(c) 6–10 s, $\frac{\text{change on y-axis}}{\text{change on x-axis}} = \frac{16\,ms^{-1}}{4\,s} = 4\,ms^{-2}$

(d) Acceleration was very rapid in the first 4 seconds ($9\,m^{-2}$) and the slope was also steepest; acceleration was less in next 2 seconds and less again in the next 4 seconds.

7 Note 2 cm = 20 mm;
so rate of growth = 20 mm/5 days = 4 mm/day

8 $\frac{\text{change in velocity}}{\text{change in time}} = \frac{30\,ms^{-1}}{10\,s}$ = acceleration of $3\,ms^{-2}$

Workbook 9: BCP p 16 Dealing with numbers

Prefixes: 1 (a) 1/100, (b) 1/1000

2 Move digits relative to the decimal point: (a) 3 left, (b) 4 right, (c) 2 left, (d) 2 right, (e) 6 right, (f) 6 left

Rounding: 1 (a) 60, (b) 70, (c) 100, (d) 770

2 (a) 700, (b) 600, (c) 3500, (d) 8400

3 (a) 0.0329, (b) 437, (c) 0.550, (d) 459

4 (a) 43, (b) 57, (c) 0.056, (d) 0.46

Significant figures: 1 Most precise are: (d) and (g)

2 (a) 2, (b) 3, (c) 2, (d) 3; **3** (a) 344, (b) 0.567

4 (a) 24.3, (b) 0.557; **5** (a) 132, (b) 136

Standard form: 1 (a) 4.6×10^2, (b) 7.37×10^4, (c) 3.90×10^{-1}, (d) 4.3×10^{-2}

2 (a) 8900, (b) 527, (c) 0.055, (d) 0.000843

3 (a) 1.032×10^4; **4** (a) 4.831×10^4

5 (a) 4.3208×10^2; **6** (a) 1.1618×10^1

Workbook 9: BCP p 17 Answers to multiple-choice items

1 **D** 2 **A** 3 **D** 4 **B** 5 **C** 6 **B** 7 **B** 8 **C** 9 **C** 10 **A**
11 **B** 12 **B** 13 **D** 14 **A** 15 **C** 16 **C** 17 **B** 18 **A**
19 **C** 20 **B** 21 **A** 22 **C** 23 **B** 24 **D** 25 **D** 26 **B**
27 **A** 28 **C**

Crossword puzzle p 18

Answers across
5 ACCELERATION 8 nm 9 SPEED 10 ICT
11 DIGIT 12 PREFIX 13 mm 17 COMPOSITE
19 MASS 21 mg 22 SIGFIG 24 HIGH
26 BYTE 27 LINE 29 EDP 30 SISYSTEM

Answers down
1 VELOCITY 2 DENSE 3 ENGINEERS
4 UNIT 6 CENTI 7 AREA 12 PI 13 MB
14 FORCE 15 LENGTH 16 VARIABLE
18 PROBLEMS 20 TIME 23 SHAPE 25 Gm 28 cm

Unit 16 Transport in living things

Workbook 9: BCP p 20–21 Cross-sections: plants

4 (a) vacuole or cell sap, (b) cell membrane, (c) nucleus, (d) cell wall, (e) or (f) water in by osmosis, (f) or (e) mineral salts in by diffusion.
5 (a) root hair, (b) epidermis, (c) root storage tissue, (d) xylem, (e) phloem.
6 (a) epidermis, (b) stem storage tissue, (c) phloem, (d) cambium, (e) xylem, (f) packing cells, (g) vascular tissue or vein.
7 (a) cells containing chlorophyll, (b) main vein, (c) upper epidermis, (d) xylem, (e) phloem, (f) vein.

Workbook 9: BCP p 23 LS of heart

4 (a) vena cava or venae cavae, (b) pulmonary artery, (c) aorta or dorsal aorta, (d) pulmonary vein, (e) left atrium, (f) left ventricle, (g) right ventricle, (h) right atrium.

Workbook 9: BCP p 24 Simple circulation

1 (a) vein from body, (b) artery to lungs, (c) capillaries in lungs, (d) vein from lungs, (e) artery to body, (f) capillaries in body, (g) lot of carbon dioxide, (h) heart, (i) lot of oxygen, (j) right side, (k) left side.

Workbook 9: BCP p 25 Circulation

3 (a) renal vein, (b) hepatic vein, (c) vena cava, (d) pulmonary vein, (e) vena cava, (f) artery to head and arms, (g) pulmonary artery, (h) aorta or dorsal aorta, (i) hepatic artery, (j) hepatic artery.
Questions: (f) The pulmonary artery is the only artery that contains de-oxygenated blood, from the heart to the lungs.
(g) The pulmonary vein is the only vein that contains oxygenated blood, from the lungs to the heart.

Workbook 9: BCP p 28 Answers to multiple-choice items

1 **B** 2 **D** 3 **B** 4 **A** 5 **B** 6 **A** 7 **B** 8 **C** 9 **D**
10 **C** 11 **A** 12 **C** 13 **D** 14 **A** 15 **D** 16 **A**
17 **C** 18 **B** 19 **A** 20 **B** 21 **D** 22 **D** 23 **A**
24 **C** 25 **A** 26 **D** 27 **B** 28 **A** 29 **C** 30 **C** 31 **D**
32 **C** 33 **D** 34 **A** 35 **D**

Crossword puzzle p 29

Answers across
1 HEART 2 AMOEBA 7 CIRCULATORY 9 VEIN
11 AORTA 14 OXYGEN 16 RED 17 AIDS 19 CELL
Answers down
1 HYPERTONIC 2 A PULMONARY 3 BLOOD
4 TRANSPORT 5 XYLEM 6 TRANSPIRATION
7 CARBON DIOXIDE 8 ARTERY 10 PLASMA
12 ROOT 13 FOOD 15 GAIN 18 IN

Unit 17 Sensitivity and co-ordination

Workbook 9: BCP p 30 Sense organs

1 Eyes (a) – (f). (b) Nose (a), (b), (d), (f). Tongue (d), (f). Ears (b), (c), (d). Skin: anything that is close or safe enough to touch: (b), (c), (d), (f).
3 (a) nerve endings in sense organ, (b) nerve fibre covered by a sheath, (c) impulse, (d) nucleus, (e) cytoplasm, (f) nerve endings in the spinal cord or brain

Workbook 9: BCP p 30 (cont.)

4 (a) receptor, (b) cord, (c) hearing/sight, (d) sight/hearing, (e) impulses, (f) centres, (g) brain.

Workbook 9: BCP p 31 Touch, taste, and smell

4 (a) dead cells, (b) epidermis, (c) muscle, (d) oil gland, (e) hair, (f) dermis, (g) fat layer, (h) pressure sensor, (i) sweat gland, (j) heat sensor, (k) cold sensor, (l) pain sensor, (m) hair, (n) sweat pore, (o) touch sensor.
6 (a) bitter, (b) sour, (c) salt and sweet.

Workbook 9: BCP p 32 Eye and seeing

1 (a) conjunctiva, (b) cornea, (c) pupil, (d) aqueous humour, (e) iris, (f) ciliary muscle, (g) suspensory ligament, (h) lens, (i) optic nerve, (j) blind spot, (k) vitreous humour, (l) retina, (m) choroid, (n) sclera, (o) eye muscle.
3 (a) Rays cross at the pinhole to form inverted image (b) rays converge to a point (c) rays spread (diverge).

Workbook 9: BCP p 33 Ear and hearing

1 (a) ear flap, (b) ear canal, (c) eardrum, (d) hammer, (e) anvil, (f) stirrup, (g) ear bones, (h) oval window, (i) semi-circular canals, (j) auditory nerve, (k) cochlea, (l) Eustachian tube, (m) round window.
4 (a) Largest amplitude A, (b) highest frequency C, (c) quietest sound B, (d) lowest pitch D, (d) same amplitude C and D; C has the higher pitch, (e) same frequency A and B; A is louder.

Workbook 9: BCP p 34 Central nervous system

1 (a) skull, (b) brain, (c) spinal cord, (d) central nervous system, (e) backbone, (f) nerves, (f) peripheral nervous system.
2 (a) cerebrum (forebrain), (b) cerebellum (midbrain), (c) medulla oblongata (hindbrain) (See SB9: BCP p 73.)
4 (a) stimulus (heat), (b) receptor (sensory nerve endings in skin), (c) sensory nerve fibre (to spinal cord), (d) spinal cord (relay fibre), (e) motor nerve fibre (from spinal cord), (f) effector (muscle in the arm), (g) response (arm and hand removed from hot object).

Workbook 9: BCP p 36 Endocrine system

1 (a) pituitary gland (e.g. growth hormone), (b) thyroid (thyroxine), (c) pancreas (insulin), (d) adrenal glands (adrenaline), (e) ovaries (oestrogen and progesterone), (f) testes (testosterone).

Workbook 9: BCP p 37 Answers to multiple-choice items

1 **A** 2 **C** 3 **A** 4 **B** 5 **D** 6 **B** 7 **D** 8 **C** 9 **B**
10 **D** 11 **D** 12 **C** 13 **C** 14 **D** 15 **C** 16 **B** 17 **A**
18 **D** 19 **D** 20 **C** 21 **C** 22 **B** 23 **A** 24 **D**

Crossword puzzle p 38

Answers across
1 RODS 7 RETINA 8 AMPLITUDE 11 LENS
12 ENERGY 13 SENSORY 15 RECEPTOR 17 TESTES
19 REFLEX 20 EARS 21 SPINAL CORD
Answers down
2 STIMULI 3 FREQUENCY 4 IN 5 TASTEBUD
6 MUSCLE 9 DIVERGE 10 EYE 13 SMELL
14 SENSES 16 RAY 18 HEAD

Unit 18 Embryo development and birth control

Workbook 9: BCP p 39 Embryo development

1 Sperm: (a) nucleus, (b) mitochondria, (c) tail; Egg: (a) egg membranes, (b) nucleus, (c) cytoplasm, (d) yolk.
2 See SB9: BCP p 85. (a) identical twins develop from one zygote so always either 2 girls or 2 boys; (b) non-identical twins from two zygotes, so both girls, both boys or one of each; (c) triplets can form from one zygote and are identical, but otherwise from two zygotes and all boys, all girls, 2 boys and 1 girl, or 2 girls and 1 boy. The two that form from one egg are identical. Students can make models to show the alternatives.
3 (a) Fallopian tube or oviduct, (b) foetus, (c) muscles of uterus wall, (d) plug of mucus in neck of cervix, (e) vagina, (f) amniotic sac, (g) amniotic fluid, (h) umbilical cord, (i) placenta.

Workbook 9: BCP p 45 Answers to multiple-choice items

1 **A** 2 **C** 3 **B** 4 **B** 5 **C** 6 **A** 7 **A** 8 **D**
9 **A** 10 **D** 11 **B** 12 **D** 13 **C** 14 **B** 15 **B** 16 **D**
17 **A** 18 **C** 19 **D** 20 **C** 21 **B** 22 **D** 23 **A** 24 **B**
25 **C** 26 **A** 27 **C** 28 **C** 29 **A** 30 **D** 31 **B**

Crossword puzzle p 46

Answers across
3 CONTRACEPTIVE 9 IUD 10 NATAL 11 EGG
14 TWO 16 LOHOCLA 17 BIRTH 18 FOETUS
19 SGURD 21 VEIN 22 SPERM
Answers down
1 CONDOM 2 FERTILISATION 4 TWINS
5 AMNIOTIC 6 VASECTOMY 7 DIET 8 PLACENTA
12 GROWTH 13 SMOKING 15 EMBRYOS 20 HIV

Unit 19 Chemical bonding, reactions and equations

Workbook 9: BCP p 47 Groups of elements

1 (a) Names: see SB9: BCP p 114–15, Periodic table.
(b) Group 0: helium, neon and argon.
(c) Group 1: lithium, sodium and potassium.
(d) Group 2: beryllium, magnesium and calcium.
(e) Group 6: oxygen and sulphur.
(f) Group 7: fluorine and chlorine.
2 and **3** see SB9: BCP p 116–17.
4 (a) 2 (lithium and beryllium) or 8; (b) 8. The outer shells become full with 2 or 8 electrons.

Workbook 9: BCP p 48 Ionic bonding

1 (a) few, (b) outer, (c) lose, (d) positively, (e) ions, (f) lot, (g) electrons, (h) shell, (i) electrons, (j) negatively.
2 Check the drawings by looking at SB9: BCP p 117, Ionic bonding.
3 Group 1 (metal), outer electrons and combining = 1, Group 2 (metal), outer electrons and combining = 2, Group 6 (non-metal), electrons 6, combining power = 2,
Group 7 (non-metal), electrons 7, combining power = 1.
4 (a) ionic, (b) negative, (c) attract, (d) ions, (e) charges, (g) ion, (h) two.

Workbook 9: BCP p 48 (cont.)

5 (a) $LiCl$, (b) $BeSO_4$, (c) $AlCl_3$, (d) $CaSO_4$, (e) KNO_3, (f) K_2SO_4, (g) $Zn(NO_3)_2$, (h) $Cu(OH)_2$, (i) NH_4HCO_3, (j) $(NH_4)_2SO_4$, (k) $(NH_4)_2CO_3$, (l) $Mg(HCO_3)_2$, (m) $Al_2(SO_4)_3$, (n) $ZnCl_2$, (o) $Al(OH)_3$, (p) Na_2CO_3

Workbook 9: BCP p 49 Covalent bonding

1 (a) sharing, (b) outer, (c) 8, (d) non-metals, (e) gases, (f) electrons, (g) combining, (h) electrons, (i) outer.
2 (a) Combining power: C, Si (4), N, P (3), O, S (2), F, Cl (1)
(b) Electrons in shells (see Workbook, p 47).
(c) (i) C and Si have 4 electrons in their outer shell, (ii) Si has an additional shell of 8 electrons than C.
(d) (i) O and S have 6 electrons in their outer shell. (ii) S has an additional shell of 8 electrons than O.
3 (b) oxygen, (c) chlorine, (d) hydrogen chloride, (e) water, (f) carbon dioxide are shown in SB9: BCP p 119. (g) methane is a carbon atom surrounded by 4 hydrogen atoms, so each hydrogen shares 2 electrons, and the carbon shares 8.

Workbook 9: BCP p 50 Chemical reactions: Oxidation

1 Fill-ins: (a) reaction, (b) reactants, (c) products, (d) mass, (e) reactants/ products, (f) products/ reactants, (g) exothermic reaction.
3 Sodium with water is a violent, exothermic reaction. Potassium or ammonium nitrate, and ammonium chloride all react with water in endothermic reactions.
4 Salt: dissolves, no energy change, physical change. Calcium oxide: exothermic, chemical change.
5 Magnesium burns brightly in air to form magnesium oxide (exothermic reaction) that turns damp litmus blue. Magnesium does not react with cold water but rapidly produces gas (hydrogen) with hydrochloric acid.
6 Sulphur burns brightly in air to form sulphur dioxide (exothermic reaction) that turns damp litmus red. Sulphur floats but does not react with water or hydrochloric acid. No reaction with a lighted splint.

Workbook 9: BCP p 51 Synthesis and decomposition

1 Fill-ins: (a) combination, (b) simple, (c) larger, (d) elements, (e) exothermic.
2 (a) Mixture: Iron attracted by magnet, sulphur floats and iron sinks in water, iron releases hydrogen with hydrochloric acid. Grey and yellow parts can be seen. (b) Compound: Not attracted by magnet, sinks in water, makes a smelly gas (hydrogen sulphide) with hydrochloric acid, black solid. Fe + S + FeS. Chemical reaction: requires heat and gives out heat; new product that has its own different properties
3 (a) $Na + Cl_2 = 2NaCl$ (sodium chloride)
(b) $2H_2 + O_2 = 2H_2O$ (water)
(c) $C + O_2 = CO_2$ (carbon dioxide). Also $2C + O_2 = 2CO$ (carbon monoxide) with incomplete combustion where there is not enough oxygen.
4 Fill-ins: (a) single, (b) breaks, (c) simpler, (d) energy, (e) electricity, (f) endothermic.

Workbook 9: BCP p 51 (cont.)

5 (a) Green copper carbonate when heated decomposes to carbon dioxide gas and black copper oxide.
$CuCO_3$ — heat → CO_2 + CuO
(b) White calcium carbonate when heated decomposes to carbon dioxide gas and white calcium oxide.
$CaCO_3$ — heat → CO_2 + CaO

Workbook 9: BCP p 52 Displacement and metal reactions

1 Fill-ins: (a) metal, (b) displace, (c) less, (d) compound, (e) displacement, (f) swap.
2 Before: magnesium (grey), copper sulphate (blue). After: copper (orange), magnesium sulphate (clear).
$Mg + CuSO_4 = MgSO_4 + Cu$
3 Before: both solutions are clear. After: zinc chloride is clear and barium sulphate is a white precipitate.
(a) $ZnSO_4 + BaCl_2 = ZnCl_2 + BaSO_4$
(b) $Na_2SO_4 + BaCl_2 = 2NaCl + BaSO_4$
4 Fill-ins: (a) metals, (b) reactive, (c) reactivity, (d) metals, (e) magnesium, (f) reactive, (g) copper.
5 (a) calcium is the most reactive and (b) iron is the least reactive of the three metals.
6 (a) combine explosively with air, (b) with cold water, calcium reacts but magnesium does not, (c) become coated with a layer of oxide and do not corrode, (d) copper, as it does not react with cold or hot water, (e) as an acid it can interact with metals and carbonates.

Workbook 9: BCP p 53 Balancing chemical equations

1 3– N; 2– O, S, (CO_3), (SO_4); 1– F, Cl, (NO_3), (OH), (HCO_3); 1+ H, Li, Na, K, (NH_4); 2+ Mg, Ca, Be, Cu (common), Zn; 3+ Al. (Note: Fe is not included as it is either 2+ or 3+.)
2 Varied answers in the table.
Matching rules: 1 $ZnSO_4$: (f), 2 LiCl: (a), 3 $ZnCl_2$: (c), 4 CaO: (b), 5 $Cu(NO_3)_2$: (g), 6 HNO_3: (i), 7 $(NH_4)_2SO_4$: (j), 8 Na_2S: (d), 9 $NaHCO_3$: (e), 10 K_2SO_4: (h).
3 (a) $AlCl_3$, (b) $Al(NO_3)_3$, (c) NH_3, (d) $Al_2(SO_4)_3$

Workbook 9: BCP p 54 Balancing equations

4 (a) $Mg + Cl_2 = MgCl_2$,
(b) $CuO + H_2SO_4 = CuSO_4 + H_2O$,
(c) $Na_2CO_3 + CaCl_2 = 2NaCl + CaCO_3$,
(d) $2Na + 2H_2O = 2NaOH + H_2$,
(e) $Ca(OH)_2 + 2HNO_3 = Ca(NO_3)_2 + 2H_2O$,
(f) $BaCl_2 + K_2SO_4 = BaSO_4 + 2KCl$,
(g) $2H_2 + O_2 = 2H_2O$
5 (a) Spectator ions: $2Na^+$ and $2Cl^-$;
Ions making the precipitate: Ba^{2+} and SO_4^{2-}
(b) $Fe^{3+} + 3OH^- = Fe(OH)_3$;
(c) $Cu^{2+} = 2OH^- = Cu(OH)_2$

Workbook 9: BCP p 55 Answers to multiple-choice items

1 **C** 2 **A** 3 **B** 4 **C** 5 **D** 6 **C** 7 **B** 8 **A** 9 **D**
10 **D** 11 **C** 12 **A** 13 **D** 14 **B** 15 **A** 16 **D** 17 **C**
18 **C** 19 **C** 20 **D** 21 **B** 22 **B** 23 **A** 24 **C** 25 **D**

Crossword puzzle p 56

Answers across
4 SO2 5 MOLECULE 8 BE 9 FE 10 TLAS (SALT backwards) 12 METAL 13 CO2 15 ATOM 16 AR 17 OUT 18 IONIC 20 PPT 22 ION 24 MASS 27 VALENCY 29 OH 31 NON 32 RADICAL 34 HE 35 DIS
Answers down
1 ELEMENT 2 CU 3 SHELL 4 SUBSCRIPT 5 MG 6 COVALENT 7 ELECTRONS 11 H_2O 14 POSITIVE 19 COMBINE 21 TEST 23 NA 25 SYN 26 BOND 28 ENDO 30 CL2 33 CA 34 H2 36 IN

Unit 20 Acids and alkalis

Workbook 9: BCP p 57 Acids, alkalis and indicators

2 (a) red, (b) dyes were soluble in alcohol, (c) dye, alcohol, plant cells, (d) (i) red, (ii) dark green/black, (e) Yes or No, (f) Other groups probably the same.

Workbook 9: BCP p 58 Reactions of acids

2 Calcium, magnesium, aluminium and zinc all give hydrogen with hydrochloric acid (in order of activity – most active first); no reaction with copper.
3 (a) All the carbonates bubble and produce carbon dioxide. (b) $CO_2 + Ca(OH)_2 = CaCO_3 + H_2O$
(c) All. (d) $Na_2CO_3 + 2HCl = 2NaCl + CO_2 + H_20$

Workbook 9: BCP p 59 Reactions of alkalis

2 (a) No reaction. (b) They give carbon dioxide.
3 (b) and (c) Ammonia turns damp litmus blue: it is the only alkaline gas. (d) $NH_4Cl + NaOH = NH_3 + NaCl + H_2O$
4 (a) Precipitates of iron hydroxide (brown) and copper hydroxide (blue) in colourless solutions are formed.
(b) (i) $FeCl_3 + 3NaOH = Fe(OH)_3 + 3NaCl$
(ii) $CuSO_4 + 2NaOH = Cu(OH)_2 + Na_2SO_4$
5 (a) $Fe^{3+} + 3OH^- = Fe(OH)_3$ (charges balance),
(b) $Cu^{2+} + 2OH^- = Cu(OH)_2$ (charges balance)

Workbook 9: BCP p 60 Neutralisation

2 (a) $HCl + NaOH = NaCl + H_2O$,
(b) $HNO_3 + NH_4OH = NH_4NO_3 + H_2O$,
(c) $H_2CO_3 + 2NaOH = Na_2CO_3 + H_2O$,
(d) $H_2SO_4 + Mg(OH)_2 = MgSO_4 + 2H_2O$,
(e) $2HCl + CuO = CuCl_2 + H_2O$,
(f) $HNO_3 + KOH = KNO_3 + H_2O$,
(g) $H_2SO_4 + FeO = FeSO_4 + H_2O$,
(h) $H_2CO_3 + Cu(OH)_2 = CuCO_3 + 2H_2O$.

Workbook 9: BCP p 62 Making salts

1 (a) $2HCl + MgO = MgCl_2 + H_2O$,
(b) $HNO_3 + NH_4OH = NH_4NO_3 + H_2O$,
(c) $H_2SO_4 + Na_2CO_3 = Na_2SO_4 + CO_2 + H_2O$,
(d) $H_2SO_4 + Zn = ZnSO_4 + H_2$,
(e) $2Na + Cl_2 = 2NaCl$, (f) – (h) varied.
2 See SB9: BCP p 157. (a) Answers vary, (b) Baking soda: sodium hydrogen carbonate (NaHCO3), washing soda: sodium carbonate (Na_2CO_3).

Workbook 9: BCP p 63 Answers to multiple-choice items
1 **D** 2 **C** 3 **C** 4 **D** 5 **A** 6 **A** 7 **B** 8 **C** 9 **D** 10 **B** 11 **A** 12 **C** 13 **B** 14 **C** 15 **A** 16 **B** 17 **A** 18 **A** 19 **D** 20 **A** 21 **C** 22 **A**

Crossword puzzle p 64

Answers across
4 NEUTRALISATION 8 CA 9 BASE 12 ACIDS 13 AQ 14 WATER 17 CARBON 20 EQUATION 23 NO 24 DIOXIDE 27 STATE 28 LITMUS
Answers down
1 METALS 2 ATOM 3 RADICAL 5 ALKALI 6 INDICATOR 7 NEUTRAL 10 SALT 11 PH 15 AMMONIA 16 RED 17 CHEMICAL 18 GNORTS 19 ION 21 NO3 22 BLUE 25 PPT 26 14

Unit 21 Electricity and magnetism

Workbook 9: BCP p 65 Static electricity
1 Plastic (pen, balloon, spoon) rubbed with woollen or cotton cloth will gain electrons and become –vely charged. It attracts paper, hair, the wall and a flow of water. A metal spoon does not develop a surface charge.
2 A Perspex rod rubbed with cotton cloth loses electrons to become +vely charged.

Workbook 9: BCP p 66 Conductors and insulators
2 (a) – (d) Conductors are metals: used where we want to conduct electricity; insulators are non-metals: used where we want to be protected against electricity (and heat).
(e) Graphite is a non-metal that conducts electricity.
(f) Air is an insulator: because an open switch is not a complete circuit.

Workbook 9: BCP p 67 Comparing series and parallel
Refer to SB9: BCP p 176–9.

Workbook 9: BCP p 68 Series circuits
1 (a) If bulb **X** is unscrewed, none of the other bulbs can work because there is only one circuit.
(b) **A** is like circuit S (b), and **B** is like S (c).

No. of cells	Total volts	No. of bulbs	Volts used per bulb	Bulbs
S(a) 1	1.5 V	1	1.5 V	Bright
S(b) 1	1.5 V	2	0.75 V	Dim
S(c) 1	1.5 V	3	0.5 V	? No light
S(d) 2	3.0 V	1	3.0 V	Brightest
S(e) 2	3.0 V	2	1.5 V	Bright
S(f) 2	3.0 V	3	1.0 V	Normal

3 Increase in number of cells increases the brightness.
4 Increase in number of bulbs decreases the brightness.
Note: The results will depend on the ratings of the bulbs. Relative brightness is worked out by the ratio of dry cells to bulbs: if this is high, the bulbs will be bright. If the ratio is low, the bulbs will be dim. Try out all the circuits beforehand and decide for yourself whether the descriptions in the last column of the table agree with your observations.

Workbook 9: BCP p 69 Parallel circuits
1 (a) If bulb **X** is unscrewed, the other bulbs still work as they each have their own circuit to the dry cell.
(b) **C** is like circuit P (a), and **D** is like P (b).

No. of cells	Total volts	No. of bulbs	Volts used per bulb	Bulbs
P(a) 1	1.5 V	2	1.5 V	Bright
P(b) 1	1.5 V	3	1.5 V	Bright
P(c) 2	3.0 V	2	3.0 V	Brightest
P(d) 2	3.0 V	3	3.0 V	Brightest
P(e) 3	4.5 V	2	4.5 V	May 'blow'
P(f) 3	4.5 V	3	4.5 V	May 'blow'

3 Increase in number of cells in series increases the voltage and the brightness of the bulbs.
4 Increase in number of bulbs in parallel (with the same number of cells) does not affect their brightness.
Note: The results will depend on the ratings of the bulbs.

Workbook 9: BCP p 70 Meter readings
1 For each dial record the lowest number the pointer is between: (a) 06165 (b) 05213 (c) We are charged for the amount of electricity we convert to other forms as our appliances work.

Workbook 9: BCP p 71
2 (a) handle (I): so we do not get heat and electricity conducted into us. (b) covering (I): to stop electricity coming out of the wire. (c) wire (C): to conduct electricity from the mains supply to the iron. bimetallic strip (C): to conduct heat: (d) above, brass to expand more and make the strip bend away from the bar; (e) below, steel to expand less. (f) base of iron (C): to conduct heat from the iron to press the clothes.
(g) heating element (C): conducts electricity and becomes worm; conducts heat to base of iron.
(h) bar (C); part of the electrical circuit.
(i) case (I): insulates against electricity (so no electric shock), and against heat (so we don't burn ourselves).
3 (a) 2-pin plugs with appliances with low wattage, or encased in plastic (e.g. an electric jug) which doesn't need an earth wire.
(b) 3-pin plugs with appliances with higher wattage and metal parts.
(c) Third pin is the earth pin for safety.
(d) Thin metal that will melt if excess current flows.
(e) Thickness: thinnest allows least current to flow before it breaks.
(f) The fuse must melt before damage is done to expensive appliances.

Workbook 9: BCP p 72 Safe use of heat and electricity
5 (a) Pan with hot food has its handle where a child could reach it. The hot food might spill and cause burns. Handles should be placed away from the edge.
(b) Mains circuit is switched on while a person is changing a light. The person might get a shock. Turn off the switch when working on an appliance.

Workbook 9: BCP p 72 (cont.)

(c) Too many plugs attached to one socket. It is 'overloaded'. This can heat up the cables and cause a fire. Put no more than two plugs in a socket.
(d) Top insulation has been removed, so the inner wires are exposed This could cause a fire or short circuit. Re-wire the plug.
(e) Outer insulation and inner wires have been cut and taped together. Risk of electric shock or a fire. Re-install a new cable.
(f) Water can conduct electricity, so an electric appliance and cable should not be near water. The person could get an electric shock. Remove the heater.
(g) The iron is burning the cloth. This could start a fire. Adjust the control on the iron.
(h) The circuit needs 10 A fuse wire, but someone has used 30 A. The 30 A wire will not protect the appliances in this circuit, so they may be damaged with excess current. Fit the correct fuse wire.

Workbook 9: BCP p 73 Magnetism

1 Fill-ins: (a) iron, (b) steel, (c) poles, (d) north, (e) compass, (f) repel, (g) magnetic.

Workbook 9: BCP p 74 Magnetism

6 While the wire or magnet is moving: current is induced; while still: no current is induced. What happens is that the system that is set up is able to change kinetic energy of movement into flow of electrons: current.
All of the actions increase the current induced.

7 (a) An electric current flowing in an insulated wire coiled around an iron nail can make an electromagnet. The effect stops when the current is stopped.
(b) A magnet being moved into and out of a metal coil can induce a flow of electrons: an electric current. This is how a dynamo and a generator work.

Workbook 9: BCP p 75 Answers to multiple-choice items

1 **B** 2 **D** 3 **C** 4 **B** 5 **A** 6 **B** 7 **A** 8 **B** 9 **C**
10 **D** 11 **A** 12 **C** 13 **C** 14 **B** 15 **D** 16 **A**
17 **B** 18 **D** 19 **C**

21 Bulb (b) goes out (as it is in series with bulb (a): in the same circuit). Bulb (c) stays alight (as it is in parallel with bulb (a): with its own connection to the dry cell).

Crossword puzzle p 76

Answers across
3 OHMS 5 RESISTANCE 10 CHARGE 12 LIT 14 CELL 16 DYNAMO 17 ING 18 PLUG 22 SWITCH 24 IN 25 CURRENT 26 ELECTRON 27 UNITS
Answers down
1 BI 2 PARALLEL 3 OUT 4 MAGNET 5 RESISTOR 6 STATIC 7 SERIES 8 CIRCUIT 9 SAFETY 11 PMA 13 CONDUCT 15 LIGHTN 16 DRY 19 FUSE 20 kWh 21 LIVE 23 TRAN

Circuits below Clues: B is dimmest (1:3 ratio of cells to bulbs), C is next (1:2 ratio), D is next (2:3 ratio) and A is brightest (1:1 ratio).

Unit 22 Thermal energy

Workbook 9: BCP p 77 Kinetic energy

1 Water in beaker **B** has twice the volume of **A**, so twice as many particles to increase their kinetic energy.

2 (i) Hot water loses heat to its surroundings and cools.
(ii) Cold water gains heat from its surroundings and warms.

4 (b) Liquid **C** (30 × 250 = 7500) has more thermal energy than **D** (25 × 200 = 6000).
Note: the temperature readings are the average kinetic energy, so to make a fair comparison we multiply these by the volumes to get the total kinetic energy = thermal energy of the liquids.
(c) Heat energy flows from liquid **F** to **E**: from a higher to a lower temperature.

Workbook 9: BCP p 78 Conduction

1 (f) Important to use spoons all of the same size.

3 (a) Water boils, (b) ice does not melt, (c) heat is not conducted in the water from the top to the ice at the bottom. Water at the top heats by convection.

4 The insulated can (A) loses less heat than can B, because air is a good insulator (poor conductor).

Workbook 9: BCP p 79 Convection

1 (a) When heated the air expands, becomes lighter and rises up into the balloon.
(b) Cooling and contracting occur. (c) Warmer, less dense air rises; cooler air sinks.

3 The ice cubes will slowly melt as they are warmed up by the surrounding water; the colour will mix very slowly.

4 (c) No: you would expect convection currents to also form close to large lakes where the temperatures of land and water would be different in the day and night.

Workbook 9: BCP p 80 Radiation

1 (c) A thermometer left in a black car will show a higher temperature than one in a white car. Note: if it rains for a short time on both cars, the water will evaporate most quickly from the black car. Black absorbs and emits more heat than white or colours.

Workbook 9: BCP p 81 Heating and cooling

2 Labels: (a) evaporation or boiling, (b) condensing, (c) melting, (d) solidifying or freezing, (e) sublimation.

Workbook 9: BCP p 82 Answers to multiple-choice items

1 **C** 2 **D** 3 **A** 4 **B** 5 **A** 6 **A** 7 **D** 8 **C** 9 **D**
10 **D** 11 **A** 12 **B** 13 **B** 14 **C** 15 **A** 16 **B**
17 **B** 18 **C** 19 **B** 20 **D** 11 **D**

Crossword puzzle p 83

Answers across
3 CONDUCTION 7 NIGHT 9 UP 10 AIR 11 SEA 14 RADIATION 16 LIQUID 18 ENERGY 20 STATE 21 FLUID 22 ATMOSPHERE
Answers down
1 IN 2 SOLID 3 CONVECTION 4 TEMPERATURE 5 METAL 6 CURRENT 8 HEAT 12 KINETIC 13 OUT 15 THERMAL 17 DOWN 19 GAS

For Worksheets: 1–30

Introduction: Working like a scientist (3)

Worksheet 1 The scientific method (p 84)

1 Order: 1 (e), 2 (a), 3 (c), 4 (b), 5 (f), 6 (d)
2 (a) Ten similar seeds in the light with dry cotton wool. (b) Ten similar damp seeds but left in the dark.
3 Fill-ins: (a) hypothesis, (b) prediction, (c) fair, (d) independent, (e) variable, (f) control, (g) variables, (h) dependent, (i) variable(s), (j) prediction, (k) hypothesis, (l) independent, (m) variable, (n) x-, (o) dependent, (p) variable, (q) y-

Worksheet 2 Engineering design process (p 85)

1 Order: 1 (a), 2 (c), 3 (f), 4 (b), 5 (e), 6 (d)
2 See p 10 in SB9: BCP for steps in the EDP.

Worksheet 3 Measuring physical quantities (p 86)

1 (a) 1.1 cm, (b) 2.4 cm, (c) 3.8 cm, (d) Length, (e) 1 mm
2 (a) 370 g, (b) 310 g, (c) 240 g, (d) Mass, (e) 10 g
3 (a) 54 cm^3, (b) 42 cm^3, (c) 18 cm^3, (d) Volume, (e) 2 cm^3
4 (a) 36.3 °C, (b) 37.4 °C, (c) 37.9 °C, (d) Temperature, (e) 0.1 °C

Worksheet 4 Working with numbers (p 87)

Prefixes: 1 (a) $\frac{1}{100}$, (b) $\frac{1}{10}$, (c) $\frac{1}{1000}$
2 (a) 0.05 kg, (b) 500 mg;
3 (a) 1 km, (b) 10 000 dm
4 Move the digits (a) 1 left, (b) 2 right, (c) 3 right
5 (a) 10^{-1}, (b) 10^{6}, (c) 10^{-3}, (d) 10^{3}, (e) 10^{9}, (f) 10^{-2}

Area and volume:
2 (a) 36 cm^2, (b) 8 m^2, (c) 6 cm^2
3 Cube: a^3, Cuboid: $a \times b \times c$, Sphere: $\frac{4}{3}\pi r^3$, Cylinder: $\pi r^2 \times b$
4 (a) 125 cm^3, (b) 523.6 cm^3 to 1 d.p., (c) 126 cm^3

Significant figures: 1 Most precise: (d) and (h)
2 (a) one, (b) two, (c) two, (d) three, (e) two, (f) two
3 (a) 7.65, (b) 0.0238, (c) 0.137, (d) 24.0
4 (a) 172, (b) 32.2; **5** (a) 671, (b) 40.2

Standard form: 1 (a) 4.5×10^3, (b) 6.37×10^4, (c) $5.6\ 10^{-1}$, (d) 7.8×10^{-2}
2 (a) 234, (b) 570, (c) 0.083, (d) 0.000623
3 (a) 7.68×10^6, (b) 5.681×10^{-3}
4 (a) 3.888×10^4, (b) 2.46×10^{-3}
5 (a) 2.11692×10^{-1}, (b) 3.9715×10^{-6}
6 (a) 1.5×10^3, (b) 2.48×10^1

Worksheet 5 Line graphs and gradients (p 88)

1 (b) (i) $\frac{50}{10} = 5\,ms^{-1}$, (ii) zero gradient or stationary, (iii) $\frac{50}{5} = 10 ms^{-1}$ (iv) The object begins travelling, then stops; then it moves again at a faster speed.
2 (b) (i) $\frac{10}{10} = 1\,ms^{-2}$. (ii) no change in velocity or no acceleration or steady velocity of 10 ms^{-1}, (iii) $\frac{20}{5} = 4\,ms^{-2}$, (iv) Object accelerating and then travels at steady velocity before accelerating faster.

Worksheet 5 (cont.)

3 (a) The flat part of a distance–time graph means no distance is being travelled; the object is stationary; (b) The flat part of a velocity–time graph means there is no change in velocity; no acceleration; steady velocity.

Unit 16: Transport in living things

Worksheet 6 Diffusion and osmosis (p 89)

1 Matches: (a) 3, (b) 4, (c) 2, (d) 1
2 Matches: (a) 2, (b) 3, (c) 1
3 (i) Fill-ins: (a) vibrate, (b) move, (c) liquids, (d) solvent, (e) diffuse, (f) concentration, (g) lower, (h) concentration, (i) gradient.
(ii) Fill-ins: (j) Osmosis, (k) diffusion, (l) higher, (m) gradient, (n) small, (o) membrane, (p) Larger, (q) enters.

Worksheet 7 Transport in plants (p 90)

1 Matches: (a) 1 C, (b) 3 A, (c) 4 B, (d) 2 B
2 Matches: (a) 3, (b) 2, (c) 3, (d) 4, (e) 1
3 (a) water and salts, (b)/(c) xylem, and water and salts, (d) sunlight energy, (e) transpiration pull, (f) carbon dioxide, (g)/(h) phloem, and food, (i) root push.

Worksheet 8 Blood and the heart (p 91)

1 Matches: (a) 2, (b) 1, (c) 5, (d) 4, (e) 3
2 Labels: (a) venae cava, (b) right atrium, (c) right ventricle, (d) pulmonary artery, (e) aorta, (f) pulmonary vein, (g) left atrium, (h) left ventricle; (i) blood from body to right atrium, (j) blood to lungs from the right ventricle, (k) blood to body from the left ventricle, (l) blood from lungs to left atrium

Worksheet 9 Circulation in humans (p 92)

1 Matches: (a) 3 A, (b) 1 C, (c) 2 B
2 (a) heart pumps blood, (b) arteries carry blood from heart to capillaries, (c) veins carry blood from capillaries to heart, (d) oxygen and food diffuse into cell, (e) carbon dioxide, heat and wastes diffuse out of cell, (f) oxygenated blood, (g) de-oxygenated blood, (h) body cell
3 Fill-ins: (a) alveoli, (b) artery, (c) carbon dioxide, (d) oxygen, (e) vein

Worksheet 10 Problems with circulation (p 93)

1 Matches: (a) 3 D, (b) 4 C, (c) 2 A, (d) 1 B
2 Matches: (a) 3, (b) 2, (c) 4, (d) 1
3 Choices: Positive √: 1, 3. 6; negative X: 2, 4, 5
4 See SB9: BCP p 51–3.

Unit 17: Sensitivity and co-ordination

Worksheet 11 Sense organs: Skin, tongue, nose (p 94)

1 Matches: (a) 2 C & E, (b) 4 D (+ C & E), (c) 1 D, (d) 5 A, (e) 3 B;
2 Matches: (a) 2, (b) 1, (c) 3
4 Matches: (a) 4, (b) 3, (c) 5, (d) 1, (e) 2

Worksheet 12 Sense organs: Eye and ear (p 95)

1 Matches: (a) 4, (b) 14, (c) 11, (d) 6, (e) 1, (f) 2, (g) 9, (h) 5, (i) 7, (j) 15, (k) 3, (l) 12, (m) 10, (n) 8, (o) 13
2 Matches: (a) 5, (b) 11, (c) 10, (d) 7, (e) 2, (f) 3, (g) 1, (h) 12, (i) 4, (j) 8, (k) 13, (l) 9, (m) 6

Worksheet 13 CNS and reflex actions (p 96)

1 (a) 1 A and H, and (a) 5 B and G; (b) 2, and (b) 4 C and E; (c) 3 D and F
2 Matches: (a) 3, (b) 1, (c) 2
3 Fill-ins: (a) sensory, (b) reflex, (c) hindbrain, (d) involuntary, (e) forebrain, (f) voluntary
4 Matches: (a) 6, (b) 5, (c) 2, (d) 4, (e) 7, (f) 3, (g) 1

Worksheet 14 Nervous and endocrine systems (p 97)

1 Comparison of systems, see SB9: BCP p 76.
2 Matches: (a) 2 D, (b) 5 B, (c) 3 F, (d) 6 A, (e) 4 C, (f) 1 E
3 (i) Fill-ins: (a) nervous, (b) electrical, (c) short, (d) endocrine, (e) hormones, (f) long-lasting
(ii) Fill-ins: (g) adrenaline, (h) quick, (i) fight, (j) oxygen, (k) muscles, (l) insulin, (m) diabetes

Unit 18: Embryo development and birth control

Worksheet 15 Before and after birth (p 98)

1 Matches: (a) 5, (b) 3, (c) 2, (d) 7, (e) 1, (f) 6, (g) 4
2 Labels: (a) and (b): food and oxygen; (c) and (d): food and oxygen; (e) and (f): carbon dioxide and other wastes; (g) and (h): carbon dioxide and other wastes; (i) umbilical vein, (j) umbilical artery
3 Matches: (a) 2, (b) 3, (c) 5, (d) 4, (e) 6, (f) 1

Worksheet 16 A healthy pregnancy (p 99)

1 Matches: (a) 4, (b) 3, (c) 5, (d) 1, (e) 2
2 Matches: (a) 7, (b) 3, (c) 1, (d) 6, (e) 9, (f) 10, (g) 4, (h) 2, (i) 8 (j) 5

Worksheet 17 Birth control methods (p 100)

1 (a) 2, (b) 3, (c) 4, (d) 1
2 Matches: (a) Natural: 2, 4, 5, 7; (b) Barrier: 1, 6, 8, 9; (c) 3, 12, 14, 16; (d) 10, 11, 13, 15

Unit 19: Chemical bonding, reactions and equations

Worksheet 18 The periodic table (p 101)

1 Information on elements to complete the squares.

Element	Symbol	Number of protons	Number of neutrons	Mass number
Lithium	Li	3	4	7
Potassium	K	19	20	39
Helium	He	2	2	4
Argon	Ar	18	22	40
Fluorine	F	9	10	19
Oxygen	O	8	8	16

2 Information for atoms of elements. All the values in the table for a particular element are the same: Atomic number = number of protons = number of electrons.
3 Matches: (a), (c) and (f): 1 C; (b), (e) and (h): 2 A; (d) and (g): 3 B

Worksheet 19 Ionic and covalent bonding (p 102)

1 Information on atoms (neutral) or ions (charged).

Element	Symbol	Number of protons	Number of electrons	Atom or ion?
Magnesium	Mg	12	10	Ion 2+
Sodium	Na	11	10	Ion 1+
Chlorine	Cl	17	17	Atom
Chlorine	Cl	17	18	Ion 1–
Potassium	K	19	18	Ion 1+
Fluorine	F	9	10	Ion 1–

2 Calcium ion is without its two electrons in the outer shell.
Chloride ion gains an electron into its outer shell.
3 $Ca^{2+} + 2Cl^{1-} = CaCl_2$ (calcium chloride)
4 Show outer shells with eight electrons (2 shared).
5 Ammonia, see SB9: BCP p 119.

Worksheet 20 Chemical reactions and equations (p 103)

Oxidation: 1 $2Mg + O_2 = 2MgO$,
2 $S + O_2 = SO_2$,
3 $C + O_2 = CO_2$, **4** $2C + O_2 = 2CO$

Decomposition: 1 $CuCO_3 = CuO + CO_2$,
2 $CaCO_3 = CaO + CO_2$,
3 $2NaHCO_3 = Na_2CO_3 + CO_2 + H_2O$

Synthesis: 1 $Fe + S = FeS$, **2** $2Na + Cl_2 = 2NaCl$,
3 $6CO_2 + 6H_2O = C_6H_{12}O_6 + 6O_2$

Displacement: 1 Mg + CuSO4 = MgSO4 + Cu,
2 $BaCl_2 + ZnSO_4 = BaSO_4 + ZnCl_2$,
3 $Ca + 2H_2O = Ca(OH)_2 + H_2$

Worksheet 21 Balancing chemical equations (p 104)

1 Matches: (a) 1 B; (b) 1, 2 and 5 B; (c) 4 D; (d) 3 C; (e) 5 B
2 Combining power: 3- N; 2- O, S, CO_3, SO_4; 1- F, Cl, NO_3, OH, HCO_3; 1+ Na, K, NH_4; 2+ Cu, Zn, Mg, Ca; 3+ Al
3 (a) 12, (b) 18, (c) 24, (d) 16
4 (a) $Mg + F_2 = MgF_2$,
(b) $2NH_4Cl + Na_2SO_4 = (NH_4)_2SO_4 + 2NaCl$
(c) $Ca + 2HCl = CaCl_2 + H_2$
(d) $2Na + 2H_2O = 2NaOH + H_2$
(e) $NaHCO_3 + HCl = NaCl + CO_2 + H_2O$
(f) $CuSO_4 + 2NaOH = Cu(OH)_2 + Na_2$SO4

Unit 20: Acids and alkalis

Worksheet 22 Acids, alkalis and indicators (p 105)

1 Matches: (a) 1 A, (b) 2 C, (c) 1 B, (d) 2 D
2 Matches: (a) 1 B, (b) 4 D, (c) 4 A, (d) 2 C
3 (a) See SB9: BCP p 141 and 143. Hibiscus is red in acid and dark green, almost black, in alkali.
(b) Universal indicator distinguishes pH 1 to 14.
4 Fill-ins: (a) pH, (b) ions, (c) strong, (d) hydrogen, (e) ions, (f) pH, (g) 1–2, (h) strong, (i) hydroxide, (j) ions, (k) pH, (l) 12–14, (m) acids, (n) alkalis, (o) skin, (p) neutral, (q) 7.

Worksheet 23 Reactions of acids and alkalis (p 106)

1 Acids: 1, 3, 6, 7, 11, 12, 15, 16, 18, 19, 20, 21, 22; Bases: 2, 4, 5, 7, 8, 9, 10, 11, 13, 14, 17, 21, 23, 24

2 (a) $Ca + 2HCl = CaCl_2 + H_2$, (b) $Mg + 2HCl = MgCl_2 + H_2$, (c) $2Al + 6HCl = 2AlCl_3 + 3H_2$

3 (a) $Na_2CO_3 + 2HCl = 2NaCl + CO_2 + H_2O$, (b) $CaCO_3 + 2HCl = CaCl_2 + CO_2 + H_2O$, (c) $NaHCO_3 + HCl = NaCl + CO_2 + H_2O$

4 (a) $CuSO_4 + 2NaOH = Cu(OH)_2 + Na_2SO_4$ (b) $FeCl_3 + 3NaOH = Fe(OH)_3 + 3NaCl$ (c) $Ba(NO_3)_2 + 2NaOH = Ba(OH)_2 + 2NaNO_3$ (d) $NH_4Cl + NaOH = NaCl + NH_3 + H_2O$

Worksheet 24 Neutralisation and making salts (p 107)

1 Fill-in: (a) base, (b) concentration, (c) neutralise, (d) hydrogen, (e) hydroxide, (f) radical, (g) metal, (h) salt.

2 Matches: (a) 2 B, (b) 1 C, (c) 3 A

3 (a) $HCl + NaOH = NaCl + H_20$, (b) $2HNO_3 + Ca(OH)_2 = Ca(NO_3)_2 + 2H_2O$, (c) $HNO_3 + NH_4OH = NH_4NO_3 + H_2O$, (d) $H_2SO_4 + Mg(OH)_2 = MgSO_4 + 2H_2O$

5 (a) $2HCl + CaO = CaCl_2 + H_2O$, (b) $H_2SO_4 + 2NH_4OH = (NH_4)_2SO_4 + 2H_2O$, (c) $2HNO_3 + Na_2CO3 = 2NaNO_3 + CO_2 + H_2O$, (d) $2HCl + Mg = MgCl_2 + H_2$, (e) $Fe + S = FeS$

Unit 21: Electricity and magnetism

Worksheet 25 Static electricity (p 108)

1 Fill-ins: (a) neutral, (b) electrons, (c) plastic, (d) electrons, (e) negative, (f) paper, (g) negative, (h) positive, (i) Metals, (j) charges.

2 (a) 1 A, C and E, (a) 2 B and D.

3 See SB9: BCP p 172.

4 (a) Static electricity is the build-up of charge on a surface; current electricity is charge on the move.
(b) Metals cannot keep a charge on their surface as it is quickly conducted away; when part of a circuit, the electrons in metals become part of the electric current.

Worksheet 26 Electrical circuits (p 109)

1 Drawings: (a) wire, (b) bulbs, (c) dry cell, (d) switch, (e) battery

2 Bulbs that light: (a) Switch 1: A and B, (b) Switch 2: C and D, (c) Switch 3: E only, (c) Switches 3 and 4: E and F, (d) Switch 5: none, (d) Switches 5 and 6: G, (d) Switches 5, 6 and 7: G and H.

3 Fill-ins: (a) voltage, (b) resistance, (c) bulbs, (d) voltage, (e) increased, (f) bulbs, (g) brighter, (h) resistance, (i) voltage, (j) current.

Worksheet 27 Series and parallel circuits (p 110)

1 Fill-ins: (a) series, (b) unlit, (c) current, (d) parallel, (e) unchanged, (f) dimmer, (g) series, (h) parallel.

2 Fill-ins: (i) series, (j) dimmer, (k) bulbs, (l) brighter, (m) parallel, (n) unchanged.

Worksheet 27 (cont.)

3 (a) Series; the combined voltage of the dry cells is part of the circuit.
(b) Check the bulb: see if the wire is broken – if it is, then replace it with a new bulb; check the dry cells: ensure they are both facing the same way and there is no gap between them – if necessary get new dry cells; check the contacts near the bulb and the base that there is good contact.

Worksheet 28 Magnets and electromagnets (p 111)

1 On (a) arrows drawn should show repulsion; on (b) and (c) arrows should show attraction.

2 Compass (a) poles are N on the left, and S on the right; compass (b) poles are N on the left and S on the right.

3 Fill-ins: (a) steel, (b) electromagnet, (c) coil, (d) current, (e) electromagnet, (f) current, (g) bells, (h) iron, (i) steel.

4 (a) A, (b) D

5 See SB9: BCP p 190–5.

Unit 22 Thermal energy

Worksheet 29 Conduction, convection and radiation (p 112)

1 Matches: (a) 2 D and (a) 3 B, (b) 1 C and (b) 4 A

2 Conduction: 1, 5, 7, 9, 12; Convection: 3, 4, 8, 10, 14, 16; Radiation: 2, 6, 11, 13, 15

3 (a) B, (b) A

4 See SB9: BCP p 210–11.

Worksheet 30 Kinetic energy, heating and cooling (p 113)

1 Matches: (a) 2, (b) 1, (c) 4, (d) 3

2 (a) Temperature is the average kinetic energy, so we multiply this by the volume to get the total kinetic energy.
(b) The tea starts hot and loses heat to the cooler surroundings.
(c) The colder ice gains heat from the lemonade and melts.
(d) The metal is cooled, there is less kinetic energy and it contracts to become a firmer fit.
(e) The hot water adds kinetic energy to the particles that move apart and the metal expands; the lid can be removed.
(f) When heated the gas in the balloon expands, becomes less dense and rises; when cooled the air is heavier and the balloon sinks.
(g) The solid chocolate takes heat from my hand and the surroundings, and particles start to move – the solid melts.
(h) The glass surface is cold, and the water vapour in the air is cooled so that the gas changes to drops of water.
(i) A thermos is designed to reduce heat transfer by conduction, convection and radiation. So a hot liquid will tend to stay hot, and a cool liquid will tend to stay cool.
(j) The microwaves make water molecules in the food vibrate and this means that the food becomes warmer and quickly cooked from the inside.

Great Clarendon Street, Oxford, OX2 6DP, United Kingdom

Oxford University Press is a department of the University of Oxford. It furthers the University's objective of excellence in research, scholarship, and education by publishing worldwide. Oxford is a registered trade mark of Oxford University Press in the UK and in certain other countries

First published in 2019

British Library Cataloguing in Publication Data
Data available

978 0 19 842165 8

10 9 8 7 6 5 4 3 2

Paper used in the production of this book is a natural, recyclable product made from wood grown in sustainable forests.
The manufacturing process conforms to the environmental regulations of the country of origin.

Printed and bound by CPI Group (UK) Ltd, Croydon CR0 4YY.

Acknowledgements

Cover: Shutterstock.com

Artwork by Q2A Media Services Pvt. Ltd. and OUP.